The Wizards of Ozymandias

The Wizards of Ozymandias

Reflections on the Decline and Fall

BUTLER SHAFFER

MISES
INSTITUTE
AUBURN, ALABAMA

Published by the Ludwig von Mises Institute
518 West Magnolia Avenue
Auburn, Alabama 36832
mises.org

ISBN: 978-1-610160-252-4

Dedication

To the memory and spirit of Sophie and Hans Scholl and the White Rose, who reminded us what it means to be civilized.

Table of Contents

Preface

When I first decided to chronicle the collapse of Western Civilization, I assumed I would have a sufficient amount of time to observe and comment upon the transformations taking place. I shared T.S. Eliot's sentiment that: "This is the way the world ends, Not with a bang but a whimper."[1] Surely a vibrant culture that took centuries to develop would have to experience a prolonged demise. I could not imagine that its downfall would be as precipitous as it has proven to be. Because of the complexities involved, it is difficult to identify a specific date or period when the descent began. Suffice it to say that the process was well underway by the time Henry Kissinger was awarded the Nobel Peace Prize!

The sense of civility that helps give meaning to a "civilization" is in full retreat. Our institutionalized social behavior has reverted to its reactive, reptilian origins; our thinking has become dominated by the political imperative that all of life is to be subjected to the exercise of collective power. Indeed, the formal systems through which we have organized and identified ourselves could be described as being in an ever-escalating war with life itself. As the creators of sophisticated technologies, we have made ourselves increasingly machine-like; robotic servants of institutional

---

1   T.S. Eliot, *The Hollow Men*, 1925.

systems we have been conditioned to revere, whose purposes we neither understand nor control, and of which we are afraid to ask questions. Our corporate-state world plunders, enslaves, controls and destroys us, all in the name of advancing our liberty and material well-being. Most of us are dominated by an unfocused fear of uncertainty, a longing for the security of emptiness.

The reasoned intelligence and spiritual inspiration that would otherwise power life energies, remain suppressed within us. Our current art, music, and literature largely entertain and amuse us ("amuse" being a way of distracting us from the meditative influences provided by the muses). What we refer to as "classical music" was often the popular music of earlier centuries. A century or two from now, which "rock" musician is likely to stand alongside Bach, Beethoven, Wagner, and Mahler as expressions of the inner spirit of mankind? What modern writers will be compared to Shakespeare, Dante, Emily Dickinson, or Walt Whitman?

If there is one period in Western history that I think reflects what we have become, it would be the French Revolution. What could be a more fitting symbol for that period of collective madness, destruction, and inhumanity than the guillotine, ever busy searching for new victims? Whatever visions of mankind in society have been offered by the numerous creators of Western Civilization are being lost as the culture, itself, disappears into history's "black hole." My oldest daughter, Bretigne, may have most succinctly encapsulated the changes occurring during her lifetime when she wrote: "I don't know who the people around me are anymore."[2]

Long before having children of my own, I embraced the idea that one had a moral obligation not to allow his or her children to live under tyranny. I continue to hold to this principle, even as I acknowledge my failure to accomplish that end. I continue in my efforts, insisting upon such peaceful means as writing, speaking, and teaching, for there are no shortcuts to the transformation of consciousness upon which such a task depends. My current writing is directed to a select audience of five people: my grandchildren. I share Albert Jay Nock's purpose of writing for the benefit of the Remnant, to whom will be left the task of helping to restore civilized society after the end of our destructive one. Still, my own efforts are motivated more by the presence of these five people, in the hope that they—and all the other children and grandchildren of the world—can walk away from

---

2   Bretigne Shaffer, "Mere Anarchy Loosed Upon the World," in *Why Peace*, Marc Guttman, ed. (Marc Guttman: East Lyme, Conn., 2012), pp. 118–26, at 124.

the organized bondage others have planned for them; that they can live in a truly civilized civilization based upon the self-directed, self-serving, creative, free, and peaceful behavior that it is their nature to enjoy as human beings.

Is it possible that the world my generation will leave to the next can be transformed; that society can become decent and supportive of life? Can conditions of peace and liberty replace the wars, coercive regulation, and worship of violence that have combined to destroy our present civilization? The book ends with such questions, and invites the reader to contemplate how such a life-centered culture might arise.

It is inherent in all writing that the author of a work bears the responsibility for its substantive content. It is also the case that a book does not get into print without a great deal of help from others. This work is no exception to this fact. Among those who provided me with such assistance were Spencer and Emalie MacCallum and David Gordon, three friends who were kind enough to review and provide constructive criticism of the manuscript. Judy Thommesen, Chad Parish, and Lew Rockwell at the Mises Institute also provided invaluable assistance in bringing the book to publication. Above all, I must thank my editor-in-chief, Jane Shaffer, for her page-by-page efforts—including her questions and suggestions—while the writing was still in progress. I suppose I could also thank the politicians, government officials, and other defenders of statism for their actions that provided me with endless material; but that might be pushing the acknowledgments too far.

Ozymandias

I met a traveller from an antique land
Who said: "Two vast and trunkless legs of stone
Stand in the desert. Near them, on the sand,
Half sunk, a shattered visage lies, whose frown,
And wrinkled lip, and sneer of cold command,
Tell that its sculptor well those passions read
Which yet survive, stamped on these lifeless things,
The hand that mocked them, and the heart that fed;
And on the pedestal these words appear:
My name is Ozymandias, King of Kings:
Look on my works, ye Mighty, and despair!
Nothing beside remains. Round the decay
Of that colossal wreck, boundless and bare
The lone and level sands stretch far away."

—*Percy Bysshe Shelley* (1817)

Introduction

Civilizations begin, flourish, decline, and disappear—or linger on as stagnant pools left by once life-giving streams.

—Will Durant

These essays began as part of a continuing contribution to an E-Book titled *The Wizards of Ozymandias: Reflections on the Decline and Fall.* Written over a period of several years, they are intended as a collection of personal observations accompanying what I consider the dissipation of the systems and characteristics of Western culture. In my first book, *Calculated Chaos: Institutional Threats to Peace and Human Survival,*[1] I used *The Wizard of Oz*[2] to illustrate how the characters' dependencies upon external authority provided a metaphor for what I regard as the greatest threat to human well-being: the institutional structuring of society. This book extends the inquiry to consider the impact institutionalism may have on the decline of civilization. My explanations for the major societal transformations now occurring—as well as the prospects for reviving the life-serving qualities of our culture—are offered as

---

1   *Calculated Chaos: Institutional Threats to Peace and Human Survival* San Francisco: Alchemy Books, 1985; republished Coral Springs, Fla.: Llumina Press, 2004).

2   L. Frank Baum, *The Wonderful Wizard of Oz* (Chicago: George M. Hill, 1900).

speculative impressions rather than as an empirical study of the causes of such changes.

The poet Shelley introduced us to Ozymandias in his poem of the same name, providing the picture of a tyrant whose arrogance of power led him to historical oblivion. Ozymandias is a reminder of the fragile nature of every system—be it biological, institutional, or galactic in character. As we are learning from the advanced course in history in which we seem now to be enrolled, this uncertain existence also applies to so-called civilizations. There is disagreement among historians as to the number and identity of civilizations around which so much of mankind has organized itself. While the values and practices of many past cultures continue to have a diluted influence—both good and bad—on modern societies, Western Civilization has lost much of its once-vibrant character. It is difficult for intelligent minds to dispute that this current system is in the process of joining Ozymandias in the dust-bin of history.

Western culture has added much to the quality of human existence. From the various arts, literature, and philosophy, to systems for producing and exchanging the means for enhancing the material well-being of mankind, to more sophisticated scientific understanding and its technological offspring and revelations in mathematics that have allowed us to take abstract reasoning into dimensions our ancestors could not have fathomed, the well-being of mankind has been greatly advanced during this epoch. We have even imagined ourselves capable of restraining the appetites of the Ozymandiases with written constitutions and structures designed to limit power.

Because of our nature as social beings, and having experienced the productive benefits of a specialization of labor, we have long known the advantages of organizing ourselves into groups to accomplish common purposes. Once in a while, a multitude of factors converge to create what is later recognized as a "civilization." Western Civilization is the most recent example, having been preceded by, among others, such cultures as the Babylonian, Egyptian, Greek, Hittite, Minoan, Persian, Phoenician, Roman, Mayan, and Incan. Students of human history have tried to unravel the elements that both *produced* and brought about the *demise* of past civilizations. Because civilizations are characterized by multitudinous networks of complexities, historians invariably encounter the uncertainties that inhere in complication.

The study of chaos informs us that complex systems are subject to far too many interconnected and inconstant variables to make it possible to control events in order to achieve predictable outcomes. The ability to predict outcomes in a complex system rests on a "sensitive dependence on initial conditions," meaning an awareness of the presence and strength of every factor that could affect the result.[3] In other words, our efforts to describe or to prescribe those patterns of regularity we define as "order" are limited by complexity itself. Events in our world are generally produced by countless networks of influences that make it difficult to identify causation. What may appear—if seen at all—as an inconsequential factor can produce damaging results (thus the nursery rhyme about "the want of a nail" leading to the loss of the war). We also discover that our faith in linear processes to produce anticipated results is often upset by the intervention of nonlinear influences ("the straw that broke the camel's back"). The hubris that attends all political programs of central planning is fueled by an ignorance of the forces of chaos.

For the same reasons, explanations for historic behavior prove just as difficult. That so many factors have been identified by so many observers concerning both the origin and demise of civilizations, is a confirmation of the uncertainties that lie hidden within the dynamics of chaos and complexity. While there is no consensus of opinion as to the causes of the *birth* or *death* of civilizations, there are a number of common components upon which various historians focus.

As we better understand how *chaos* underlies so much of what we experience as both *order* and *disorder* in the world, we begin to discover the presence of what are referred to as *attractors* within systems. An attractor represents the organizing principle that brings regularity to a system (i.e., "attracts" orderliness). An earthquake fault line can be regarded as an attractor for geologic forces operating in an area subject to plate tectonics while, on a social level, an estate sale can be regarded as an attractor for antique dealers.

There are many who believe the marketplace is a form of undisciplined, disordered confusion, and that political intervention is required to protect the public from such unpredictable conduct. To those who understand the dynamics of the marketplace, however, the seeming chaos is

---

3   See, e.g., James Gleick, *Chaos: Making A New Science* (New York: Viking Penguin, 1987); Ilya Prigogine and Isabelle Stengers, *Order Out of Chaos: Man's New Dialogue With Nature* (Boulder, Colo.: Shambhala, 1984); Erich Jantsch, *The Self-Organizing Universe* (New York: Pergamon Press, 1980); and John Briggs and F. David Peat, *Turbulent Mirror* (New York: Harper & Row, 1989).

underlain with processes through which the interplay of competing interests provides incentives for orderly behavior. In the language of "chaos," the pricing system is an "attractor" that brings buyers and sellers together to engage in transactions that benefit both. The study of chaos and complexity make us aware that simplistic, linear explanations no longer suffice for our understanding of a complicated world. Scientific inquiry has helped us move beyond superficial explanations of behavior, and to examine less-apparent influences.

That said, is it possible to identify causal factors that bring about the creation and the demise of a civilization? Are there *elements* and *processes* that serve as attractors for the development of a culture? Such inquiries into the "how" and "why" of civilizations are difficult to assess, given the multifaceted variables involved. Like efforts to identify the mechanisms that trigger biological evolution, they are too dependent on abstract speculation. How, for instance, does *individual* behavior influence *collective* outcomes? Like the proverbial tale of the blind men reporting on their examination of an elephant, are we too locked in to our particular experiences to be able to communicate to others anything of verifiable substance? Because of my personal history, the focus of this book will be upon that period known as Western Civilization. What can be said of the dynamics of this epoch that distinguishes it from other societies in other periods of time?

Creative and vibrant civilizations do not come into being in some haphazard manner, nor are they the products of careful planning on the part of self-appointed "leaders." They seem, rather, to have emerged from the convergence of various conditions, whose syntheses provided the opportunity for great numbers of people to pursue their respective interests in mutually-supportive ways. A culture thrives when it is capable of producing the values that define it. While some civilizations were grounded in agriculture, the success of Western Civilization can be traced, to a great extent, to the processes of industrialization, which essentially resolved the problem of how to sustain the lives of millions of people. It is important to note that a *civilized* society does not necessarily mean an *industrialized* society. The decline of our present civilization may be abetted by the emergence of an *information* based culture which might provide the basis for an even more prolific civilization.

The origins of any productive system seem to be traceable to conditions in which the self-interest driven purposes of individuals are allowed expression. These include the respect for autonomy and inviolability of personal boundaries that define liberty and peace and allow for cooperation for mutual ends. Support for such an environment has led to the flourishing of human activity not only in the production of material well-being, but in the arts, literature, philosophy, entrepreneurship, mathematics, spiritual inquiries, the sciences, medicine, engineering, invention, exploration, and other dimensions that fire the varied imaginations and energies of mankind. Our subjectively defined self-interests become energized within a social matrix that both encourages and reinforces novelty through informal, undirected processes.

Civilizations are not mandated by authorities, nor are they the products of systemic planning. People did not get together and say to one another "hey, let's start a civilization!" Such cultures have been, rather, the unintended consequences arising from the interplay of creative forces that sustain and enhance life. The variability and cross-fertilization of ideas and techniques that can arise in pluralistic settings conducive to diversity and spontaneity, have been indispensable to the life of modern civilization. In much the same way that "brainstorming" sessions provide synergistic opportunities for individuals to come together to produce solutions to problems that none could have brought about on their own, a culture supportive of individuality can generate values and systems at exponential levels of creativity.

It is difficult to think of the dynamics of Western Civilization without identifying its *individual* creative producers. When mention is made of this culture, do not the names and accomplishments of Aristotle, Plato, Shakespeare, Gutenberg, Beethoven, Galileo, Sophocles, Leonardo, Roger and Francis Bacon, Homer, Austen, Dante, Edison, Kepler, Carnegie, Michelangelo, Alcott, Locke, Curie, Rembrandt, Thomas Aquinas, Adam Smith, Emerson, Orville and Wilbur Wright, Milton, Bach, James Watt, van Gogh, Montessori, Pasteur, Darwin, Van Eyck, Einstein—to identify but a scant few individuals[4]—immediately come to mind? Do we not think of such persons as the *creators* of our civilization?

While the works of such people make up so much of the substance of our culture, their efforts, standing alone, would have been insufficient to produce a civilization. What other conditions were necessary to such ends? A factor I have long considered a major contributor to the emergence of highly productive societies can be found in what I call the "power of place."

---

4   I use the word "individual" *not* to denote activity isolated from other persons, but to refer to persons acting as autonomous, self-owning beings who, more often than not, voluntarily associate and cooperate with others, but who are free not to do so.

Why, for instance, did technological inventiveness, standing alone, not produce industrialized societies in such places as ancient Greece, Baghdad, and Rome? In the 1st century AD, the Greek scientist, Hero, invented what we now know to be a steam-engine. He drew upon the works of earlier Greeks Vitruvius (80 BC-15 AD), and Ctesibius (285-222 BC) to create an instrument which, as far as is known, was used only to open and close temple doors. Another Greek invention, the Antikythera mechanism, was created in the second century BC, as a system of gears and cogs used, apparently, to calculate astronomical phenomena. While this device is often referred to as the earliest known computer, its appearance did not transform the pre-Christian world into a "Silicon Valley." Was the two-thousand year-old copper cylinder found near Baghdad—believed by some to be an ancient electrical device—just another technological cul-de-sac that would await development centuries later? Did the glass industry of ancient Rome suffer from governmental restraints on technological innovation, thus impeding its development?[5]

My curiosity about the role that "place" might play in the creative process led me to inquire into the underlying conditions that attracted inventive and productive energies to *Manchester,* rather than *Marseilles,* as the birthplace of the Industrial Revolution; or *Florence,* instead of *Naples,* as the center for the Italian Renaissance. Why did the Roman empire decline in its western region, but continue to prosper in its eastern domain? What forces converged to bring such creative minds as Emerson, Thoreau, Louisa May and Bronson Alcott, and Nathaniel Hawthorne, to live within walking distance of one another in Concord, Massachusetts? Why did an interest in individual liberty develop so strongly in *America,* and not in *Russia*? The "places" that provide settings for those outbursts of life-sustaining creativity we call "civilizations," obviously involve more than just geography.

In order to more deeply explore the dynamics involved in the development of this culture, I would like to focus on one of the major contributors to Western Civilization, one that had a profound impact on my own life. At some point in my youth, I became aware of the long-standing practice in such countries as Austria of many students graduating from college and then going on to law school. Following their legal studies, they would undertake careers that may or may not have involved the practice of law. During my college years, I became very interested in going on to law school,

---

5   Henry Hodges, *Technology in the Ancient World* (New York: Barnes & Noble Books, 1970), pp. 209–10.

although at no time—whether before, during, or after law school—did I have any intention of practicing law. I wasn't certain as to what kind of work I wanted to do, but law practice was not one to which I gave serious attention: law school, for me, was to provide the opportunity to synthesize disparate subject areas of learning—what used to be termed a "liberal arts" education—and to develop critical, analytical thinking. This approach was well-expressed by one nineteenth-century writer who observed that the study of law was "a sort of search for truth, carried on by teacher and student in common, and which they feverishly undertook, opening up an endless field for philosophic speculation."[6]

While I was aware of this fairly common practice in Austria, I was only later able to put names and faces to those who had actually done so. Various musical composers, painters, poets, philosophers, inventors, writers, journalists, found the study of law an integral part of their intellectual development. These major contributors to the life of Western Civilization included such Austrian students of the law as two of the fathers of sociology, Max Weber and Ludwig Gumplowicz; major figures of the "Austrian School" of economics, Carl Menger, Eugen von Bohm-Bawerk, Ludwig von Mises, and Nobel laureate Friedrich Hayek, as well as the economists Friedrich von Wieser and Leopold Kohr (who authored the phrase "small is beautiful"); philosophers Anton Menger, Otto Bauer, Max Adler, Fritz Mauthner, Adolf Stohr, Gottfried Leibniz, and Gustav Bergmann; lawyers and philosophers Erik von Kuehnelt-Leddihn, and Hans Kelsen; the inventor Wolfgang von Klempelen; journalist Karl Kraus; artist and psychologist Anton Ehrenzweig; art historian Alois Riegl; the poet Hugo von Hofmannsthal; music composer Emil von Reznicek; and students of music, Guido Adler and Eduard Hanslick. The world-renowned symphonic conductor, Fritz Reiner, provided another example. Throughout my years of law school teaching, I have often wondered why men and women with backgrounds in music tended to do so well. Perhaps in the interconnectedness of Austrian culture can be found insights lost in modern student concerns over grade-point averages and bar exams! Nor can I overlook the major contributions made to civilization by such erstwhile students of the law as the literary giants Kakfa and Goethe.

The study of law is but one example of the creative nature of the metamorphic powers of an integrative culture. Those who pursued other

---

6   Paul Bonnefon, *Oeuvres Completes d'Etienne de la Boetie* (Bourdeaux: C. Gounouilhou, and Paris: J. Rouam et Cie., 1892), p. xlvi.

inter-disciplinary studies illustrate a similar influence. Such dynamics—rather than the modern reductionist emphasis on specialization—helps us understand why Austria became a focal point for the creativity that found expression in such music composers as Haydn, Schubert, Mozart, the two Johann Strausses, Schonberg, Beethoven, and Mahler; such scientific minds as Gregor Mendel, Freud, Alfred Adler, Konrad Lorenz, Ernst Brucke, Theodor Meynert, Erwin Schrodinger, Ludwig Boltzmann, Arthur Schnitzler, Ernst Mach, Fritjof Capra, and Paul Feyerabend; the novelist and first woman to win the Nobel Peace Prize, Bertha von Suttner; the writer and inventor Josef Popper-Lynkeus; as well as such prolific thinkers as Edmund Husserl, Viktor Frankl, Joseph Schumpeter, Karl Popper, Arthur Koestler, Franz Brentano, Bernard Bolzano, Eric Voegelin, and Ludwig Wittgenstein; and actress and inventor Hedy Lamarr. While not all of these persons were students of multiple subject areas, the more holistic, integrated Austrian culture in which they and other individuals worked doubtless produced an environment that added to their creativity.

The processes that allow the genius and creative energies of individuals to merge into a prolific civilization, include such powerful domains as *frontiers*. The course of American history has led many of us to think of a frontier in *geographic* terms, as an unknown and uncertain territory existing beyond the known and established. Frederick Jackson Turner has written of the pivotal role played by a politically unstructured environment in which people were free to explore and innovate and, as a consequence, generate a free and productive society.[7] States whose political systems were too restrictive and structured found themselves in competition with an ever-expanding "west," to which creative persons were attracted. The presence of reasonably accessible and less-regulated environments also served to temper state efforts for control.

Of greater significance than geographically defined frontiers are the psychological and intellectual dimensions—the "state of mind"—of people who either *accept* or *disregard* the restraints placed upon their behavior by external authorities. As Alfred North Whitehead expressed it, "the vivid people keep moving on, geographically and otherwise, for men can be provincial in time, as well as in place."[8] There is a vibrancy in the life process

---

7   Frederick Jackson Turner, *The Frontier In American History* (New York: Henry Holt and Company, 1920).

8   Lucien Price, *The Dialogues of Alfred North Whitehead* (Boston: Little, Brown and Company, 1954), p. 50.

that manifests itself along the boundary lines that separate the known from the unknown; the stable from the changeable; the familiar from the novel. In the interplay between the *conscious* and *unconscious* minds—often experienced when the brain is in an alpha state—we can experience this dynamic of creativity.

One can see this same creativity where the boundaries of various intellectual disciplines meet. The study of "history," "economics," "law," "physics," etc., takes place within realms whose inviolabilities are often fiercely guarded by certified professors within each field. Not unlike the nature of political "peace" talks, so-called "inter-disciplinary" conferences frequently encounter resistance from participants dedicated to the defense of their respective "turfs." The historian who invades the territory of the physicists, or the economist who incorporates legal doctrine into his presentation— and, I must add, vice-versa—risks attack from the home-guard.

But it is precisely where such boundary lines meet that much creativity occurs. Looking across the boundary line into the neighbor's space can reveal a frontier to be explored. One might discover qualities on the other side that can be synthesized with their own discipline to create an expanded understanding of the world. Cross-disciplinary similarities might also be found, helping to confirm one's prior thinking. As one noted historian has observed, nineteenth century medical practice in Austria was premised on allowing natural processes of healing to take precedence over interventionist procedures. This attitude also prevailed among many Austrians regarding politics, as well as in the Austrian economics—pioneered by Carl Menger and Ludwig von Mises—that eschewed government interference with the marketplace.[9] Did earlier principles from the realm of *medicine* influence *economic* thought, or might this common principle have a deeper basis of understanding that surfaced within each of these fields?

All creative actions confront the energies that seek to stabilize existing systems, practices, and thought. Elsewhere, I use the metaphor of the "cutting-and-filling" functions of rivers to illustrate the constant interplay between forces of *stability* and *change* that pervade nature.[10] On the *cutting* side—where its energy is greater—the river eats into the surrounding bank, bringing earth, plants, and other debris into the stream. On the

---

9   William M. Johnston, *The Austrian Mind: An Intellectual and Social History, 1848–1938* (Berkeley: University of California Press, 1972), pp. 228–29.

10   Butler Shaffer, *Boundaries of Order: Private Property as a Social System* (Auburn, Ala.: Ludwig von Mises Institute, 2009), pp. 307–09.

weaker *filling* side, dirt and silt collect, and it is here where new plant life forms. In this interaction is found the synthesis between the forces of destruction and consolidation that is the essence of creativity.

We are beginning to develop a better understanding of how the turbulence of chaotic systems produces order in the world. From this enhanced awareness comes a growing appreciation for the individualized and spontaneous nature of the creative process. Privately owned property; personal liberty; respect for contracts—which, in turn, is dependent upon longer-term time preferences; and the decentralization of decision-making, provide the necessary social environment for such inventiveness. The creative energies that gave birth to Western Civilization arose from within individuals who were able to transcend the lines that constrain our understanding and practices to within established boundaries. As has always been the case, within free and independent minds are to be found the frontiers for the creation of new ideas and forms to help us live humanely.

We have seen how civilizations are *created* by individuals. In the following pages, we shall discover how they are *destroyed* by collectives[11] which are good for little more than the destruction of what others have created. We see this in the sharp contrasts between *market* economies and *state socialism*; between the Industrial Revolution and the Soviet Union. In many ways does history remind us of the continuing struggles between the creative energies unleashed by liberty, and the repressive forces of politics. The members of collectives are too dominated by "dark side" forces of mob psychology to ever undertake the prolonged and highly-focused inquiries necessary to the creation of anything fundamentally original. Collectives provide mirror images of minds in the default mode, capable of only reflecting the shared ignorance and prejudices upon which the institutionalized control of humans depends. Because we are unable to identify the names of distant ancestors who produced so much of what we modernly embrace as our common understanding, we are inclined to imagine a collective genesis for the insights of ancient individuals. We gaze, in awe, upon 32,000-year-old handprints found in ancient caves in Spain and France, forgetting that these represented the efforts of *individuals* to communicate something of themselves to others. Even folk-music and ballads were

---

11   I am using this word as it relates to the socio-political concept of "collectivism," namely "a doctrine or system that makes the group or the state responsible for the social and economic welfare of its members." (*Webster's Third New International Dictionary of the English Language, Unabridged* (Springfield, Mass.: G&C Merriam Company, 1971), p. 445.

the creation of unknown individuals rather than collective groups. In the words of H.L. Mencken, there is the "sheer impossibility to imagine them being composed by a gang of oafs whooping and galloping around a May pole."[12]

Returning to the Austrian microcosm that reflects the fate of Western Civilization generally, when collectivism—in the form of German National Socialism—infected that country, many of its more creative individuals fled to such less-repressive frontiers as America, Switzerland, and England. Gresham's law finds expression beyond the more familiar confines of government monetary practices. Arnold Schonberg, Franz Werfel, Sigmund Freud, Erwin Schrodinger, Leopold Kohr, the brothers Ludwig and Richard von Mises, Kurt Godel, Karl Popper, Otto Loewi, Olga Hahn-Neurath and her husband Otto Neurath, Anton Ehrenzweig, Lise Meitner, Rudolf Carnap, novelist Stefan Zweig, Rose Rand, Walter Mischel, Edgar Zilsel, Philip Frank, Nobel laureates (in physics) Viktor Francis Hess, Wolfgang Pauli, and (in chemistry) Walter Kohn; painters Herbert Bayer and Georg Mayer-Marton; noted lawyer Hans Kelsen, Fritz Lang, Josef Frank, Gustav Bergmann, Robert Stolz, and Billy Wilder, were among the better known to depart Austria. They joined with such refugees from other European countries as the writers Vladimir Nabokov, James Joyce, and Nobel laureate Thomas Mann; painters Marc Chagall, Max Ernst, and Piet Mondrian; conductor Georg Solti, composer Darius Milhaud, anthropologist Claude Levi-Strauss, film-stars Marlene Dietrich and Conrad Veidt; along with Nobel laureates Max Born and Albert Einstein (physics), Fritz Haber (chemistry), and Bernard Katz and Hans Krebs (medicine). In such highly personal ways have civilizations continued the dance between the life-enhancing creativity of individuals, and the collective forces of death and destruction.

Mindful of the historic interplay of forces at work in the creation and death of civilizations, I am of the opinion that Western Civilization—with particular attention directed to its American franchise—has about run its course. While this book focuses on such a prognosis, I also address the question: what is likely to follow from this imminent "decline and fall?" Might the remnants of our terminal culture—like an estate bequeathed us by a rich benefactor—provide the foundations for a fundamentally transformed culture; one that does not cannibalize itself?

---

12   H.L. Mencken, *A Mencken Chrestomathy* (New York: Alfred A. Knopf, 1967), p. 472.

Previous civilizations continue to exert their influences, long after their death-certificates have been signed by historians. Philosophy students still begin their studies by reading the ancient Greeks; Roman law and engineering retain their influences into the twenty-first century; Western Civilization, itself, also finds its foundations greatly influenced by the Saracens, whose contributions to mathematics, science, and the replacement of Roman with Arabic numerals, helped lay the foundations for the Renaissance. The evolution of human language, biology, and culture, has arisen through millennia of interconnected, cross-fertilizing relationships. The influences of our ancient, primitive ancestors—who learned how to organize with fellow tribesmen either to hunt for food, or to destroy their neighbors—continue to direct our thought and behavior. Our lineage is traceable both to Attila the Hun and Homer; to Machiavelli as well as Shakespeare; while the contrasting images of Ozymandias and Botticelli's "Venus" speak to passionate emotions.

Western culture has produced material and spiritual values that have done so much to humanize and civilize mankind. It has also produced highly-structured institutions and practices that not only impede, but reverse these life-enhancing qualities. Is it possible for us to energize our intelligence in order to rediscover, in the debris of our dying civilization, the requisite components for a fundamentally transformed culture grounded in free, peaceful, and productive systems that *sustain* rather than *diminish* life?

CHAPTER 1

On the Decline and Fall

As events inform us, it is not a pleasant experience to witness the decline and fall of a once vibrant civilization. There is a sadness in any deathwatch, particularly when one's vigil is interrupted by memories of a once robust parent, aunt, or uncle—with whom one learned and enjoyed so much of life—now in a weakened and terminal state. Whether we are considering a relative or the society in which one lives, there is no joy to be found in the final days of either. In either instance, one realizes that his or her life experiences, if not sense of being itself, are connected with others. As with any relationship, each of us helps to fashion the other, such that the sadness and joys of one sadden and delight the other.

The society in which I was born, raised, and work, and into which my wife and I brought our children, is now in a state of rapid decline. But as most of us are wont to do when informed of the impending death of a loved one, we desperately reach out for a remedy that we hope will reverse the fatal condition. Surely there is some new "leader" or political/religious ideology that can reinspire us, or some as yet undiscovered legislative nostrum which, if unable to reverse our apparent fate, may at least disguise the symptoms for a period of time.

Because civilizations transcend individual lives, we are unaccustomed to thinking that the society in which we live could ever have an end point or, if it did, that we might find ourselves in its final days. I strongly suspect that those who lived in the civilizations that preceded our own, were thoroughly convinced that their social structures, practices, and culture would endure forever. But history teaches us otherwise. Just as small children must eventually confront the mortality of their parents—and, in the process, theirs as well—there is nothing remarkable in the pattern of civilizations, like human beings, being born, growing into adulthood, and eventually dying.

What defines a great civilization, and what conditions are necessary to its existence? Is it wondrous buildings and monuments to its political leaders, or a succession of military conquests and elaborate systems of social control? These are the features that government schools have trained us to consider, characteristics that define the aspirations of political institutions.

To my mind, such a view is far too *noun*-oriented, conceiving of greatness more in terms of the *things produced,* rather than the *verb*-oriented *processes* by which such civilizations function. Has Western Civilization been great because of the *works* of such people as Shakespeare, Michelangelo, Beethoven, and Einstein, as well as the life-enhancing products of industrialization, or because of the existence of *conditions* in which such creativity could take place?

Because the principle of *entropy* maintains its constant influence in the world, all living systems must generate new energy (or "negative entropy") if they are to resist—at least temporarily—their collapse into their ultimate fate. We eat, in other words, *not* because someone has prepared an attractive meal for us, but because our continuing failure to do so will soon bring about our death.

The health of any system—be it an individual or a society—depends upon the production of those values necessary for that system's survival. The production and distribution of goods and services, technology, the sciences, medicine, the arts, and agriculture, are just a few of the more prominent examples of the values upon which Western societies have depended.

If we misfocus our attention, we may erroneously conclude that our material well-being is dependent upon the creation of the "things" that we consume in our efforts to sustain ourselves. In so doing, we tend to ignore the underlying conditions that make the production of such values possible. The Industrial Revolution was a humanizing epoch because it taught us how to produce the material wealth that can sustain the lives of millions of people. It would take a misanthropic disposition to deny the benefits to mankind arising from this period. But when our mind connects up the *benefits* with the *organizational systems* that created them, we are inclined to regard them as inseparable. We come to value, and depend upon, the goose that lays the golden egg, rather than upon the *processes* by which creative individuals might produce more geese, or more efficient means of generating gold.

Western Civilization is in the crisis it is *because* we have sacrificed more profound values than the immediate and quantifiable consequences we tend to associate with the pursuit of our material interests. Among these are peace; liberty; respect for property, contracts, and the inviolability of the individual; truthfulness and the development of the mind; integrity; distrust of power; a sense of spirituality; and philosophically-principled behavior. But when our culture becomes driven by material concerns, these less tangible values recede in importance, and our thinking becomes dominated by the need to preserve the organizational forms that we see as having served our interests.

In such ways do we create *institutions*. In order to clearly distinguish one form of organization from another, I define an "institution" as "any permanent social organization with purposes of its own, having formalized and structured machinery for pursuing those purposes, and making and enforcing rules of conduct in order to control those within it." In short, an "institution" is a system that has become its own reason for being—rather than just a means for producing life-sustaining values—with people becoming fungible resources to be exploited for the accomplishment of collective ends.

The very existence of institutions depends upon people developing a collective identity for themselves, a topic I explored in depth in *Calculated Chaos*. We learn to associate our very being with the herd(s) of which we are part and to which we consider ourselves subservient. While organized behavior is both natural and beneficial to us as social beings, institutions invert the role of social systems: organizations that began as tools of cooperation to foster the mutual interests of individuals, get twisted into systems that become their own reasons for being (i.e., institutions).

Having accepted the primacy of such agencies over our lives, most of us express nary a doubt about the necessity of taxpayers coming to the rescue of such systems when they face difficulties. When banks faced substantial losses as a result of New York City's financial crisis in the 1970s, only a handful of people found any flaw in having the taxpayers bail them out. So, too, with major corporations, or professional baseball and football franchises calling upon the taxpayers to underwrite their expenses. The government schools have also relied upon our worship of institutions to get taxpayers to continually fund a system that should have been allowed to die its entropic death decades ago. In the aftermath of the September 11, 2001 attacks at the World Trade Center (WTC), airlines, insurance companies, and various other institutions managed to get whisked through Congress, legislation to force the taxpayers to recompense them for *their* losses. Even commercial advertising can dredge up no more meaningful response to these events than for us to equate spending our money—with such advertisers, of course—as acts of patriotism! More recently, the major recession of the Bush/Obama years led the federal government to provide major corporate interests with billions of dollars of loans and bailouts on what so clearly expressed the institutionalist premise: "too big to fail."

"But what is wrong with coming to the rescue of these institutions?," it may be asked. "Think of all the money that has been invested, and all the men and women who are employed by such firms." The same argument might well have been made, a century ago, when the buggy whip and carriage manufacturers, horse ranchers, and hay farmers, were faced with bankruptcy as a consequence of the automobile. Or what of the motion picture industry, which has regularly sent lobbyists to Washington to fight the "threat" of television, then cable television, and then VCR's—all of which ended up being *boons* to Hollywood: should they have, as they continue to demand, government support for their enterprises?

The problem with all of this, as historians advise us, is that the *institutionalization* of the systems that produce the values upon which a civilization depends, ultimately bring about the *destruction* of that civilization. Arnold Toynbee observed that a civilization begins to break down when there is "a loss of creative power in the souls of creative individuals," and, in time, the "differentiation and diversity" that characterized a *dynamic* civilization, is replaced by "a tendency towards standardization and uniformity." The emergence of a "universal state," and increased militarism, represent later stages in the disintegration of a civilization.[1]

Will and Ariel Durant reached similar conclusions, observing that the health of a civilization depends upon "individuals with clarity of mind and energy of will . . . capable of effective responses to new situations."[2] Carroll

---

1   Arnold J. Toynbee, *A Study of History* (New York: Oxford University Press, 1958), pp. 244–45, 364, 552, 555.

2   Will and Ariel Durant, *The Lessons of History* (New York: Simon & Schuster, 1968), p. 91.

Quigley demonstrated how the maintenance of static, equilibrium conditions can lead to the collapse of civilizations, a process he directly relates to the institutionalization of what he calls the "instruments of expansion."[3]

A creative civilization, in other words, is dynamic, not stable; adaptive to change, not seeking equilibrium. It is characterized not by those who seek to preserve what they have, but by those who seek to produce what their minds tell them they *can* have. Individual liberty abounds in such a society, as men and women advance new ideas, new technologies, and new practices.

The explanation for the interrelatedness of institutionalism and the collapse of civilizations is not difficult. Because of their size and bureaucratic sluggishness, institutions tend to become less adaptable to the constancies of change inherent in all living systems. Life is a continuing process of making adjustments and creative responses in a world of complicated inexactitude. But institutions insist not only upon their illusions of predictability, but their systems of control by which they imagine they can direct the world to their ends. This is why institutions have always aligned themselves with the forces of *power*, in order to compel the rest of nature—particularly mankind—to conform to their interests.

But power wars against life, for power seeks to force life to become what it does not choose to be. Because "life" expresses itself as autonomous and spontaneous activity, it is inextricably dependent upon the *liberty* of individuals. Liberty is not simply a proposition designed to placate intellectuals who want to protect the expression of their opinions. It is, rather, the condition in which individuals—and the societies in which they live— can remain resilient, adaptive to changing conditions, and thus maintain the creative impulses necessary for their vibrancy.

The *individual*, with his or her uniqueness and self-directed nature, is the expression of life on this planet. As such, a condition of liberty tends to generate variation and non-uniformity, with social order arising as the unintended consequence of individuals pursuing their varied self-interests. Manners, customs, the dynamics of the marketplace, cooperation, negotiation, and other social pressures, help to regularize human behavior while keeping it flexible. The antisocial conduct of the few is met with ostracism, boycotts, and other refusals to deal.

3　Carroll Quigley, *The Evolution of Civilizations* (Indianapolis, Ind.: Liberty Press, 1979), pp. 101 ff.

But most institutions tend to be uncomfortable with liberty, for the processes of change that are implicit therein run counter to their purposes of a structured permanency. Because of their size and scope of operation, institutions deal with people on a *mass*, rather than *individualized*, basis. As our world becomes more institutionalized, standardization and uniformity become more dominant values. The informal systems and practices that connect people to one another get replaced by coercive rules, hierarchically-structured organizations, violence and the threats of violence, SWAT teams, torture, enhanced punishments, and longer prison sentences for an ever-widening group of offenses. As such coercive practices proliferate, there is a continual weakening of the informal social mechanisms and, like muscles that fall into disuse after a serious illness or injury, begin to atrophy. Manners and social habits soon give way to speech codes, "hate" crimes, and other forms of institutionally-mandated standards of conduct. When a civilization reaches the point at which only coercive force is capable of holding it together, it is finished as a viable system.

Civilizations die out for the same reason organisms do: their failure to maintain a sufficient resiliency that will permit them to overcome entropy. As the Durants put it, they then "linger on as stagnant pools left by once life-giving streams."[4] Still, there is no historical determinism at work that would make the collapse of Western Civilization inevitable. The health of any system depends on its being sufficiently resilient to allow it to adapt to the constancy of change that is inherent in all of life. A vibrant system—whether an individual, a business firm, or a civilization—will incorporate the need for self-corrective behavior into its methods. Such thinking is contrasted with what preceded the construction of highly-structured open-hearth steel mills or automobile assembly lines in those American cities that are now referred to as the "rust belt." When the need for adaptability is ignored or resisted, stagnation is a likely consequence.

In any society, there has always been an underlying current of energy through which the life processes seek expression. Political systems, grounded in coercion and violence, have always represented a continuing war against such life processes. But it is institutionalism—the belief that established organizations are ends in themselves whose interests must be preserved and protected—that makes political systems so dangerous and destructive to the liberty upon which life forces depend. Just as water can

---

4   Durant, *The Lessons of History*, p. 91.

be dammed up for only so long until it either bursts through or circumvents the structure kept in its way, life energies will continue to seek their expression. To the extent a civilization welcomes such expression, it will prosper and extend its beneficent influences to the rest of mankind. Indeed, in recent decades, Western society has been exhibiting a sufficient resiliency to overcome many of the institutionalizing tendencies of a pyramidally-structured world. Organizations have been moving from systems of *centralized*, vertical authority, to *decentralized* horizontal networks. The *pyramid* has been collapsing in favor of what I call a *holographic* organizational model, wherein authority is distributed throughout the system rather than concentrated at the top.

Well-managed business firms now recognize the greater productivity and profitability of having increased decision-making decentralized into the hands of employees. Alternative health care, educational, religious, and dispute resolution systems have been challenging the Kafkaesque bureaucratic structures of the institutional order. The recent proliferation of private schools and homeschooling reflect such transformations. The Internet, and other computerized technologies, have decentralized the flow of information, as well as banking, consumer-driven retailing, and other business practices.

These decentralizing changes have been occurring in the political realm as well, with the collapse of the Soviet Union providing the most vivid example. The monolithic USSR splintered into *fifteen* independent countries, while the erstwhile Yugoslavia fractured into *five* separate countries. Elsewhere, *fourteen* additional subdivisions have been created, producing a total of *thirty-four* new countries since 1990 alone, and with more apparently on the way.[5] Secession movements are challenging centralized political authority in cities, states, and countries throughout the world. The previous solidity of a mass-minded culture—exemplified in the phrase *e pluribus unum*—has centrifuged into numerous hyphenated identities based upon race, gender, religion, nationality, or lifestyles of various groups.

While these changes were taking place long before the terrorist attacks of September 11, 2011, the events of that day portend a much deeper psychic meaning than most of us have begun to realize. As brutal and horrific as these atrocities were, the shock they brought on goes far beyond the numbers of casualties. Nor does the trauma lie in the fact that America, it-

---

5.   See "New Countries of the World," http://gheography.about.com/cs/countries/a/newcountries.htm

self, had been attacked by terrorists: the bombing of the World Trade Center in 1993, the downing of Pan Am Flight 103, and the suicide attack on the U.S.S. Cole, preceded September 11th.

It is in the *symbolism* of the World Trade Center's demolition that the deeper psychological meaning is to be found. On one level, of course, the WTC symbolized private capitalism, whose virtues and efficiencies had so recently won out over socialism and other forms of state planning as the system best able to maximize the material well-being of humanity. This may have been a contributing consideration, on the part of the terrorists, in its being selected as the principal target.

But the central factor in these buildings being selected as targets was their being symbols of the American government practices through which wars and other military operations have been conducted throughout the Middle East. It was not *laissez-faire* capitalism or other expressions of liberty that were attacked that day, but corporate-statism, through which major business interests control the destructive machinery of the state to achieve ends they are unable to obtain in free markets.

The World Trade Center symbolized something more, something that I suspect its brutish attackers would never have sensed, but which, I believe, underlies the deeper shock all of us are experiencing. Almost like a pair of Jungian archetypes, the WTC buildings stood, at the base of Wall Street, as towering symbols of a *vertically* structured, institutionalized world. Such symbols were utterly destroyed by a handful of box-cutter-armed terrorists, who symbolized to the world that war, itself, had become decentralized. For Americans who still think of "defense" in terms of nuclear missiles; fleets of battleships, aircraft carriers, and atomic submarines; and tens of thousands of hierarchically disciplined soldiers, the confluence of these symbolic forces has generated much turbulence within our minds.

The present "war against terrorism" goes much deeper than simply trying to eradicate cadres of maniacal butchers—as desirable as such ends would be *if* capable of being realized through warfare. The decentralizing influences that have been at work throughout our world for a number of years—and whose processes are becoming better understood through the study of chaos and complexity, marketplace economics, biological systems, psychology, and systems analysis—are proving to be incompatible with the hierarchically-structured forms through which institutions have come to dominate Western Civilization. Institutions tend to lack resiliency. They are generally less interested in adapting their systems and methodologies to a changing environment, than in forcing the environment—including people—to adapt their behavior to conform to institutional interests.

It is just such attitudes, as we have seen, that have brought down prior civilizations. Considered from a broader historical perspective, it becomes evident that *terrorists* have not been the *cause* of the decline of Western Civilization any more than were the invading barbarians the cause of the fall of the Western Roman Empire. Each such group was but a *symptom*, among many, of the *vulnerability* of a civilization that had become weakened by its own contradictions and lack of responsiveness to the conditions upon which life depends.

Understood in its broader context, this war could more properly be defined as a War for the Preservation of Institutional Hierarchies, a war against the processes of change that are working against vertically-structured, command-and-control social systems. That this has been declared to be a "permanent" war against humanity in general (i.e., "if you're not with us, you're against us") should awaken us to its broader implications. It is ironic—but understandable—that, at a time when the world is becoming more *decentralized*, institutional interests are hard at work to expand upon their mechanisms of *centralized* control. Whether flying the banner of the "New World Order," or NATO, or the United Nations, or the European Community, or the World Trade Organization, the institutional order continues to insist upon its command-and-control mechanisms.

As this war continues, those of us who persist in conducting our lives outside institutional walls, or who continue to use the Internet as though it were a tool by which free minds communicate with one another, or who insist upon the privacy of our lives and business transactions, will discover ourselves thrown into the new suspect class of "terrorists." As the state increases its demands for national identity cards, secret trials conducted by the military (rather than by untrustworthy juries), the use of torture against suspects, the assassination of Americans, greater surveillance of our lives—including having police enter our homes without our knowledge or consent—and military patrolling of American streets, we should become aware of the truth of Pogo Possum's observation: "we have met the enemy and he is us."[6]

Though our civilization finds itself in a state of turbulence, it is not fated to collapse. While the institutional order lacks resiliency, there is a

---

6   Walt Kelly, *The Pogo Papers* (New York: Simon and Schuster, 1953).

life force within nature that insists upon adaptability. In a material sense, this life force may find expression as DNA, which all living things have in common. Biological evolution fosters the variability that allows living systems to respond to changes in their environments. But such processes are at work beyond—albeit interconnected with—biology. In the dynamics of the *marketplace* we find the most vibrant expression of the creative, life-sustaining nature of resilient behavior. When institutional interests conspire against change, they have declared themselves to be in a state of war with life itself!

But you and I are part of this same life force, and our resiliency may be the means through which our civilization reenergizes itself and allows all of the institutional entropy to work its way out of a fundamentally new social system. Just as the creative energies of the Industrial Revolution replaced the rigidly structured and stultifying system of feudalism, our present civilization may—if you and I are up to the task—transform itself into an even more productive society.

But to do so, we must be prepared to move beyond the vertically-structured, institutionalized thinking in which we have been carefully conditioned. You and I can bring civilization back into order neither by *seizing* political power, nor by *attacking* it, but by *moving away* from it, by diverting our focus from marbled temples and legislative halls to the conduct of our daily lives. The "order" of a creative civilization will emerge in much the same way that order manifests itself throughout the rest of nature: *not* from those who fashion themselves *leaders* of others, but from the interconnectedness of individuals pursuing their respective self-interests.

In the institutional order's war to preserve itself against the life-sustaining processes of change, the most treasonable of propositions will be that which affirms that *life belongs to the living, not to institutional power structures!* We must learn to love our *children* more than we do the dehumanizing agencies of restraint and destruction that now threaten their futures with announced plans for an endless war against all. The time is now upon us, as individuals, to assert that life is going to prevail on this planet; that we shall reclaim our free and creative spirit and, in so doing, revitalize Western Civilization; and that those structured systems that insist upon exploiting and destroying life in the course of advancing their own interests must now stand aside. What if a fundamentally transformed civilization—one that expresses decentralized, autonomous, and peaceful behavior, while discarding its destructive, anti-life, institutional structures—is already unfolding before you? Would you be prepared for it?

CHAPTER 2

The Life and Death of Civilizations

I n my view, many Americans could qualify as collective recipients of a Darwin Award: the recognition given to those "who contribute to human evolution by self-selecting themselves out of the gene pool through putting themselves (unnecessarily) in life-threatening situations."[1] While the awards are given to those who perish through some "astonishing misapplications of judgment," it may be the American branch of Western Civilization that will cease to exist as a consequence of the combined judgments and practices of most of us.

Only the most vacuous minds—whose opinions are grounded in conventional delusions rather than empirical evidence and rational analysis—can fail to recognize that modern civilization, as we have known it, has reached a terminal state. No amount of public opinion polling can restore any former greatness. The only question is whether its remnants can be transmuted into fundamentally new forms and practices making for a more free and productive society, or whether it shall continue its downward spiral.

Western Civilization appears to be at a bifurcation point; one of those conditions that eventually confronts complex systems. The study of "complexity," or "chaos," informs us that a complex system can be thrown into

---

1   Wikipedia.org/wiki/Darwin_Awards

turbulent states to which it might respond either by actions (or inaction) that hasten its collapse into total entropy[2]; or by the development of practices that allow it to adapt to the complexities it encounters. Such processes are seen in the efforts of biological systems to sustain themselves; in the mind's debate between learning and ignorance; in the competitive success or failure of businesses; or in the life and death of entire civilizations.

Modern society is in a state of turbulence brought about, in large part, by political efforts to maintain static, equilibrium conditions; practices that interfere with the ceaseless processes of change that provide the fluctuating order upon which any creative system—such as the marketplace—depends. Institutions, being ends in themselves, have trained us to resist change and favor the status quo; to insist upon the certain and the concrete and to dismiss the uncertain and the fanciful; and to embrace security and fear risk. *Life*, on the other hand *is* change, *is* adaptation, creativity, and novelty. But creativity has always depended upon a fascination with the mysterious, and an appreciation for the kinds of questions that reveal more than answers can ever provide. When creative processes become subordinated to preserving established interests; when the glorification of systems takes priority over the sanctity of individual lives, societies begin to lose their life-sustaining vibrancy and may collapse.

It is the nature of complex systems to be subject to both unforeseen and unknowable influences and irregularities. As a consequence, the factors contributing to either the emergence or decline of civilizations are too incomprehensible to allow for precision in predicting or accounting for the occurrence of either. The history of civilizations has always involved a struggle between the forces of *life* and *death*. To continue as a vibrant system, a civilization must generate practices allowing for the production of the life-sustaining values that define itself. Our modern, industrialized civilization arose—and has managed to maintain itself—through practices conducive to the creation of new technologies, methods of production and distribution, and the free exchange of material and intellectual resources. By remaining resilient and adaptive to the inconstancies that define life, marketplace systems have placed human action in harmony with life itself.

But once social systems began producing vibrant, life-sustaining values, the forces of death began to ooze up from the depths of humanity's

---

2   Because of the second law of thermodynamics, every *closed* system moves from a state of *order* to *disorder*. Because living systems are *open*, they can temporarily resist entropy by ingesting negative entropy (i.e., external sources of energy).

"dark side." People who were incapable of creative acts themselves, or were envious of the successes and rewards enjoyed by others, resorted to violence to despoil others. From simple acts of piracy and pillaging, clever minds developed formal systems (i.e., governments) and intellectual rationales (i.e., political philosophies) that would *institutionalize* theft and the violent methods upon which thievery depends.

It should come as no great news to report that when "dark side" forces begin to prevail—whether within an individual or a society—life-promoting qualities and values go into a decline. When incentives for creativity subside in favor of schemes for plundering others—i.e., when wealth is increasingly transferred not by voluntary exchange, but by coercion—the civilization exhibiting such traits has begun its entropic decline. The benefits of innovation—particularly when financed with one's own resources—become less attractive than the rewards to be reaped from street-smart maneuverings for a government subsidy, legislative restraints on a competitor, or a multimillion dollar lawsuit engineered by shallow lawyers against corporate "deep-pockets." Whether such a course can be reversed depends upon whether the thinking of those who comprise that civilization can be transformed.

Western Civilization was spurred by an admittedly uneven embrace of life-enhancing values and practices. The Renaissance, in rediscovering classical Greece, helped shift the focus of thinking and behavior to human well-being. Renaissance historian Jacob Burckhardt chronicled the transformation in consciousness that took place in post-medieval years. From a period in which people thought of themselves in *collective* terms (e.g., "a race, people, party, family, or corporation—only through some general category"), there emerged the "man [who] became a spiritual *individual* and recognized himself as such."[3] The arts, scientific inquiries, the enlightenment—with its emphasis on individualism and reason—and the Industrial Revolution, were the more significant life-sustaining influences of modern civilization. To what extent has the modern emphasis on *group* identities and legal rights (e.g., race, gender, lifestyle, religion, etc.) impeded the creative processes that arise from individualism?

The creative richness of a civilization derives from the behavior of individuals, not from some imagined collective genius. The creative process depends upon men and women being free to experiment; to generate and

---

3   Jacob Burckhardt, *The Civilization of the Renaissance in Italy* (New York: The Modern Library, 1995; originally published 1878), p. 100.

pursue any of a variety of options; to be mistaken; and to offend the habits, tastes, sensibilities, or established interests of others. Individuals may combine their efforts with others but, as one experiences in brainstorming sessions, it is the interplay of individual insights and responses that gives birth to the new.

Individuals have produced the art, music, literature, philosophies, scientific discoveries, inventions, engineering and technological innovation, that underlie great civilizations. The statue of David was conceived and sculpted by Michelangelo, not by an artists' guild. The Mona Lisa derived from the genius of Leonardo da Vinci, not from some corporate "paint-by-the-numbers" kit.[4] The writings of Shakespeare and Milton were the products of individual minds, not a government-funded writers' workshop. It was Thomas Edison, not a local labor union, who worked in his simple workshop for long hours, often at subsistence levels, to invent many of the technological underpinnings of modern civilization.

We ought to have learned from basic biology that the individual is not only the carrier of DNA (hence, life itself) from one generation to the next, but also the carrier of the values upon which a civilization depends if it is to retain its vigor. A moment's reflection should suggest that there is more than an allegorical relationship here. But what are the conditions that are conducive to individual creativity and productiveness?

Our inquiry ought to begin with a clear assessment of the nature of life itself. We need to strip away a lot of foolish thinking and recognize that the pursuit of self-interest goes to the very essence of all living things. As such, we need to become aware that spontaneity and autonomy are vital to life processes. Coercion is thus anti-life, for it forces life to go in directions it doesn't want to go. Neither can the creative process be commanded or directed by others, but must arise within individuals who are disposed to inventiveness. I once visited a government school classroom and saw a primary grade teacher clap her hands and announce to her conscripts: "all right, it is time for self-directed learning!" The idea that one's creative motivation can be mandated by another is as absurd as ordering another to "be spontaneous!"

A civilization cannot remain creative unless its members are free to control their own energies and to convert some portion of the material

---

4   Some painters and sculptors occasionally worked with assistants on projects (e.g., Michelangelo and the Sistine Chapel fresco), but the process was under the control and direction of the individual artist.

world to their self-interested purposes. This fact of existence—which various ideologies have managed to distort but not refute—gives rise to a need for the private ownership of property. One would have thought that the utter failure of Marxist systems to provide for mankind's material well-being would have been sufficient to disabuse gullible souls of the fallacy—woven into the social fabric by socialist obscurants—that "human rights are more important than property rights." This notion continues to erode the conditions essential to the well-being of societies.

State regulatory systems are the most pervasive means by which coercion restrains the creative process. Government mandates and restraints are always directed against the property interests of persons. They function as imposed, nonproductive costs—a form of entropy—to the efforts of actors to pursue their interests. To the extent of their imposition, they provide disincentives to creativity.

A current example illustrates the point. The costs of state regulation have been a major factor in the decisions of many businesses to relocate some of their operations to foreign countries. It is illusory to believe that the self-interest pursuits of some people can be hindered by others without consequences. To the degree state policies increase the costs or reduce the benefits of a course of action desired by someone, the actor will try to circumvent such restraints in the least costly manner. In the same way, a dammed-up river may eventually burst the constraints humans have designed for it; but rather than condemn the river—or, as an exaggeration of our hubris, build a bigger dam!—we ought to make ourselves aware of the anti-life implications of interfering with irresistible flows of energy. Our failure to respect the autonomous processes by which life creates its well-being, will prove as destructive to our civilization as it was to those that preceded it.

Because life processes involve continuing transactions with nature—which, contrary to the biases of many, includes human beings—the viability of a civilization depends on its having a healthy working relationship with reality. It is no coincidence that the enlightenment and the scientific revolution were central influences in the emergence of Western Civilization. The "age of reason" helped us appreciate that, while "truth" had an ephemeral and amorphous quality to it, its pursuit was critical to the health of a society. From such a perspective, freedom of speech and religion can be seen not as sops conferred upon dissidents in order to confirm the liberal sentiments of the established order, but qualities upon which the vibrancy of a system depends. Freedom of inquiry and expression are not so much to be *tolerated* as to be actively *encouraged*.

But the relevance of truth to a civilization has a much broader reach than this. Our world is an interconnected labyrinth shrouded in causal uncertainties. But because we must act in the present in anticipation of desired consequences, we need all the truth we can get. Lies, deceptions, inaccuracies, and other errors, compound the difficulties associated with the pursuit of efficacious behavior in an inherently uncertain world. The well-being of both individuals and societies are restrained by incorrect information, a fact that can be quickly confirmed by any physician.

While the health of individuals and civilizations depends upon the value of truth, all political systems are firmly grounded in lies, illusions, and false promises. Almost all who support the state do so out of a conditioned belief that it will protect our lives and property; and yet it is the essence of the state to coerce with threats of punishment or death, and plunder through taxation, its alleged beneficiaries. Unlike a productive civilization, a healthy state cannot coexist with truthfulness.

A synonym for living in harmony with reality is "integrity." To live with integrity is to live the integrated life, without contradiction or conflict. Have we not seen enough of the pyramiding of lies, fabricated "evidence," meaningless distinctions, and other conscious acts of deception leading to the U.S. invasion of Iraq to cause any decent human to question the integrity of both the state and its leaders? There is a common phrase among the British that reflects such dishonesty: "do not accept something as true until it has been officially denied." How long would you have maintained a business partnership with a person who behaved in this manner? How profitable would your enterprise be if you had to spend half your time countering the influence of falsehoods generated from within your organization?

The death of civilizations is facilitated by a movement from individualized to collective patterns of thinking. It is mass-mindedness that produces the state's deadliest expressions: wars and genocides. The indiscriminate slaughter of people and the massive destruction of cities, factories, transportation systems, and other forms of material wealth are inconsistent with the creative processes of civilizations. To bring about our participation in such devastating activities requires the systematic conditioning of how we view ourselves.

When we move from a more personal sense of who we are to such collective identities as race, religion, nationality, ideology, gender, or other groupings, we have prepared our minds to be energized on behalf of institutionally-defined causes. The state has long been the primary conductor of such practices. As Carl Jung and others observed, our willingness to identify with groups of any sort, produces a herd-mentality that is easily mobilized on behalf of destructive, collective purposes. Evidence of such dynamics can be seen in the sudden emergence of American flags after 9/11, and the continued willingness of many Americans to support their government's enraged, high-handed reaction to this event by attacking and killing innocent Iraqis.

Still, I remain optimistic. I believe that the American civilization has about run its course, and is collapsing into a dehumanizing destructiveness. Nonetheless, I suspect that we may be able to extricate ourselves from our present turbulence by rediscovering the conditions that make for a free and productive world, and learning to walk away from those systems and practices that are destroying us. We may end up fundamentally *transforming* our world. To do so will require us to do more than tinker with the details of our well-organized madness.

The history of our language may provide us with insights for unraveling our confused and conflict-ridden minds. While reading an etymological dictionary a number of years ago, I discovered that the words "peace," "freedom," "love," and "friend" had common ancestries.[5] Perhaps our intuitive energies will permit us to rediscover the more harmonious vision of society held by our predecessors. Whether the forces of life can overcome our present lemming-like death march is the question now confronting the mind and soul of mankind.

A metaphor may prove useful in making my point. For decades, the federal government has poured tens of billions of dollars into the space program, in an effort to extend the militarization of mankind beyond Earth itself. More recently, private enterprises have arisen to conduct space exploration for productive, life-enhancing ends. One such entrepreneur is Burt Rutan who designed and produced the "Voyager," a plane that was the first to make a non-stop, non-refueling flight around the world. Later, Rutan successfully launched SpaceShipOne, the first non-governmental spacecraft to leave Earth's atmosphere.

---

5   Eric Partridge, *Origins: A Short Etymological Dictionary of Modern English* (New York: Greenwich House, 1983), p. 235.

These alternative approaches to space flight provide a fitting contrast between *institutionalized* and *individualized* ways of living. We are beginning to more fully understand the dysfunctional nature of larger systems, and to appreciate the advantages associated with relatively smaller organizations, a comparison I explored in my *In Restraint of Trade*[6] book, and taken up herein. This is not to suggest that increased organizational size will inevitably make a system less resilient to change and less creative. But larger organizations are subject to increased internal forces that encourage bureaucratization, ossification, and other moderating influences that make effective responses more difficult. A visual expression of this distinction was made after the landing of SpaceShipOne, as this tiny plane taxied past a number of huge, major airline jets that were quietly parked on adjoining aprons. What more poignant example of the *human*, rather than the *institutionalized*, scale of creative action; a contrast made even more apparent when, after his plane had landed, Rutan held up a large sign—produced by a friend of mine, Ernie Hancock—that read: "SpaceShipOne, Government Zero."

But the comparative analysis of organizational size did not end there. When SpaceshipOne completed its orbit around the earth, a more profound, spiritual meaning of the flight was expressed by its pilot, Mike Melvill who, while coming in for his landing, yelled out "hoo-ha!" This is the kind of response we were accustomed to making as children while experiencing the thrills of a roller-coaster ride, or speeding on a bicycle, or other acts that allowed us to exceed the ordinary. In our institutionalized world, however, we have learned to suppress our emotions; to not run on school playgrounds; and, if we want to continue working as NASA astronauts, not to express ourselves as Melvill did. This man's spirited outcry reflected the emergence of a space program mobilized by human *passion* rather than *robotic* conditioning.

The spiritual dimensions of travel into outer space have been expressed by some NASA astronauts. If spirituality is experienced as a personal sense of transcendence (e.g., of moving beyond the confines of one's present physical, emotional, or intellectual consciousness), wouldn't the act of leaving the earth—seeing the base from which one's life and understanding has literally been grounded—be expected to generate such sensations? Might

---

6   Butler Shaffer, *In Restraint of Trade: The Business Campaign Against Competition, 1918-1938* (Lewisburg, Penn.: Bucknell University Press, 1997, republished Auburn, Ala.: Ludwig von Mises Institute, 2008).

viewing the launch of these spacecraft provide us some two-dimensional vicarious sense that astronauts experience in three dimensions?

But it is not the purpose of NASA—or, for that matter, any other governmental programs—to promote the spiritual enrichment of people's lives. The dreary curricula of government schools demonstrates the state's hostility to such elevating purposes. Burt Rutan is not alone in grasping that space travel is too spiritually uplifting an experience to be monopolized by the bureaucratically-structured and dispirited nature of governmental agencies.

NASA's programs were never designed to provide ordinary men and women the opportunity of experiencing space flight; an individual who wanted to have such an experience had to pay the Russian government twenty million dollars to be taken to its space platform. By contrast, Rutan's company is working toward the creation of space flights for individuals who want to experience space and, he added, at prices that will eventually be within the reach of most of us.

Institutions dislike spontaneity, emotional responses, and other unpredictabilities whose energies cannot be made to serve organizational purposes. This is why institutions have a uniform dislike for individual liberty; why, in the course of some social or natural disturbance, we are admonished to "stay calm" and "not get emotional." Human actions that do not further institutional interests are a form of "entropy;" of energy unavailable for productive work.

As I watched—and delighted in—Mike Melvill's reaction to his SpaceshipOne trip, my mind recalled the earlier Challenger disaster. Immediately following the explosion, the institutional reporting of what had occurred failed to match the release of emotions with which the rest of us responded. In perfunctory style, the NASA spokesman continued to provide a linear reporting of telemetric readings and other data, telling us of down-range distances, velocity, and other facts that had just been proven irrelevant. He performed his job correctly, just as he had been trained and expected to do, without the expression of any emotion or break in the established mantra. Only later did he calmly report that there was "obviously a major malfunction."

The calmness with which the institutionalists spoke that day contrasted sharply with newscaster Herbert Morrison's live reporting of another spacecraft explosion: the 1937 fiery destruction of the Zeppelin "Hindenburg." The classic news footage of Morrison's reporting reveals the depth of his emotions over the catastrophe: "oh, my," and "oh, the humanity" are intermixed with his tears, leading him to finally tell us "I can't talk." For his emotional involvement in the event, Morrison was fired from his job! Even in 1937, the institutional order could not abide the passions of individuals.

How much of such attitudes carry over into our daily work, whatever that may be? We have conditioned ourselves to regard material costs and rewards as the paramount standard by which to judge the propriety of our actions. Spiritual and emotional expressions—the unconscious inner voices we have learned to ignore and suppress—will be tolerated as long as they do not interfere with our commitments to institutional purposes. But what is the quality of a job that trains us to give mechanistic reports on the behavior of machines, even as human beings are being killed in the malfunctioning of the machines? Is life enhanced or diminished by the kind of work that deadens or eradicates the inner sense of humanity from its performance, and why ought we to care?

Such questions carry us far beyond the excitements of space travel, but bring us back to what most of us have come to regard as the default position of our "humdrum" lives. Can we become as determined to walk away from our conditioning as organizational servo-mechanisms as the institutional order was in so training us? Can we find a kind of work, or play, or learn how to raise our children, or plant a garden, or engage in any other activity, that will provide us the spontaneous outburst that Mike Melvill expressed that day? Can we rediscover that "recreation" is far more meaningful than simply joining the company's bowling team; that it means to "re-create"—not just expend—our energy; to reenergize our creative ways? Can we come to think of "success" in our work as more than just an increase in salary or net receipts over expenses, or the accumulation of billable hours, but of the enjoyment of the work as an end in itself? Can we re-learn what we knew as children but have been trained to forget, namely, that whatever we do should energize the human spirit; that the meaning of life is to be found in the "hoo-ha!"?

Burt Rutan will not transform Western Civilization, anymore than Michelangelo created the Renaissance. Each is only representative of a vision of mankind's capacity for a greatness that has always lain light-years beyond the grasp of kings and emperors. But whether the exploration of space will continue to be dominated by the militaristic and political control premises that underlie NASA, or the humanity-serving purposes of Rutan's undertaking, will be one of many indicators of the broader direction our society will take. This is just one area of human activity in which each of us will—whether by conscious act or by default—channel our energies and other resources into systems of *death* or of *life*. The best of what it means to be human is not to be found in improving the systems of death, destruction, coercion, torture, and control that define political behavior. It is only when we are free to explore, question, innovate, and cooperate with one another that we can experience the fullest sense of what it means to live as human beings.

That the state must employ violence to achieve its ends is, perhaps, the best evidence for the presence of a life force that insists upon its expression in the world regardless of the barriers placed in its path. The individuals and societies who are able to transcend barriers will be the ones who will survive and prosper. Whether Americans will continue to insist upon our civilization's freefall into history's black hole, or whether we shall transform our practices into life-sustaining systems, is a question that only you and I can answer. But as I said, I remain optimistic. I am betting my life on the Burt Rutans, the Mike Melvills, and our inner sense of "hoo-ha!"

CHAPTER **3**

Consuming Our Capital

It must be admitted that there is a degree of instability which is inconsistent with civilization. But, on the whole, the great ages have been unstable ones.

—Alfred North Whitehead

A sure-fire sign of a business enterprise in decline is when it begins using its invested capital to pay operating expenses. Such signs of ill-health are not confined to the world of commerce and industry, but can exhibit themselves in the life of any system. We are witnessing the practice in the collapse of Western Civilization, as we scurry to meet short-term demands by sacrificing the foundations upon which our culture has long been grounded.

Neither the Industrial Revolution nor the emergence of the factory system were sufficient to account for the greatness of Western culture. There were numerous practices, attitudes, ideas, and other factors that provided the necessary conditions for this culture to flourish. It has been the preoccupation with the material benefits of our civilization—accompanied by an increasing belief in the irrelevance of its intangible foundations—that has contributed so much to the collapse of Western society. Because of the centrality of institutionalism in our lives, it can safely be said of our culture that whatever is *non*material has become *im*material. Whatever does not contribute to institutional purposes in our modern world is regarded, at best, as a harmless diversion or, at worst, an interference to be enjoined. But the cost of maintaining institutional primacy often becomes a weakening—or even destruction—of the conditions that allowed creative energies to produce the civilization.

Western culture is not to be praised only because it allowed creative geniuses to produce what they have, but because it has allowed all of us to live better lives than would otherwise have been available to us. Even the poorest among us enjoy technologies beyond the powers of monarchs of old to command: central heating and air conditioning, electric light and appliances, automobiles, telephones, television and computers, to name just a few of the more familiar examples. Contrary to the lingering complaints and economic ignorance of socialists, mankind has learned how to produce and distribute wealth without having recourse to looting and other forms of violence. While many continue to employ political coercion as a means of disrupting the peaceful and voluntary systems that have done so much to benefit and humanize mankind, the knowledge for how life-enhancing ends are accomplished remain available to all thoughtful minds.

What are the intangible qualities upon which a prolific society is based? As suggested earlier, they seem to include the importance of conditions such as individual liberty, the inviolability of private property, and respect for contractual obligations: factors that must exist if self-interest-driven pursuits are to be energized. While no civilization has yet to embrace these values with consistency—the powerful sentiments of the Declaration of Independence, for instance, did not extend to slaves or American Indians—the creative well-being of any society can be measured by the degree of their influence. The collapse of the Soviet Union was occasioned by its continuing war against the self-directed nature of life.

While the works of creative individuals make up so much of the substance of our culture, their efforts depended upon conditions that encouraged—or at least did not discourage—their efforts. The marketplace system of voluntary transactions facilitated exchanges that allowed people to benefit exponentially from one another's efforts. To the degree respect for the principles of property ownership prevailed, men and women enjoyed the means for acting freely within the world. The importance of liberty and the distrust of power led to efforts (e.g., constitutionalism) it was thought could restrain political systems. A focused interplay of the intellectual and spiritual dimensions of our minds provided a base from which to analyze and evaluate human action.

It has been this underlying social environment, wherein the self-interest motivations of individuals are able to express their autonomous and spontaneous energies, that represents the capital of a healthy civilization. The *products* of such a culture—as much as they contribute to human well-being—are of far lesser import than the respect for intrinsic principles that allow for the production of creative works. For the same reason that erosion of the capital structure of a firm can hasten its demise, sacrificing the fundamental values of a civilization can bring about its death.

It is difficult for rational minds to look at our present societal plight and see it as only a temporary downturn. We are close enough in time to the "Great Depression" that plagued America for more than a decade, that many of us imagine that, like this earlier period, there will be a full recovery to both our economic and other social systems. We might think of our current problems as akin to a bad case of the flu that our immune system will soon subdue. Perhaps a hangover from an evening of self-indulgence provides a more comforting metaphor.

Whatever analogy we choose, our current cultural decline runs to much deeper explanations than what confronted us some eight decades ago. The hangover of prior generations has advanced to cirrhosis of the liver, and rather than facing the need for a change in lifestyle, we look for an organ donor to absorb the costs of our profligacy. Our illness, in other words, is of terminal dimensions; our erstwhile immune system—made up of those personal and social attributes that sustain a healthy organism—has been depleted through decades of ignorant and unfocused dissipation.

The creative well-being of a civilization depends upon individuals enjoying the liberty to pursue their respective self-interests. Protecting this process involves a continuing struggle against the efforts of collectives to promote *their* interests by coercively restraining the autonomous behavior of *others*. In our case, the institutionalized collective, backed by the power of the state, has often found the most expedient course of action to be found in consuming the capital upon which Western Civilization has long thrived. Like a spendthrift heir to an estate—whose upbringing has provided him with little sense of responsible behavior—far too many of us have been eager to scuttle the values that have kept us relatively free and prosperous. Being willing to play the political game of accepting short-term benefits in exchange for long-term costs—particularly if such are to be borne by others—we have helped to destroy the capital of our basic social system.

The principles of the marketplace no longer discipline economic behavior as they once did. Firms that lack the creativity and competence to withstand the rigors of competition, now call upon the government to bestow gifts of billions of dollars upon them. Just as the state has long subsidized its failures (e.g., government schools, police protection, military defense), major businesses will have their failures subsidized. They are also able to take advantage of the state's powers of eminent domain—a practice inconsistent with the principle of private property—to force others to incur the costs of building factories, shopping malls, apartment complexes, and sports stadia. Following the invention of the automobile, there have been close to *two-thousand* car manufacturers in America who succumbed to the disciplines of the marketplace and became defunct. There was a time when it was understood that the opportunity to *succeed* in the marketplace carried with it the risk of *failure*. Today, firms plead for government funding under the rationale that they are "too big to fail."

While the Constitution neither limited government power nor guaranteed individual liberty, there was a time when most people shared the illusion that it did—or, at least, that its language ought to be so interpreted. Today, the Constitution no longer has any definitive meaning: presidents can declare wars on their own initiative, or appoint "czars" to regulate whatever sectors of society they choose; legislation need not be completely drafted before being enacted into law; Bill of Rights requirements for public trials, habeas corpus, restraints on searches and seizures, are routinely violated whenever it suits government officials to do so. Administrations now openly admit to their authority to assassinate Americans whom they unilaterally select for extermination. The chief offense at the Nuremberg war-crimes trials involved the starting of a war; today, such an act is a cause for celebration among patriotic Americans. The Constitution neither protects individuals, nor empowers government: state power is now grounded in pure usurpation.

Truth-telling; respect for the obligations of contracts; stable currencies; and a willingness to overcome immediate time preferences—all of which are necessary for longer-term investments—are qualities in decline in our world. The lies that precipitated wars in Afghanistan and Iraq no longer trouble most Americans, who seem prepared to accept a new set of official falsehoods about Iran; courts have long been willing to rewrite—or refuse to enforce—contracts they deem "unfair" to one of the parties; while inflationary monetary policies encourage short-term time preferences among both investors and consumers.

Such phenomena reflect the dysfunctional and destructive attributes often associated with organizational size. In his important book, *The Breakdown of Nations*, Leopold Kohr identified what he called "the *size theory of social misery*;" that "whenever something is wrong, something is too big."[1] As Gabriel Kolko observed in *The Triumph of Conservatism*,[2] large business organizations have a tendency to become too bureaucratic and rigidified to retain the resilience necessary to make adaptations to changes in their world. Complexity feeds upon itself, producing more complex situations for which additional rules and procedures are adopted in an effort to stabilize the system. While having resort to state power is not an inevitable consequence of an organization's enhanced size, any reduced capacity to adapt to changing conditions increases the pressures to pursue such an option.

Because of the inconstancies and uncertainties inherent in our world, a tension is generated between creative persons who seek to take advantage of the processes of change, and those with established interests to protect. The latter group responds to the specter of change with conservative, moderating proposals. The sense of security associated with permanency—particularly as to systems and practices that have proven beneficial in the past—fosters tendencies for restraint and regularity and opposition to liberty and spontaneity. Such preservationist efforts add to the complexity with which people must contend in their actions. To the degree human action interferes with such regularizing purposes, more rules and bureaucratic procedures are introduced, creating more stabilizing complexity. In the words of George Orwell's Emmanuel Goldstein, such dynamics create "the persistence of a certain world-view and a certain way of life. . . . Who wields power is not important, provided that the hierarchical structure remains always the same."[3]

It must be noted that there is nothing intrinsic about size or complexity that necessarily devitalizes an organization. The benefits arising from economies of scale and the specialization of labor are well-established. Business historian Alfred Chandler has analyzed the economic advantages size played in such developing industries as electricity, automobile manufacturing, and other industries. In his view, a combination of technological

---

1   Leopold Kohr, *The Breakdown of Nations* (New York: E.P. Dutton, 1978), pp. xviii, 26 (emphasis in original).

2   Gabriel Kolko, *The Triumph of Conservatism* (Glencoe, Ill.: The Free Press, 1963).

3   George Orwell, *1984* (London: Penguin Books, 1950), chap. 1.

innovations and organizational changes contributed to the development of large, nationally organized industries.[4] On the other hand, the general failure of both voluntary cartels and the merger movement to stabilize prices and other competitive conditions in industries[5] helps to refute intuitive notions about inherent powers associated with size. The 165 million years in which dinosaurs dominated the earth—compared to the 1–2 million years of humans—should make us reluctant to assume that great size is necessarily dysfunctional. It is simplistic to conclude that organizational size and preferences for maintaining the status quo make collapse inevitable. Nonetheless, the history of business organizations as well as civilizations demonstrates how size *tends* to foster conservative, less resilient, bureaucratic, and stabilizing practices that make a system less able to make creative responses to change. The observations of one student, Joseph Tainter, help to explain Carroll Quigley's views:

> Sociopolitical organizations constantly encounter problems that require increased investment merely to preserve the status quo. This investment comes in such forms as increasing size of bureaucracies, increasing specialization of bureaucracies, cumulative organizational solutions, increasing costs of legitimizing activities, and increasing costs of internal control and external defense. . . . As the number and costliness of organizational investments increases, the proportion of a society's budget available for investment in future economic growth must decline.[6]

When "continued investment in complexity" produces a decline in marginal returns, "a complex society reaches the phase where it becomes increasingly vulnerable to collapse."[7]

Neither is there anything in social organization that mandates institutional arrangements. As Kohr and others have observed, there are forces associated with size that increase the pressures for institutionalization. One such influence has been the movement from what Joseph Schumpeter identified as *owner*-controlled to *manager*-controlled business firms. This transformation produces a shift in perspective from longer-term to shorter-term

---

4   Thomas K. McGraw, ed., *The Essential Alfred Chandler: Essays Toward a Historical Theory of Big Business* (Boston, Mass.: Harvard Business School Press, 1988), pp. 69, 263.

5   See my *In Restraint of Trade*, pp. 45–46, 75, 122, 200, 204, 209–10.

6   Joseph Tainter, *The Collapse of Complex Societies* (Cambridge: Cambridge University Press, 1988), p. 195.

7   Ibid.

considerations in decision-making.[8] I encountered this tendency when, in law practice, I witnessed owners of businesses considering the impact their actions might have on their children and grandchildren who might one day own their enterprises; while managers—whom Schumpeter correctly characterized as having the mindset of employees—tended to focus the scope of their actions only upon immediate concerns. Politicians and bureaucrats typify such thinking, looking only to the next election or their own retirement to define their time-frames.

This should remind us that social organizations, like religions, ideologies, or other belief systems, are the products of our minds. Why do so many mergers and consolidations continue to take place when the empirical record so often attests to their ineffectiveness in increasing market shares, profits, or growth for the firm?[9] Part of the answer may lie in Schumpeter's analysis, which triggers an explanation grounded in the concept of property, in which "ownership" and "control" are severed from one another, creating differing motivations for each. Two students of the subject have offered an explanation for the phenomenon that goes more to psychological and ego satisfaction: "managers prefer to control larger enterprises, because social prestige, salary and perquisites increase with the

---

8   Joseph Schumpeter, *Capitalism, Socialism, and Democracy*, 3rd ed. (New York: Harper and Brothers, 1950), pp. 156 ff.

9   See, e.g., Dennis C. Mueller, "Mergers and Market Share," *The Review of Economics and Statistics* 67, no. 2 (May, 1985): 259–67; Lawrence G. Goldberg, "The Effect of Conglomerate Mergers on Competition," *Journal of Law and Economics* 16 (April, 1973): 137–58; Kenneth M. Davidson, "Looking at the Strategic Impact of Mergers," *The Journal of Business Strategy* 2, no. 1 (Summer, 1991): 13–22; Michael Firth, "The Profitability of Takeovers and Mergers," *The Economic Journal* 89, no. 354 (June, 1979): 316–28. One observer commented upon the "considerable agreement that the conglomerate merger-making peaking in 1968 led to widespread failure. . . ." (See, F.M. Scherer, "Corporate Takeovers: The Efficiency Arguments," *Journal of Economic Perspectives* 2, no. 1 (Winter, 1988): 69–82, at 71.) Another observed that "[s]even or eight years on average following merger, acquired units' profitability had declined sharply relative to pre-merger levels," while "similarly profitable small companies that remained independent managed to sustain even more rapid growth." (See, David J. Ravenscraft and F.M. Scherer, "The Profitability of Mergers," *International Journal of Industrial Organizations* 7 (1989): 101–16, at 115. A study done in the United Kingdom suggested that "the effect of mergers on company profitability has frequently been negative, on average most studies suggest that mergers have if anything lowered the profits of amalgamating firms." (See, A.D. Cosh, A. Hughes, K. Lee, and A. Singh, "Institutional Investment, Mergers and the Market for Corporate Control," *International Journal of Industrial Organization* 7 [1989]: 73–100, at 74.)

size of the enterprise managed."[10] Doesn't this separation of ownership and control underlie all of politics, as men and women seek to exercise control over what they do not own?

As I have developed elsewhere,[11] an institutionalizing imperative begins to dominate our thinking; we learn to identify ourselves with and attach ourselves to organizations that produce the values upon which we believe our well-being depends. At this point, the *organizations* become transformed into *institutions*; they become a doppelganger, a shadowy counterpart of ourselves; we transfer to them the fears of our own mortality; they become "too large to fail."

What we fail to understand when we elevate the *products* of our actions above the free and creative processes that *generated* them, is how the vibrancy that defines life itself gets diminished, taking our culture with it. If we were to take our children or grandchildren to a taxidermist to have them forever preserved in the cuteness of their infancy, we would at once see that it is their life-sustaining *energy* we want to perpetuate, not some momentary form in which such dynamism finds expression.

To relate such distinctions to current political behavior, the creative health of the American economy would be fostered by allowing Detroit auto manufacturers to go out of business, rather than having their insufficiencies subsidized by the state. Did the auto industry really suffer when the Brush, the Omaha, the Stanley Steamer, the Moon, the Maxwell, or the Eldredge Runabout failed to survive? Were such enterprises regarded as so significant as to be bailed out by the government? Certainly, the deadly virus of institutionalism had already infected that industry when, by the late 1940s, established firms were able to call upon the federal government to thwart the competition from Preston Tucker's innovative car.

Historians have warned us of the threats to a civilization arising from treating its productive institutions as ends-in-themselves, whose interests are to be stabilized through standardization and the structuring of the conduct of others. It is through resiliency and adaptability—not the preservation of established forms and practices—that a culture can remain productive. Can we learn, from history, to see through the destructive and debilitating nature of our attachments, and to focus our thinking upon fostering the

---

10   Lana Hall and Jan Sweeney, "Profitability of Mergers in Food Manufacturing," *Applied Economics* 18 (July, 1986): 709–27.

11   See my *Calculated Chaos* and *In Restraint of Trade*.

endless processes of liberty which, alone, make for a creative society? Or, shall we continue mouthing our institution-serving catechisms that tell us how major industries are "too big to fail;" that state and local governments are "too big to fail;" or, that the American Empire is "too big to fail"? At what point do we begin to understand that the printing of money does not create wealth?

After the illusory nature of money no longer sustains even short-term political thinking, and the political establishment intensifies its perpetual war upon human beings, will we continue to allow our gullibility to be exploited? When we are then told that "Western Civilization is too big to fail," to whom will we look for a bailout? Having consumed the capital upon which our civilization was grounded, what printing presses, or military forces, or legislative enactments, will the state have at its disposal to restore what has been destroyed?

CHAPTER 4

A World Too Complex to be Managed

What an immense mass of evil must result . . . from allowing men to assume the right of anticipating what may happen.

—Leo Tolstoy

The cable newscaster chirped: "what is the cause of rising gasoline prices? That depends upon your point of view." By this standard, the causal explanations offered by any nit-witted galoot achieve a credibility equal to that of the most carefully-informed student of the subject. In an age in which public opinion polls weigh more heavily than empirical and reasoned analyses in evaluating events, the communal mindset of dullards may prevail by sheer numbers.

If, according to this newscaster, my "point of view" is that sun spots are "the cause of rising gasoline prices," I have explained the current pricing phenomenon. Because such a theory would exceed the boundaries of what even the collective clueless would tolerate, more plausible—though equally erroneous—explanations must be sought. Those looking for simplistic answers to complex problems will find greater comfort in "oil company price gouging" as the underlying reason for fifty-dollar visits to neighborhood gas pumps.

One of my students—picking up on the "price gouging" theme—opined that monopolistic oil company greed was to blame for these price increases. "First of all," I responded, "why do you characterize the petroleum industry as 'monopolistic'? It is highly competitive. Secondly, why do you think that it took a century for 'greedy' oil company leaders to figure out that the demand for gasoline was so inelastic that customers would be willing to pay over $3.00 per gallon to buy it? Furthermore, have you ever asked yourself why the prices of gold and oil have consistently paralleled one another over the years? Why do you suppose this is? Has the petroleum industry also cornered the gold market?" When one's thinking is not informed by intellectual principles, it is possible to concoct any causal explanations of events.

The eagerness of so many people to accept superficial answers to complex problems, is what keeps the political rackets in business. People are aware that they have insufficient information upon which to make predictions about intricate economic and social relationships and, presuming that the state has access to such knowledge, allow it to take on this role. What these individuals generally fail to understand is that state officials are equally unable to chart or direct the course of complex behavior.

Current society is rapidly being transformed from vertically-structured, institutionally-dominant systems into horizontally-interconnected networks. Our world is becoming increasingly decentralized, with questions arising as to the forms emerging social systems may take. The study of chaos informs us that the multifaceted, interrelated nature of complex systems renders our world unpredictable. As our understanding of chaos deepens, our faith in institutional omniscience will likely be abandoned.

Our experiences with the state should make us aware of how misplaced has been our confidence in the centralized planning and direction of society. It is commonplace to speak of the "unintended consequences" of political intervention. This is just a way of acknowledging the inconstancy and unpredictable nature of complexity. Minimum wage laws, for instance, create increased unemployment, a problem to which the state responds by the enactment of unemployment compensation legislation. This program, in turn, generates the problem of welfare fraud, to which the state makes further responses. Minimum wage laws increase the costs of doing business, making firms less competitive in a world market. This leads to political pressures to increase protective tariffs and self-righteous campaigns against foreign countries whose economies are not burdened by minimum wage legislation.

In this sense, politics functions the way much of traditional medicine does: to repress troublesome symptoms with remedies that produce exponential increases in other symptoms requiring additional medications or surgery. If you look inside an elderly person's medicine cabinet and see the many drugs that are used to suppress symptoms brought on by previous drugs, you will see a perfect parallel to the expansion of governmental "solutions" to politicogenic "problems."

The succession of problems occasioned by state action is reflected in other areas. Americans who fail to understand the causal relationship between decades of violent American foreign policies and the attacks on the World Trade Center, will be eager to accept such simplistic explanations of 9/11 as the product of "terrorists" bent on destroying America out of "evil" or "envious" motivations. Any deeper inquiry will prove too troublesome for those challenged by complexity or for their political attachments, and so they settle for the lies and deceptions of political authorities.

The future is the product of so many interconnected variables that it is presumptuous for any of us to portray its features. Furthermore, our understanding—even of the present—is forever burdened by our past. Kierkegaard was aware of the problem of trying to correlate prior learning and future conduct. "Philosophy is perfectly right," he declared, "in saying that life must be understood backward. But then one forgets the other clause—that it must be lived forward."[1] A penumbra of ignorance will always enshroud both the historian and the prophet.

Ignorance and fear are closely entwined and, as Thoreau and others have observed, "nothing is so much to be feared as fear."[2] There is probably no greater drain on our psychic energies than fear of the unknown. I see this in my students, and advise them, on their first day of classes, to learn to be comfortable with uncertainty; that an awareness of one's ignorance is a catalyst for learning. As the Austrian economists tell us, we act in order to be better off after acting than if we hadn't acted at all. So, too, learning occurs only when we are uncomfortable with not knowing something we would like to know.

But fear can debilitate us, making us susceptible to the importunities of those who promise to alleviate our fears if only we will give the direction of our lives over to them. In this way does the institutional structuring of our

---

1   Soren Kierkegaard, *Journals and Papers, vol. I*, trans. by Howard V. Hong and Edna H. Hong (1843).

2 · Henry David Thoreau, *Journal* (September 7, 1851).

lives begin, with the state demanding the greatest authority over us, and promising release from our uncertainties.

But the state has no clearer crystal ball into the future than do you or I. To the contrary, it is more accurate to suggest that you and I are less prone to error in the management of our personal affairs, than is the state in trying to direct the lives of hundreds of millions of individuals. In addition to our separate interests, the variables confronting events in your life and mine are less numerous, and more localized, than those with which the state deals in its efforts to collectively control all of humanity. If you or I make an error in judgment, you or I suffer the consequences. When the state errs in its planning, mankind in general will suffer.

Our world is entangled in too many undiscoverable details to be centrally managed. If we are to livewell in an inconstant and unpredictable society, we need all the personal autonomy and spontaneity that we can muster. Perhaps in the same way that our ancestors learned to shift their thinking from a geocentric to a heliocentric model of the universe, our children and grandchildren will discover that human society functions better when it is organized horizontally rather than vertically. In words that have become increasingly familiar to us, "nothing grows from the top down."

CHAPTER 5

The Common Good = Collectivism

In recent weeks—as the present administration and most of congress continue to propose the expansion of state power over people's lives—more balloon juice has been released endeavoring to justify such programs on the grounds of fostering "the common good." Any inquisitive mind should see, at once, that the idea of a "common good" is almost entirely that: an *idea*, a fiction. Those who have completed a course in microeconomics can attest to the fact that our tastes, values, and preferences vary from one person to another and, further, fluctuate within individuals. What you and I consider to be in our respective interests will sometimes coalesce and other times deviate from one another. What is to my immediate interest when I am starving becomes far less important to me after I have had a filling dinner. Add to all of this variability and uncertainty the fact that the entire notion of "good" is purely *subjective*, and it can be seen that the insistent chanting of this phrase has no more intellectual respectability to it than does the stomping of one's feet.

Is an alleged "*common* good" intended to convey the idea of a *universal* good, one that is applicable to everyone? If so, the only value I have found to which all persons would seem to subscribe, is this: *no one wants to be victimized.* I have yet to find an individual to which this proposition would not apply. No one chooses to have his or her person or other property interests trespassed upon by another. The failure to recognize both this fact and the fact that all of our values are subjective in nature, has given rise to the silly notion of *altruism*, the idea that one could choose to act contrary to his or her perceived interests. However we act is motivated by a desire to be better off after we have acted than if we had chosen a different course. I have a long-standing challenge to one of my colleagues to present me with an example—real or hypothetical—in which an individual chose to act contrary to his highest value. Even acts of charity are driven by a desire to satisfy some inner need which, to outsiders with contrary preferences, appear to be acts of self-sacrifice. Such thinking amounts to little more than this: "I wouldn't have done what he just did, therefore, he is being altruistic." The idea of altruism is grounded in the belief that values have an *objective* quality to them, a bit of nonsense perpetuated by Ayn Rand.

Transactions in a free market occur because people do *not* have a commonly shared sense of the value of things. If I agree to sell you my car for $5,000, and you agree to pay $5,000 for it, each of us places a different value upon it. To me, the car is worth *less* than $5,000 (i.e., I'd rather have the money than the car) while to you it is worth *more* than that amount. The *price* of the car is objectively defined ($5,000) but its *value* can never be known to either of us. The condition of liberty, in which property interests are respected, is inherently diverse and in constant flux, as men and women pursue their varied self-interests.

In an effort to overcome the motivation of people to pursue their individual interests, and to accept the purposes of institutions as their own, humans have been indoctrinated in the idea that there is a "common good" that expresses a more fulfilling sense of self. When we have learned to suppress our individual values and interests in favor of an institution, we have become part of the collective mindset upon which all political systems depend for their existence. With our thinking so transformed, we are easily duped into believing that what we might otherwise see as our victimization is the essence of our self-fulfillment. In this way are young men and women seduced to "be all you can be" by joining the Army and having their lives destroyed in state-serving foreign adventures.

The doctrine of egalitarianism has proven useful to the established order as a catalyst for this psychic metamorphosis. Otherwise intelligent men and women internalize the proposition that being victimized by the suppression of one's personal interests in favor of an alleged "common good" is acceptable, as long as their neighbors are being equally victimized. There is a pro-liberty sentiment in e.e. cummings' observation that "equality is what does not exist among equals."[1] The statists, however, have a far different meaning for the word: that being coerced by the state can be justified if the compulsion is shared equally by all. So considered, victimization by the state is simply a cost people must bear to bring about their allegedly "greater" personal interest in the "common good."

Such reasoning is generally good enough to entrap those who don't bother to think through the proposition. Anyone who examined the "equal protection of the laws" concept in practice would quickly realize that *no* law applies with equal force to people. Laws are enacted for the purpose of imposing restraints on *some* people for the benefit of *others*. Proposed legislation requiring everyone to pursue their self-interests would never be enacted because it would not differentiate one group from another and, in the process, provide its advocates with a comparative advantage.

But even if the "equality" principle was given its purported meaning (i.e., to have government restraints operate equally upon all), the absurdity of such an idea would at once become evident: people would be understood to have organized the state for the purpose of assuring their mutual victimization! The nonsensical nature of such thinking would become, in the words of H.L. Mencken, "so obvious that even clergymen and editorial writers [would] sometimes notice it."[2]

Nor can the case for a "common good" be rescued by an appeal to the utilitarian doctrine of the "greatest good for the greatest number." My jurisprudence professor, Karl Llewellyn, responded to this proposition in class one day by asking "what about the greatest good for the greatest *guy*?" Utilitarianism is just another variation on the collectivist theme that some may be victimized in order to benefit the group. "The greatest good for the greatest number" is the mantra of every cannibal and socialist.

The utilitarian premise has never been the operating principle in politics. It has been used as yet another diversion—like "common good," "general welfare," etc.—to mask the promotion of special interests behind the façade of collective interests. Thus have such ideas been used to advance such corporate interests as defense contractors, banks, insurance companies, auto manufacturers, pharmaceutical companies, et al., in their efforts

---

1   e.e. cummings, "Jottings," originally published in *The Harvard Wake* (1951), reprinted in e.e. cummings, *Six Nonlectures* (Cambridge, Mass.: Harvard University Press, 1962), p. 70.

2   H.L. Mencken, *Minority Report: H.L. Mencken's Notebooks* (New York: Alfred A. Knopf, 1956), p. 173.

to obtain, through state power, what they cannot obtain in a free market. Major corporations have never been advocates of a free society, preferring to side with the forces of state power to stabilize their interests against the forces of change that attend conditions of liberty. The lyrics to a song from the musical *Li'l Abner*—paraphrased from former General Motors president Charles Wilson—express the modern corporate mindset: "what's good for General Bullmoose, is good for the USA."[3]

The ugliness of collectivist thinking is not confined to the redistribution of wealth, but is also used to rationalize a mindset that rejects the individual as a self-owning, self-serving person. The war system propagates this dehumanizing idea, incorporating utilitarian premises into the notion that social benefits arise from the sacrifice of soldiers to such alleged "greater" causes as fostering liberty, ending slavery, promoting democracy, fighting communism, ending terrorism, etc.

Politically-structured collectivism, in whatever form it manifests itself, debilitates and disables individuals, depriving each of us of our biological and experiential uniqueness. This, of course, is its purpose. As long as men and women think of themselves as little more than fungible units in a group-think monolith, they and their children will continue to be ground down into a common pulp useful only to their masters. Collectivism is a religion for losers; a belief system that allows the state to marshal the wealth and energies of people for a coerced redistribution to those it favors.

Barack Obama did not invent this vulgar, anti-life concept that he works so assiduously to expand. The collectivist proposition had long been in place when George W. Bush echoed its sentiments in the phrase "if you're not with us, you're against us." Nor are the protoplasmic units (i.e., you and I) to be heard questioning the purposes or the costs of our subordination to what is the basic premise of every political system. The state shields itself from such inquiries under the pretense that "national security" would be threatened thereby. Efforts by Ron Paul and others to "audit the Federal Reserve" are met with the most arrogant of all pleas for governmental secrecy (i.e., that revealing to the public the nature of the racket being run by the Fed would jeopardize its "independence"). To the statists, such questions are no more to be tolerated than would a plantation owner feel obliged to entertain inquiries from *his* slaves about cotton prices!

3　*Li'l Abner* (Produced by Paramount Pictures, 1959).

One of my students recently asked me that most frequent of all questions: "what can I do to change all of this?" My response was this: "are you able to change anything that is beyond your control? Is the content of your thinking within your power to control? Can you become aware of the conditioned nature of your mind?"

Our problems do not have their origins in Washington, D.C., nor will their solutions be found there. We are the authors of our own dystopian worlds, and it is to our minds that we must repair if we are to save ourselves from the playing out of the ugly and destructive premises we have planted there. We might begin by acknowledging that our *individuality* is about all that we have in common with one another; and that the suppression of this quality in the name of some alleged collective purpose is essential to the creation of every political system.

CHAPTER 6

The Dysfunctional Society

L ike the *Titanic*, the American ship-of-state has hit an iceberg, and it is not timely to ask the ship's orchestra for an encore of *"America the Beautiful!"* A recurring theme in these articles is that the American branch of Western Civilization is in a state of complete collapse, and that only a fundamental change in our thinking about the nature and forms of social behavior can reverse our destructive course. I return to this topic *not* because I enjoy playing Cassandra—the "disaster lobby" is already packed—but because I am unable to count myself among the "ignorance is bliss" crowd that would prefer such probing questions as whether Janet Jackson should be fined for exposing her breast on television; the propriety of Arnold Schwarzenegger's "girly man" comment; or whether gays and lesbians should be allowed to marry.

The hurried enactment of the Patriot Act, the creation of a Department of Homeland Security, and the wholesale expansion of police powers, were reactions of the political establishment to the realization that it had lost the support and respect of millions of Americans. You may recall, in those pre-9/11 years, the increased interest in political secession; private militias; and the emergence of systems of education, health-care, and dispute resolution, that challenged politically-dominated practices. Even President Clinton lamented the fact that so many Americans "love their country but hate their government,"[1] while his wife was scheming for ways to restrain the unhampered liberty of the Internet, which functioned contrary to the establishment's institutionally-defined and controlled news and information sources.

You may also recall how, immediately after 9/11, most Americans quickly got back into line and, emulating members of Congress, fell to their knees reciting, as their new catechisms, whatever unfocused and dishonest babbling oozed from the lips of George W. Bush. Flag manufacturing suddenly became a major growth industry, as the faithful lined up to purchase and display this symbol of unquestioning obedience to state power. Fear—carefully nurtured with a steady diet of "warnings," color-coded "alerts," and, that scariest of all specters, those "unknown" forces of which we were told to be constantly aware—laid claim to the souls of most Americans. Even today, nearly three years after 9/11, a so-called "independent 9/11 commission" advises of the need for the state to centralize all of its spying, surveillance, and other information-gathering functions into the hands of *one* agency to be headed up by some born-again Lavrenti Beria, perhaps under the appropriate title "Inspector General."

There have also been trial-balloon news reports that the Bush administration will propose a national system of psychological profiling of Americans, to be followed up with appropriate drugs to alleviate identifiable "problems." The generation with which I grew up—having read Aldous Huxley's *Brave New World*—would have treated such a proposal with alarm. I suspect that the response of most prostrated Americans today would be that, as long as the drugs are FDA approved, and no groups are singled out on the basis of race, gender, lifestyle, or religion for "treatment," there would be little objection.

Watch how quickly most Americans—being carefully orchestrated by the politicians and the media—will respond with the sense of urgency into which their fear-stricken minds have become accustomed. Any men and women of libertarian sentiments who question the wisdom of allowing the American state to proceed along its planned course toward neo-Stalinist despotism, will be condemned as "America haters," or insensitive to the victims of 9/11 and their grieving families. Should the matter arise during what will be laughingly referred to as the 2004 presidential "debates,"

---

1   *Huffington Post*, February 9, 2010. www.huffingtonpost.com/mark-green/lets-call-it-pocketbook-p_b_454825.html

both Bush and Kerry will try to outdo one another in their enthusiasm for increased draconianism.

These are not temporary measures—like wartime rationing—that will be put aside when an emergency is over and "normalcy" returns. The Bush administration's allusions to the unending nature of the "war on terror" tells us that the "emergency" is a permanent one. The "terrorism" against which the state now organizes itself goes far beyond suicide bombers crashing airliners into office buildings. It is the "terror" experienced by a politically-structured establishment that has reached the outer limits of its efforts to control life processes in service to its narrow ends. A world that is becoming increasingly *decentralized* strikes terror in the minds of those who have created and become dependent upon *centralized* systems. The "terrorist" forces against which the state now mobilizes its most restrictive, punitive, surveillant, and violent mechanisms of control, is *life itself;* it is you and me, as Pogo Possum so insightfully observed a half-century ago.

"America," as a social system, simply doesn't work well anymore, and there are latent life forces that urge us in other directions. The institutional agencies around which our lives have been organized are increasingly in conflict with the interests of people grown weary of increasing burdens of taxation and regulation, and of seeking ersatz purposes in life. The political establishment's war against the American people—in which some 6.9 million are imprisoned or on probation or parole—is the most compelling evidence for the utter failure of a society dominated by the state.

But no system can last long in open hostility to its members. Trying to hold a society together through constantly reinforced fear, self-righteousness, surveillance, prison sentences, SWAT teams, expanded police forces, and increased legal and military violence, is as futile as a family trying to sustain itself through violent abuse. One of the worst symptoms of the failures of the present civilization is seen in the practice of children being criminally prosecuted and imprisoned as adults.[2] As we have been witnessing in the years after 9/11, such coercive efforts necessitate an ever-increasing use of lies, deception, and disingenuousness, for reality has a persistent way of making itself known. Such methods also eventually trigger a resentment, as even the most fervent flag-waver is found to have a

---

2   www.eji.org/eji/childrenprison

breaking point. Paraphrasing the words of *Star Wars'* Princess Leia—in confronting one of the tyrants—"The more you tighten your grip, Tarkin, the more star systems will slip through your fingers."[3]

Even the long-standing political systems and practices no longer stand in the way of establishment ambitions. Congress has been rendered little more than a rubber-stamp that approves whatever is placed before it by its masters. Despite the lies and collusions that underlay the Bush administration's determination to go to war—a war that has thus far killed some ten to fifteen thousand people, wounded tens of thousands more, and cost billions of dollars to prosecute—I have not heard a single squeak from any member of Congress to impeach any of the principals involved. When one contrasts this with the impeachment of Bill Clinton for his lies about sex— lies that led to the deaths of no one—much is revealed about the bankrupt nature of modern America.

Even the Constitution has become largely irrelevant in the political scheme of things. For the more gullible, it can be said that the Constitution is what keeps the government from doing all of the terrible things that it does; that while it is not a perfect system, it's a whole lot better than what we have! The will of the President and the Attorney General now seem to override constitutional sentiments about "due process of law" and a "speedy and public trial."

Local governments have taken to further restricting First Amendment "free speech" rights by designating "protest zones" to which criticism of the government is confined. On the eve of the Democratic national convention in Boston, a federal judge upheld such a blatant denial of free speech, even as he characterized it as "an affront to free expression." The judge admitted that the zoned area created by Boston city officials resembled a concentration camp, with a razor-wired chain-link fence surrounding it, and netting overhead. If he does regard this as such an affront—which it clearly is, as anyone who bothers to read the First Amendment will quickly discover— why did he not have the integrity to uphold his oath of office and strike down the restriction?

The answer to this question is to be found in the government's long-standing attitudes toward individual liberty in general, and freedom of expression in particular. The courts have always given an *expanded* definition to powers granted to the government, and a *restricted* definition to individual liberties.

---

3   *Star Wars* (Twentieth Century Fox, 1977).

"Freedom of expression" will be protected *only* if the speech is an ineffective challenge to state policies. *Effective* speech—no matter how peacefully expressed—will always be considered a worthy target for governmental restraint.

The "freedom of expression" about which even the politicians like to prattle, has been twisted from a celebration of pluralism into a demand for a stifling uniformity of thought and action; standardizing practices that strangle the creative forces of a culture. We live in a period of rigidly enforced "political correctness," a practice containing a glaring contradiction: an alleged belief in "diversity." But the reality of "diversity," particularly on college campuses, amounts to nothing more than the encouragement of men and women from a variety of racial, ethnic, and lifestyle groups who advocate state collectivism. If you doubt this, observe how *genuine* diversity—in the form of libertarian/free market opinion, anti-feminist women speakers, or blacks who are critical of the plantation politics of the Democratic party—is discouraged (or even prohibited) on many campuses. Freedom of expression is important to any healthy society because it challenges existing thought and practices. It is supposed to be disruptive of the status quo. But as the protestors in Boston have discovered as their messages are kept imprisoned in wire cages on an isolated street distant from the Democratic convention, "free speech" in America is now confined to speech that is comfortable to establishment interests!

The irony of it all: that such a court-enforced mockery of free expression should take place in Boston, where the voices of John Hancock and Sam Adams once made life miserable for the political establishment. The closest any of the Democratic party conventioneers will get to the spirit of Sam Adams will be what is handed them by a bartender!

People cannot get near the Boston convention center without "proper credentials," although Boston police officers plan on confronting conventioneers with protests of their own, in support of their contract demands with the city. Meanwhile, the state capitol building is surrounded by armed police officers. What better evidence than this of how distant political systems are from ordinary people, and how government officials are terrified by the very people they are supposed to "represent" and protect! But when the state increasingly compels people to do what they do not want to do, prevents them from doing what they do want to do, and forcibly takes more money from them in the form of taxes and fines, why wouldn't government officials start to worry?

About twenty years ago, I made a tongue-in-cheek suggestion that the government might—under the guise of promoting individual liberty—enact a statute mandating people to exercise their "freedom." People could be required to visit a "freedom exercise center" in their communities where, under the watchful and protective eye of policemen, they could express any opinions they wanted. This would all take place in a small room, from which others would be excluded—in the name of protecting the privacy of the speaker, of course. Only the police officers would watch to make certain that he or she had, in fact, expressed their opinions. Those who failed to do so would be prosecuted for a failure to "protect the exercise of American freedom."

I hesitate to mention this earlier proposal, given the present disposition of both Republican and Democratic politicians. I can just imagine John Kerry and George Bush racing to the microphones to be the first to propose this measure which, I am certain, would immediately be endorsed by the same gang of fools who fly flags from their homes and cars, memorize the gurglings of Bill O'Reilly, or write editorials for major newspapers.

This is what America has become, and is destined to remain unless either (a) some major metamorphosis in our thinking takes us in a different direction, or,(b) like the Soviet Union, the present dysfunctional system collapses of its inherent contradictions and hostilities to life processes. While there will always be too many question marks surrounding our questions about the future, events seem to point to option (b) as the likely prognosis, a suspicion that appears to be shared by members of the political establishment. The fate of the American civilization in such a post-collapse period will depend upon whether a sufficient intelligence and creative energy will be available to transform the culture into the kind of free and peaceful society it has long ceased to be.

CHAPTER 7

The Silence of Institutions

A few decades ago one could . . . still accept the expression "My Country right or wrong" as a proper expression of patriotism; today this standpoint can be regarded as lacking in moral responsibility.

—Konrad Lorenz

I was startled the other morning to see a cable television news headline that read: "Department of Justice studying police officer shootings." My initial response was to wonder if Will Grigg's LRC articles and blogs on the brutalities, murders, and other criminal acts by police officers[1] had generated so much attention that the political establishment was forced to deal with what appears to be a rampant problem. I later discovered that the DOJ was concerned *not* with police officers shooting ordinary people (what Will calls the "mundanes"), but with people shooting police officers. I felt a bit embarrassed having imagined, for even an instant, that modern government officials might have had occasion to regard such police assaults on individuals as the violation of a moral principle worthy of attention.

There is little doubt that political systems represent the most destructive, repressive, anti-life, and dehumanized form of social organization. If one were to consciously design and carry out a scheme that would prove disastrous to human well-being, it would be difficult to improve on what

---

1   See, generally, Will Grigg on www.*LewRockwell.com*.

we now find in place. Such entities thrive on the energies generated by the mobilization of our inner, dark-side forces, a dynamic that can be brought about only through *us*, by you and me agreeing to structure our thinking to conform to the preeminence of such institutionalized thinking.

But it is not sufficient for the state, alone, to organize and direct how we think of ourselves, others, and the systems to be employed in conducting ourselves in society. Organizations that began as flexible tools that allowed us to cooperate with one another through a division of labor to accomplish our mutual ends, soon became ends in themselves, to which we attached our very sense of being. *Tools* became our *identities*; our shared self-interests became co-opted by the collective supremacy of the organization. In this way have *institutions* been born.

How and why have we created such a destructive mindset? Why do we not understand that, in treating institutions as their own *raison d'etre*, we are creating a state of war with life processes? Are we so much the product of a lifetime of conditioning that we are unwilling to look at ourselves in the mirror? The institutional order has consistently manipulated our thinking so that we will define *their* purposes as our *own*. So inculcated have we become in this coalescence that we unthinkingly scuttle our individual sense of personhood, and give ourselves over—in both body and spirit—to collective forces that see us as no more than fungible resources to be exploited.

While the state is the most apparent and pervasive example, our institutionally-centered thinking dominates how we conduct ourselves in society. Economic organizations (e.g., business corporations, labor unions), religions, educational systems, the news media, are the more familiar forms of human activity engaged in through hierarchically-structured institutions. The values by which we measure our personal success or social benefits arising from such systems are those of particular interest to institutions themselves. These include, among others, such considerations as *material* well-being (e.g., income, employment, money, GDP); institutional *certification* (e.g., diplomas and degrees, SAT scores, professional licensing); and *social status* (e.g., fame, wealth, power, and other consequences of achieving success within institutions). In the vernacular of modern psychology, institutions are largely driven by such *left*-brained factors as linear and logical thinking, quantitative reasoning, and applied science (i.e., engineering).

Within our highly-structured world, values that do not serve institutional purposes tend to be regarded as forms of *entropy* (i.e., energy unavailable for productive work). These may include feelings and emotions, the role of fantasy and imagination, risk taking, spirituality, aesthetics, and spatial relationships. These make up what is referred to as *right*-brained expressions of our humanity. At best, such qualities are tolerated by the institutional order although, in times of turmoil, may be forcefully resisted (e.g., people being told "don't get emotional"; or to embrace "security" and "certainty" over the risks associated with liberty).

That psychologically healthy men and women incorporate both left- and right-brained influences in their lives is not to be denied. The importance of living *centered* lives—i.e., living with the *integrity* that harmonizes (i.e., integrates) our values and actions without conflict or contradiction—is what makes civil society possible. But institutionalized thinking does not allow for such symmetry. An entity that is regarded as an end in itself—its own *raison d'etre*—is immediately in conflict with the idea of individuals as self-owning beings. From a property perspective, one cannot enjoy decision-making autonomy over his or her life and, at the same time, respect an institution as its own reason for being. This is why a system grounded in liberty and private ownership of property cannot be reconciled with the state.

For such reasons, the interests of individuals and institutions are incompatible, a fact that is reflected in the tendency of members of the institutional order to converge on issues central to the maintenance of centralized authority over people. Whether we are considering the war on drugs; police surveillance; government regulation of the economy; state-funded welfare; the so-called "national defense" industry; support for government schools, wars and the expansion of empire; or numerous other state systems premised on the vertical structuring of human action, one rarely finds major institutions dissenting from established policy. Institutional entities have developed a symbiotic relationship that brings them together, as one, when the order, itself, is challenged. What business corporation, university, major religion, member of the mainstream media, corporate-sponsored "think-tank," international labor union, or other member of the "establishment," has offered a frontal criticism of war, defense contracting, the police system, or government schools?

As our institutionally-directed world continues to collapse into wars and domestic militarism; economic dislocations and corruption brought on by crony-capitalism; the failure of such state-controlled systems as education and health-care; the increasing resort to police brutality, torture, enhanced punishment, and imprisonment; increased levels of taxation and inflation; and other examples of the failure of expectations most of us have had of "the system," there is an ever-widening disconnection between institutions and individuals. There is also a growing awareness that the operational values essential to the interests of each group are not only incompatible, but beyond repair.

In the face of such a systemic bankruptcy within the institutional order—whose power we have been conditioned to embrace as the essence of social order—thoughtful minds might ask: "where is there any fundamental analysis or criticism coming from within these established entities?" What major corporations are heard speaking of the need to abandon our neo-mercantilist practices in favor of laissez-faire policies? What churches have denounced the run-away war system, daring to invoke the name of Jesus on behalf of conditions of love and peace? What colleges and universities truly tolerate the diversity of thought that could give rise to the consideration of new ideas and practices? What members of the major media offer the public anything more than propaganda useful to the political and corporate interests that own them?

It is this institutional group-think that now finds itself threatened by new technologies that do not lend themselves to centralized controls. The Internet and other unstructured tools will continue to destabilize the herds that the institutional order has worked so feverishly to keep confined to their assigned pastures. There is nothing quite so liberating as the increased flow of information, and there is nothing the establishment fears quite so much as a world of truly liberated people. Julian Assange's and Wikileaks' release of state secrets into the hands of persons political systems pretend to serve, are not the *problem* confronting the establishment: they are *precursors* of an emerging, life-sustaining social order.

In the meantime, do not expect institutional hierarchies to abandon their left-brained, linear, "bottom line" preoccupations with the accumulation of wealth and power. As George Orwell informed us, institutions may sense our right-brained needs for emotional and spiritual values, and will continue to corrupt language so as to persuade the weak-minded of an alleged commonality of purpose.

To such ends, "liberty" will become defined as a condition in which your obedience to the state will keep you out of prison. "Peace" will be what prevails among nations as long as they acknowledge the sovereign authority of the American Empire. "Life" will be a respected value as long as the living act in conformity with the collective interests of institutions. To expect anything more from the established order is to fail to understand the fundamental dichotomy between *human beings* and the *organizations* we have too long revered.

CHAPTER 8

Law as "Reason" or as "Violence"?

The other day, I received an alumni fund-raising letter from my old law school. It opened with a post-September 11th quote from a present faculty member who praised our current civilization, declaring that one of its most impressive accomplishments has been the development of a "legal order committed to resolving disputes between humans by reason and not by violence."

There is nothing particularly remarkable in this man's observations: one would find virtually unanimous agreement with such sentiments at any gathering of lawyers, judges, politicians, or other professional groups. What *is* noteworthy in his words is how far removed they are from the reality they purport to describe. Like so many of the litanies and bromides by which most people sustain their faith in systems such as the state, these words have a reassuring quality to them, at least as long as one does not examine them closely.

My experience in analyzing institutional behavior for many years has convinced me that, when those in power speak incessantly of one thing, they invariably mean its opposite. Ronald Reagan's insistence on "getting government off people's backs" was a cover for his administration expanding federal power. So, too, the current President Bush is in the process of putting together a Draconian police-state, the elements of which comprise his "Operation Enduring Freedom." Apparently what Mr. Bush has in mind is that the United States government has been "enduring freedom" long enough, and intends to bring it to an end!

The idea that modern "law" substitutes *reason* for *violence* as a means of resolving disputes is but another of these propositions that camouflages its own contradictions. That such ideas can be mouthed by their defenders with the utmost sincerity illustrates the effectiveness of the illusion.

There have been times in which "law" *was*, indeed, a means for *peacefully* resolving disputes. The ancient system known as the "Law Merchant," for example, developed among men of commerce as a way of settling quarrels in the marketplace. Judges were men well-experienced in the customs and usages that prevailed in various trades. When a dispute arose—such as when a buyer thought he had been dealt with dishonestly by a seller—it would be brought before one of these merchant judges who (a) heard the facts, and (b) rendered a decision based upon his knowledge of business custom.

What was most interesting in this tradition was that the merchant judges had no formal means of enforcing their decisions. The judges were more like arbitrators, whose decisions the losing parties were free to ignore without repercussions from the state. And yet, these judges' decisions were almost universally upheld. The pressures of the marketplace—such as the ostracism of those merchants who would not abide by a judge's decision— provided the most effective means of enforcement.

The attitudes of the merchant judges were remarkably different from modern-day judges: the former would often be heard to state that their function was to "find" the law (i.e., by discovering the customs and habits that prevailed among men of commerce), while the latter tend more to the view that their role is to "formulate" the law (i.e., to construct rules out of their *own* preferences instead of out of the common expectations of people in the community).

Over time, the political system took over the roles of these merchant judges, and "law" became more completely *politicized*. Because the state enjoys a monopoly on the use of force within a given area, its strong arm is now available to enforce decisions formulated by the legal system. Should anyone doubt that our formal system of law is grounded in violence, they need only consider the punitive prospects of refusing to abide by the decision of a court. Further evidence of the coercive nature of modern law can be found in a reading of federal or state statutes, which bear the ultimate sanction of "fine and/or imprisonment" for the violation of legislative mandates.

There is an illusion, shared by many intellectuals, that there are processes of "reasoning" which, if properly engaged in, will lead to conclusions that are free of the preferences and prejudices of the one engaging in such pursuits. What such people fail to understand is that to "reason" is to do nothing more than develop "reasons" to justify one's desired conclusions. The word "rationalize" (i.e., to attribute one's behavior to plausible motives while ignoring their true purposes) is particularly revealing. Does anyone doubt that Osama bin Laden and George Bush have articulated "reasons" for the violence each seeks to impose upon the world? The violence of the Holy Crusades, the Inquisitions, the Nazi holocaust, the Soviet and Maoist butcheries, and the nuclear slaughters at Hiroshima and Nagasaki, were all conducted by those who had clearly expressed "reasons" for their actions.

Perhaps the most significant example of the effort to produce a legal system grounded in "reason" instead of "violence" can be found in the creation of *constitutional governments*. The basic premise of constitutional systems is found in the fiction of a "social contract," whereby millions of free individuals would create a government which would, by virtue of specifically enumerated powers within the constitution, be limited in the scope of its authority. That such systems have *never* been created by unanimous agreement, but have *always* been imposed by a minority upon the rest of the population, should have been a tipoff as to the fallacies upon which they have been grounded.

But if the coercive origins of constitutional governments are not enough to convince one that violence cannot be restrained by such devices, perhaps the history of the twentieth century will provide insight. Suspicions might first be aroused by the awareness that the Soviet Union operated on the basis of a "constitution"—modeled upon the American system, complete with a "bill of rights." But further evidence can be found within the history of the United States Constitution itself.

If one reads a history of the cases decided by the United States Supreme Court, one finds the following fairly consistent patterns: (1) *powers* granted to the federal government have been given *expansive* definitions—as witness the court's "reasoning" that the "commerce clause" powers are not "limited to" economic transactions that cross state lines, but may be used to force social change, control undesirable personal conduct, and virtually any other end Congress might have in mind. Likewise, the "necessary and proper" clause has not been confined to such measures as are absolutely *essential* to some stated end, but has been expanded to embrace any means that are *convenient* to such purposes.

(2) At the same time, personal *liberties* that were supposed to have been protected by the "Bill of Rights" have been given a very *restricted* definition. Case after case reverberates with such phrases as "freedom of religion *does not include,*" or "free speech *does not mean,*" or the 13th Amendment prohibition against "involuntary servitude" *"does not prohibit military conscription or jury duty."* Perhaps the best evidence for the incessant restriction of liberties under the Constitution is to be found in the 9th Amendment, a supposed "catch-all" for *all other* liberties not enumerated within the Bill of Rights. Only a small handful of cases have ever found such additional "rights" that were subject to 9th Amendment protections.

For those who still cling to the sentiment that formal, politically-backed systems of "law" can divorce themselves from the underlying violence that defines such systems, I draw your attention to the events immediately following the World Trace Center attacks. An imperial president declares "war" upon an ill-defined "enemy," without feeling any need to have an obsequious but thoroughly marginalized Congress exercise its constitutional authority to make such a declaration. There followed a mixture of legislated enactments—usually by 100-0 Senate votes—executive orders, and proposals for practices that would allow government agencies to wiretap our telephones and Internet communications and enter our homes without our knowledge or consent; allow for the indefinite incarceration, torture, or even assassination of "suspected terrorists," as well as secret military trials for such suspects; increased inspections of our persons; as well as proposals for national identity cards, mandatory smallpox vaccinations (based upon purely hypothetical threats), and the employment of the U.S. military to police the American people. Various rationales have been offered by the defenders of such practices.

Contrary to the sentiments expressed by the aforementioned law school professor, those who have recommended "reason" in place of the "violence" now being practiced by massive government bombing abroad, and police-state mechanisms at home, find themselves accused of cowardice or appeasement. Some jingoistic militarists have gone so far as to suggest prosecuting, on charges of *treason,* anyone who opposes this now-described "permanent" state of war! To those who have watched the untold number of "Nazi holocaust" films and wondered: "how could the German people have gone along with such tyrannical measures?," they can now find the answer in the ease and quickness with which so many Americans have, with barely a whimper of doubt, rationalized the creation of tyranny in their own land.

For those who are willing to move beyond their high-school civics class conditioning, and examine what is implicit in all political behavior, it should be evident that the experiment with "constitutionalism," though offered with the best of intentions by our ancestors who believed that power could be limited by reason, has proven an illusory dream. The bloody, tyrannical history of the twentieth century gives us a perspective that requires us to abandon such naïve hopes. In the words of Anthony de Jasay, in his book *Against Politics*: "collective choice is never independent of what significant numbers of individuals wish it to be."[1] There are no principles, no matter how carefully articulated, by which the forces of *state power* can be restrained when they have their "reasons" for resorting to "violence!"

---

1   Anthony de Jasay, *Against Politics: On Government, Anarchy, and Order* (London: Routledge, 1997), pp. 59–60.

CHAPTER 9

Lest We Forget

The masses have never thirsted after truth. Whoever can supply them with illusions is easily their master; whoever attempts to destroy their illusions is always their victim.

—Gustave Le Bon

Hardly a day passes in which the reporting of political events does not bring to mind the teachings of, perhaps, the greatest of all psychiatrists, Carl Jung. He reminded us of a truth that most of us reject, namely, that there is a "dark side" to our unconscious minds which can easily be mobilized for destructive purposes to which our conscious minds would never subscribe. We are uncomfortable with the thought that we might harbor inclinations for dishonesty, violence, laziness, cowardice, killing, etc., attributes that run counter to the more praiseworthy image we would prefer having. Even though we might never act upon such negative traits, the awareness that such inner urges could come to the surface is most troubling. Eager to expunge ourselves of such fears, we may unconsciously *project* these traits upon others—"scapegoats"—against whom we can take action. Such forces often find expression when fears and perceived threats from others cause us to fall victim to mob-like thinking, capable of being organized into political or other violent undertakings. The state thrives on conflicts it has helped to generate among people, which accounts for the parallel proliferation of disputes and increased political powers. Such dynamics have been most evident during these past nine years, as the least reflective have found it easy to accept *any* group identified by political leaders as a threat to some imagined sense of security.

A virulent form of this pathology has arisen in recent weeks over the proposed construction of an Islamic cultural center a few blocks from the site of the former World Trade Center. With the same irrational, self-righteous posturing that would lead white supremacists to react to a black family moving into their neighborhood, various groups have sounded like a Greek chorus in attacking the Muslims for their alleged "insensitivity" to the "feelings" of those still traumatized by 9/11. That condemning an entire religion for the actions of a handful of its members—particularly when the 9/11 attacks were driven by *political* rather than *religious* considerations— is a form of the collectivist thinking of which Jung warned. How far might such shrieking reaction extend? Would a modern businessman properly be criticized for his plans to build a sushi restaurant near Pearl Harbor? Should the Ayn Rand Institute be charged with "insensitivity" to the religious feelings of Mormons were it to establish a facility in Salt Lake City? Is *anything* which the most neurotic person finds offensive to be defined as a "hate crime," or an act of "insensitivity?"

Is there any purpose to this tirade against an Islamic cultural center other than helping U.S./Israeli warmongering efforts against the Middle Eastern enemy-of-the-month? Can these fomenters of hatred expect to be taken seriously in posing as agents of "sensitivity" on behalf of victims of past wrongdoing? If they are truly concerned with respecting gravesites— even though the proposed Islamic center would not be located on the World Trade Center land—the Islamophobes might look further than just the dead of 9/11. They might consider providing due sensitivity to earlier victims of wrongs committed in the environs of Manhattan.

The Wall Street area is the site of an earlier cemetery that functioned for more than one hundred years. Known as the African Burial Ground, it was the final resting place for what some archeologists estimate may be as many as ten thousand former slaves and black freemen. This burial site was discovered fewer than twenty years ago, during the construction of a federal office building. Somehow, I do not expect to hear the political establishment or its mainstream media campaigning against the federal government's "insensitivity" to the victims of slavery!

For reasons that the "sensitive"-minded voices of political correctness prefer to downplay or completely ignore, Manhattan had been a major center of the African slave trade into the nineteenth century. Slaves were brought into New York City ports, there to be sold. The book, *Slavery in New York*,[1] offers this encapsulation of this slave market:

> For nearly three hundred years, slavery was an intimate part of the lives of all New Yorkers, black and white, insinuating itself into every nook and cranny of New York's history. For portions of the seventeenth and eighteenth centuries, New York City housed the largest urban slave population in mainland North America, with more slaves than any other city on the continent.[2]

It has been estimated that, by the mid-1700s, some 25 percent of the workers in New York City were slaves, while *half* the work force beyond the city was so constituted. During this same period, anywhere from 20 percent to 70 percent of New York City homes were served by one or more slaves.[3]

Many of the erstwhile slaves who had been set free prior to the Civil War saw the importance of *owning* property, rather than *being* the property of others. These persons formed a community in the mid-Manhattan area, called Seneca Village. Irish and German immigrants also bought land in this village. A number of white New Yorkers became troubled with the success of Seneca and, concerned about the impact this might have on the future development of Manhattan, called upon the New York City mayor—a Democrat—to use eminent domain to eliminate the village. The stolen land became a part of today's Central Park.

The black property owners resisted being removed from their homes, and were forcibly removed by police officers. As with later "urban renewal" projects in various cities—programs that destroyed the orderly nature of established neighborhoods, thus contributing to the modern disorder of the inner cities—the residents of Seneca Village were left to fend for themselves. Will any organized campaign of "sensitivity" to these victims of urban renewal be forthcoming from the current trumpets of bigotry?[4]

Private property interests have succumbed to the socialistic nature of eminent domain elsewhere on Manhattan. When Wall Street banking and other financial interests—particularly the Rockefellers—saw the

---

1   Ira Berlin and Leslie M. Harris, eds., *Slavery in New York* (New York: The New Press; published in conjunction with The New-York Historical Society, 2005).

2   Ibid., p. 4.

3   Ibid., pp. 4, 69–71.

4   Ibid., p. 268.

enhanced property values that would come from having a World Trade Center constructed in their neighborhood, local government employed the powers of eminent domain to forcibly deprive small businesses and other property owners of their lands. Being driven more by political interests than market demand, the resulting WTC became a white elephant unable to sustain itself without the state government. This problem was addressed, under the governorship of Nelson Rockefeller, by moving numerous state offices to this facility.

I have often wondered whether some parcels of land might be affected by a "power of place," whose influences might continue from one owner to another, and from one time period to another. It may be no coincidence that the remains of thousands of slaves—whose claims to self-ownership were so viciously denied by state and federal governments—are buried in the same area as the dead of 9/11, lands from which subsequent owners were forcibly despoiled of their property in order to serve private banking interests. Perhaps there is added symmetry in the fact that Alexander Hamilton—whose inconsistent attitudes toward slavery, and whose politically interventionist predilections would have brought him down on the side of the Wall Street banking interests—lies buried in a churchyard not far from the ruins of the World Trade Center.

Perhaps the sordid history that lies buried within this region is contributing to the playing-out of the "dark side" forces that now militate against the efforts of Muslims to build their recreation center. There is a long line of politically-generated abuses of people on Manhattan Island—and elsewhere—to be attended to before addressing the construction of a religious center that does *not* depend on violating the property interests of anyone. The inconstancy of the "sensitivity" to the claims of property ownership has been too unsightly and morally offensive for any of us to tolerate yet another denial of the principle of inviolability which, alone, can civilize us.

CHAPTER **10**

We're Going Away!

The late Arthur Koestler was of the view that mankind is an evolutionary mistake doomed to extinction. To have given a killer ape the capacity for intelligence was not, he reasoned, nature's smartest strategy.

Intelligence has been a factor that has, in many ways, set humanity apart from other species. The stabilizing influence of instinct has kept other life forms within a relatively narrow range of development: the possum, for instance, one of the oldest of animal species, has changed very little over the tens of millions of years of its presence on earth. In contrast, mankind has fundamentally changed itself and the world in what may be the first million years of its infancy.

But what has been the nature of man's development? How has intelligence informed our behavior? A view of human history—not just from the political perspective upon which historians focus—provides substantial evidence of our using the powers of the mind for both creative and destructive purposes. Sad to say, the use of our intelligence to generate tools and systems that destroy life has been in the ascendancy for well over a century. Why has this been so? Was Koestler right?

Our problems may well have their origins in the dualistic nature of our brain, which appears to be divided into "left-" and "right-"sided functions. As seen earlier, "left-brain" thinking tends to be linear, mechanistic, and analytical; it expresses itself verbally, using logic, math, and other forms of reasoning. The "right-brain" is represented by non-linear, intuitive, spiritual, emotional, and spatial thinking; it is the realm of spontaneity and the imagination. Reduced to overly-simplified terms, the "left-brain" is more dominated by a desire for *structuring*; the "right-brain" by concerns for *liberty*.

Only a handful of pathological cases could be said to be totally "left-" or "right-brained" in nature. Yet each of us tends to be more or less influenced by one side of the brain or the other. I have a number of friends who, as "left-brain" driven engineers, physicians, or business managers, are equally insistent upon defending individual liberty and unstructured ways of organizing with others. The examined and well-lived life consists not so much in *balancing* these forces, but in *integrating* them.

To the extent that our culture has become institutionalized, our thinking has come to be dominated by "left-brain" influences. This phase of our thinking has produced the inventions and discoveries, the scientific understanding, the technology, and the means by which we produce our material well-being, that reflect our mind's capacity for life-serving behavior. But as we intensify the importance of what this side of our brain produces, we tend to ignore the voices from the right-side. Seduced by the material benefits we enjoy, we relegate other values to a lower level of concern. In such ways has the *non*-material become increasingly *im*material to us.

Political systems, and the thinking that drives them, are almost entirely grounded in "left-brained" activity. For propagandistic purposes, politicians will give lip-service to such concepts as "liberty," but without any sincerity. The politician who *does* express a genuine, deeply-held concern for individual autonomy, incurs the enmity of the established interests who control the political machinery for their ends.

If one wishes to see what a world looks like when dominated by "left-brained" thinking, one need only look to recent history. Long before you or I were born, Americans gave themselves over to the structuring of their lives in service to the institutions with which they had come to identify themselves. When corporate-state interests find wars to their liking, most Americans go into a frenzied flag-waving, all the while condemning those who fail to shout "hurrah!" Most parents willingly invest their children in the sordid enterprise, emblazoning their cars with bumper-stickers (e.g., "Proud Parent of a Marine") that announce to others how much more they love the corporate-state than they do their own sons and daughters.

This country is now experiencing the logical extension of people identifying themselves with the institutional order. If major corporations are—by virtue of their incestuous relationship with the state—unable to withstand the demanding disciplines of the marketplace, the political system comes to their rescue by looting taxpayers of trillions of dollars to bail them out. In a corporate-state world, whatever the major corporations need the state will provide, regardless of the impact such activity may have on ordinary people and on the values that can only find expression on a now-excised "right" side of the brain!

The rest of the institutional order—with its own interests to advance in the structuring of the lives of people—offers its support to the corporate-state cause. The mainstream media and academia—each functioning as public-relations flacks—create and reinforce the conditioned thinking that makes us subservient to the establishment cause. In his novel, *The Chaneysville Incident*, David Bradley observed: "one of the primary functions of societal institutions is to conceal the basic nature of the society, so that the individuals that make up the power structure can pursue the business of consolidating and increasing their power untroubled by the minor carpings of a dissatisfied peasantry."[1]

I have written elsewhere of the destructive impact that institutionalized thinking has on the vibrancy of a civilization. The problem may run much deeper than this. Just as an individual, or an organization, or a civilization requires resiliency and adaptability to changing conditions—qualities that implicate such "right-brain" values as liberty and spontaneity—so, too, does the fate of a species. We ought to have learned from the dinosaurs—whose enormous size allowed them to dominate the planet far longer than the meager human timeline—that a lack of resiliency can make you extinct. The history of these giant reptiles should have taught us that investing major corporations with the coercive power of the state to structure the marketplace to their liking is not a sound policy for maintaining a productive economic system. Reptilian thinking is not conducive to creativity.

It is ironic that our successes in serving our material needs should cause us to become attached to and dependent upon the linear systems that produced such values. "Right-brained" considerations reflect the individualized nature of life, and thus are of little to no importance to the spiritless

---

1   David Bradley, *The Chaneysville Incident* (New York: HarperCollins, 1990), p. 6.

character of institutional interests. What activities are more destructive of life than wars, and the restriction of personal liberty that prevents men and women from making creative responses in an inconstant world? The study of history and economics inform us what intelligent minds can no longer doubt: privately-owned property and the economic freedom implicit in the property concept are the most effective means of maximizing the self-interests of human beings.

Nor can rationality fail to grasp that the war system—central to the well-being of the state—is antithetical to life. Beyond the millions killed in battles and bombings, as well as those who die from the destruction of the instrumentalities that produce life-sustaining goods and services (e.g., factories, office buildings, farms, etc.) there are numerous unintended consequences to warfare that hasten an end to life. Even the most entrenched military mind must begin to suspect that, when more soldiers die by *suicide* than on the *battlefield*,[2] their system of structured slaughter serves no *human* purpose. I saw a televised interview of an Army general addressing the reported problem of fourteen acts of homicide engaged in by soldiers returning to his installation during a four-year period. His response to the problem reflected a purely institutionalized mindset: the returning soldiers required more counseling and/or drug treatment to help them "adjust" to the insanity that had been made of their lives. As with children who do not conform to the mind-dulling expectations of school systems, the soldiers must endure a more intense program to silence their inner voices.

Our language reflects our attachment to war-like thinking. Almost any social condition of which we disapprove is met by a declaration of war: be it the war on poverty, the war on drugs, the war on terrorism, the war on obesity, the war on climate change, etc. Most of us are at war with life itself, regarding the exercise of institutionalized violence (i.e., politics) as the most effective means of accomplishing social change. Two decades ago, the idea of nuclear war represented a monstrous horror. Today, psychopaths in high office casually speak of initiating nuclear devastation against other nations that pose no military threat to America. What was once considered unthinkable has since become just one of many acceptable political strategies.

Fortunately, we are living at a time when decentralized social practices are weakening institutional power-structures: *vertical* authority is giving

---

2   www.disinfo.com/2011/02/for-second-straight-year-military-suicides-outnumber-combat-deaths/

way to *horizontal* networking. The Internet is but the most familiar of the means by which individuals communicate with and inform one another, rather than remaining conditioned to having institutional voices (e.g., mainstream media, governmental agencies, academia) directing the content of their thinking. President Obama's announced plan to appoint an "Internet czar" to regulate this system, as well as those statists who urge an expanded definition of "hate crimes" to include people who express distrust of government or who insist upon constitutional protections, represent the desperate responses of the political system to influences that run contrary to the primacy of institutionalism.

If the survival of a species depends upon its success in adapting to changed conditions, how much more burdensome is the task when members of that species must overcome conscious sabotage placed in their way in the name of intelligent planning? We are too much at war with the processes by which life sustains itself to be assured of our continued presence on earth. People whose minds are dominated by mechanistic linear thinking and a desire to structure all human behavior represent a lemming-like force that may make mankind the first known species to destroy itself by collective suicide. Perhaps the stated concern so many practitioners of "left-brain" regularizing have in preventing the extinction of *other* species is little more than an unconscious projection of the fears of our own removal from the grand experiment the life force has long conducted on this planet. Perhaps we humans sense what we are afraid to speak; that, in the words of the late stand-up philosopher, George Carlin, "we're going away!"

There is no determinism at work here; we are not fated to ends we are unable to influence to life-enhancing purposes. But if we are to avoid joining the dinosaurs on the sidelines, we must do what these predecessors were unable to do, namely, abandon our reptilian brains and allow our "right-brain" voices to inform our behavior.

Kenneth Boulding has expressed the problem as succinctly as anyone else: "If the human race is to survive it will have to change more in its ways of thinking in the next twenty-five years than it has done in the last twenty-five thousand."[3] At a time when both "conservatives" and "liberals" advertise their spiritual bankruptcy to a benumbed world, we have never faced a greater opportunity, or need, to explore alternative ways of

---

3   Kenneth E. Boulding, "Post-Civilization," in Paul Goodman, ed., *Seeds of Liberation* (New York: George Braziller, 1964), p. 23.

thinking. The poet Seamus Heaney has written that "we are hunters and gatherers of values."[4] It is time for us to take our search to other fields.

---

4   Seamus Heaney, *Opened Ground: Selected Poems, 1966–1996* (New York: Farrar, Straus and Giroux, 1998), p. 430.

CHAPTER 11

Fighting for Freedom

Why fight for a flag when you can buy one for a nickel.
—Ezra Pound

I grow weary of national holidays that have been converted into public relations opportunities for the celebration of the war system. In my childhood, Decoration Day was an opportunity to honor the dead by decorating graves, and I recall numerous trips to the cemetery to lay flowers at the headstones of my grandparents and aunts and uncles, including an uncle who died in World War II. While this holiday began as a way of remembering Civil War dead, its purpose, in my youth, was not so confined. It was eventually renamed Memorial Day, and its focus was narrowed to what it is today: the state-serving remembrance of military veterans. That this Memorial Day weekend was seized upon as an opportunity to open the World War II Memorial in Washington, D.C., illustrates the point. For those who still don't get the message, television stations give us a steady diet of pro-war movies.

Memorial Day weekend will soon be followed by the Fourth of July. This day—honoring the signing of the Declaration of Independence, a writing of a decidedly anti-statist nature—has likewise been co-opted by the war-lovers. Additional rounds of movies celebrating warfare will be made available to television viewers. The 1942 Bing Crosby musical,

Holiday Inn, includes a July Fourth segment with a montage of bombers, naval ships, tanks, and other weaponry—with lyrics straight out of FDR's "New Deal"—to remind audiences that what began as a day to celebrate freedom from the state was now to be understood as a day to glorify statism in its most repressive and destructive form.

November 11th was referred to as Armistice Day in my youth, a day set aside to celebrate the *end* of World War I; a day, in other words, to honor a return to *peace* in the world. By 1954, this day, too, had been hijacked by the war system, renamed Veterans Day, and once again used by the statists to remind Americans of the virtues of going off to foreign lands to kill others and to get killed or wounded themselves. And, of course, another round of pro-war films will saturate television screens. The heirs of John Wayne and Randolph Scott must receive handsome residual payments from the showing of such movies during the holiday seasons.

I have wondered how far the war establishment might go in taking over other holidays. Will Thanksgiving Day become a time to be "thankful" for all the military hardware—including some ten thousand hydrogen bombs—bestowed upon America? When, two Christmases ago, I saw a Christmas card with Santa Claus decked out in a red-white-and-blue suit, I knew the complete militarization of the culture was upon us.

These holiday celebrations of warfare are rendered even more distasteful by the nearly endless parade of speakers who praise war veterans who "fought for freedom." I have long been disinclined to criticize soldiers themselves, not because they are free from personal responsibility for their participation in institutionalized butchery, but because I prefer to focus my energies on the systemic thinking that produces such insane practices. Soldiers—most of whom were teenagers when they entered the military— are more victims of statist indoctrination in the "glory" and "heroism" of warfare than they are culprits. But just as the state found it useful to exploit their lives in wartime, it capitalizes on their deaths and sufferings in peacetime as a way of getting us to recommit ourselves to the perpetuation of the war system. To be for *peace* is to denigrate the memories of those who "sacrificed" for our "freedom."

The idea of soldiers "fighting for freedom" is an Orwellian-like concept riddled with self-contradictions. To begin with, wars have always *reduced* individual liberty, not only during but after the wars. The American Civil War was conducted *not* to free slaves, but to aggrandize state power, thus restricting liberties. Lincoln has earned the disrespect of those who value liberty for having laid the foundations of the present Leviathan state.[1] The Spanish-American War, World Wars I and II, the Korean and Vietnamese Wars, escalated the powers of the nation-state over the lives of Americans. In case these earlier episodes of organized barbarity are too distant for you, recall how quickly and easily the Bush administration was able to greatly expand the American police-state with such measures as the Patriot Act, the creation of a Department of Homeland Security, and the arbitrary holding—without trial or contact with family or attorneys—of virtually anyone the state wishes held.

How can it be seriously entertained that soldiers "fight for freedom?" They were unable to secure even their *own* freedom from the state. To allow one's life to be taken over, regimented, directed, and even destroyed by the state, hardly qualifies as a working definition of "freedom." *Slavery* is a word more befitting such a subjugated condition.

Furthermore, how can a person be said to be "free" when his or her life is embroiled in conflict? How can one be free when fighting others? Is a life fired by anger and hatred of others, along with a willingness to torture, maim, or kill anyone designated by state officials as your "enemy," consistent with a life of *freedom*?

Memorial Day speeches are filled with the prayer that "these dead shall not have died in vain." But the truth is that the victims of warfare have *always* died in vain, and will continue to die pointlessly, for war is its own reason for being. "War is the health of the state,"[2] Randolph Bourne reminded us decades ago, a health that, like the human body, is dependent upon regular exercise.

I was ten years old when World War II ended, and I recall the sense of relief in the anticipation that *peace* was to return to the world. This was not unlike the attitude that surfaced, briefly, with the end of the Cold War. But the state cannot endure peace. We should have picked up the warning when, shortly after World War II, the government changed the name of the "War Department" to the "Defense Department," and renamed our erstwhile "friends," China and the Soviet Union, as our new "enemies," while our previous "enemies"—Germany and Japan—were our new "friends." Such was the signal, had we paid attention, that war had become a permanent

---

1   See, e.g., Thomas J. DiLorenzo, *The Real Lincoln: A New Look at Abraham Lincoln, His Agenda, and an Unnecessary War* (Roseville, Calif.: Prima Publishing, 2002).

2   Randolph Bourne, *War and the Intellectuals* (New York: Harper & Row, 1964), p. 71.

system for advancing corporate-state interests by the subjugation of the American people.

If the state is to maintain power over us, it must have an endless supply of enemies with which to excite our fears. The Soviet Union served this purpose well for nearly half a century, but with its collapse, the American state went in search of a new foe. Islamic "terrorism" became the new adversary. With an expansive military presence throughout the world, the American state had assured itself of an enemy that is not likely to vanish. When the George W. Bush administration announced that the war on terror would be an endless one, it was confirming the truth of Bourne's observation.

As dangerous as terrorism is, we must acknowledge its origins and the energies that sustain it. Humanity continues to be held hostage to the deeper terrorist threat of which polite company refuses to speak, namely, the political organization of society. As we continue to recycle the destructive energies of the war system that *is* the state, the time may soon be upon us when even the most patriotic flag-waver will have to stand and say "enough!" As politicians and other participants in the war racket continue to preach of our "responsibilities" to keep this slaughterhouse stocked with sacrificial victims, we may find ourselves called to a higher responsibility. Learning how to renounce and walk away from this obscene system may be the act of responsibility each of us must take as our share of being human.

As decent and compassionate human beings, let us remember the dead and wounded of war—as well as their families—as the victims of a kind of thinking that must be transcended if humanity is to survive. But let us stop glorifying butchery with parades, medals, gaseous speeches, and the erection of war memorials. Let us have no more Tom Brokaw patronizing drivel that equates the "greatness" of people with their willingness to join in lemming-like suicidal marches. Let us stop investing the lives and souls of our sons and daughters as our commitment to this vicious enterprise. Let us learn to love our children more than we do the state that sees them as nothing more than fungible resources for the mass production of casualties.

I recall, years ago, news stories about the last Civil War or Spanish-American War veteran to die. Perhaps we shall one day have occasion to celebrate Memorial Day by remembering the final victim of the war system itself.

CHAPTER 12

Orwell Lives!

Orwell's "doublespeak" is alive and well this morning. In a nationally-televised press conference, Lt. Gen. Thomas Metz—the commander of the Multi-National Corps—kept referring to the Iraqi insurgents as "anti-Iraqi forces." Since the United States is fighting these forces, this must make the Americans the "pro-Iraqi forces." Nobody in the press called Metz on this. Corrupt systems are always preceded and maintained by the corruption of language.

CHAPTER 13

The Siege of San Fransicso

I was in San Francisco on a recent Sunday, my visit coinciding with the U.S. Navy's annual "Fleet Week" show of a portion of its arsenal of destructiveness. The most annoying part of this demonstration consisted of a prolonged buzzing of the city by at least five "Blue Angels" FA-18 fighter-bombers. This was not one of those common air-shows conducted at an airbase where Boobus Americanus could pay an admission fee for a show: in San Francisco, the entire city was the grandstand. Whether you cared to enjoy the simulated attack or not, you were subjected to the noisiest screeching, roaring, and ear-shattering sounds—with an occasional sonic boom thrown in for good measure—as these planes flew at housetop levels for a few hours. We had to keep covering our ears as these howling menaces flew a hundred feet above our heads. The planes fly in very close formation—they pride themselves in maintaining eighteen-inch separations from one another—which, on some past occasions, have led to deadly crashes. Had this occurred in San Francisco that day, hundreds of innocent people might have been added to the growing list of fungible victims of American air power throughout the world. The irresponsible nature of this undertaking was evident to any intelligent observer.

To characterize this air show as a form of entertainment is to misjudge its intended purpose. Like the annual May Day military parades conducted by the Soviet government, the objective of this exercise was to remind people of the disproportion of power that the state exercises over them. Should you harbor any sentiments of disobedience to state authority, this is what government officials have at their disposal to bring you back into line. At a time when it became known that a large body of American troops had been returned from Iraq to be deployed in American cities, the presence of such Navy hardware added to the intimidation. President Bush's threat to members of Congress—as reported by one congressman—to impose martial law should they fail to pass the infamous corporate "bailout" measure, showed the effectiveness of menacing people with violence.

War has long since ceased to be just a confrontation between competing military forces. The days in which ordinary folk would bring their picnic lunches to the hillsides surrounding battlefields to watch the mutual organized slaughter of the Lower Ruritanian army by the Slobovian forces (and vice-versa) are embedded in our past. Since at least the American Civil War, military operations have expanded far beyond attacks on forts, ammunition depots, supply lines, and other tools of warfare. The general population—what statists like to refer to as the "citizenry"—have become the targets of choice, particularly those that congregate in major cities. Those who once thought that urban areas provided safety in numbers from military attacks, now find themselves considering the advantages of isolation in under-populated areas.

The state-conducted wars and genocidal practices that consumed a very conservative figure of some 200,000,000 lives in the twentieth century, were not directed at military troops alone, but at massive populations. Thus were militarily-meaningless cities such as Dresden and Wurzburg leveled by British and American bombers in raids that killed tens of thousands of people. The attacks on Dresden were defended, by the RAF's noted war criminal, Sir Arthur "Bomber" Harris, on the grounds that there were no other cities left to bomb! The nightly "blitz" of London by German bombers served the same ends of generating massive fear among ordinary people. Likewise, the nuclear bombings of Hiroshima and Nagasaki were conducted for the primary purpose of impressing upon the Soviet Union the nature of the weaponry possessed by the United States. Whoever was responsible for the attacks on 9/11 had in mind the terrorizing of ordinary Americans—at work in their places of employment—rather than the immobilization or destruction of military installations.

Flag-waving Americans are unable to deny the fear-inspiring purposes of warfare. The United States' initial bombardments of Baghdad were carried out under the banner of "Shock and Awe," an admission that terrorizing local populations—not attacking military targets—was its purpose. What other objectives than inducing terror among innocent people could have served such constant and powerful bombardments?

While San Franciscans did not experience the death and devastation visited upon civilian Iraqis—or their counterparts in such places as Beirut and Kosovo—they were subjected to the terrorizing influences war machines provide—and are intended to provide. The war system is designed to remind people that their own governments can destroy them whenever they choose to do so, and that there are no effective repercussions to the state other than armed revolutions that end up replacing one gang of warlords with another equally rapacious group. As Randolph Bourne reminded us, war serves the intended purpose of keeping the state's compliant herd under control. As can be attested to by anyone who has watched monster films, or movies such as *Star Wars,* there is something about a screeching, powerful monstrosity—whether of a biological or technological nature—that can arouse fear and conquer even the most courageous of wills. A sci-fi movie depicting shrieking pterodactyls flying just above the rooftops of San Francisco homes served the same purposes as the real-life Blue Angels: to make the audience fearful. As with motion pictures, perhaps the Navy was presenting us with a preview of coming attractions!

As history reminds us, such domestic use of the military is not beyond the realm of possibility. The aforementioned report of government plans to deploy armed troops across America make this a genuine threat. Along these lines, my experience in the siege of San Francisco brought to mind an experience I had in my college days. At my university, male students were required to take two years of R.O.T.C. training. I opted for the Air Force franchise. Our instructor—a regular Air Force major on leave to the school—gave us an unsettling assignment. We were given detailed maps of various American cities and told to plan a bombing attack on the target chosen for us. I was given San Francisco as my targeted city, and laid out my planned assault. In doing so, I wondered whether I was to concentrate on the port, railroad facilities, manufacturing plants, or just an all-out Dresden-like slaughter of the Bay area innocents.

More than half-a-century later, I still have occasion to think back to the time when a state university and the Air Force tried to train me to conduct an aerial attack on a major American city. Had other young men been given similar assignments; men who now flew the machines that might be employed in a *real* attack? My Sunday in San Francisco was a reminder that "terrorism"—which most Americans and their government like to pretend they oppose even as they expand upon and fine-tune its tools—is the modus operandi of an ever-engorged state system. As I joined with my temporary San Francisco neighbors to protect my ear-drums, I wondered whether all of this was intended as just another round of statist entertainment—like elections—or a prediction of more serious urban sieges. That such terrorizing acts were being carried out by people purporting to be "angels" confirmed Orwell's understanding of how state power depends upon the corruption of language and, ultimately, of our thinking. Like the Air Force's slogan "peace is our profession," the Navy has its "Blue Angels" [or, perhaps, "Black-and-Blue Angels"] with which to disguise violence as civility.

CHAPTER 14

Suicide
and the Insanity of War

Tr comes a saturation point at which I can no longer listen to institutionalists (e.g., military and other government officials, academicians, members of the media) babble about what may be the most telling symptom of the anti-life nature of the state: the suicides of those entangled in its destructive machinations. Top military officials appeared this week before a congressional committee to discuss the fact that more American soldiers are dying by suicide than in combat, and to inquire into what can be done about this situation. I suspect these officers were quite sincere in their assessments and suggestions but—like institutional authorities generally—said nothing that might raise fundamental questions about the military or military thinking.

I watched about as much of this hearing as my mind could take, as one officer after another spoke of the needs for "programs" to address this problem; to help "train" servicemen and women to better handle the economic and family pressures, work-loads, and deployment in foreign countries. One military official spoke of the need to "analyze the data" to help protect the soldier who, in his view, was the military's "most valuable asset." One would fathom from the bulk of this testimony that what the young men and women who are contemplating self-destruction need most are more problem-solving skills; or perhaps another structured training program for soldiers to go through. The project could be expected to generate lucrative government-funded research grants to universities and so-called "think tanks," but no unsettling questions for the established order.

While I heard no mention of behavior modification drugs being administered to potential suicides, such an approach has been used in school systems to control young children. Might the state decide to fall back upon this strategy, perhaps to reinforce earlier conditioning, as well as to please the major pharmaceutical companies? Maybe "big-pharma" will be able to offer—at the high prices that always attend government programs—suicide-prevention drugs. As I watched this viciousness unfolding on C-SPAN, I kept recalling the Stanley Kubrick film, *A Clockwork Orange.*[1] Taken from Anthony Burgess' novel of the same name, the movie focuses on coercive methods of operant conditioning designed to overcome an individual's free will.

By its very nature, the state will persist in looking upon human beings as "assets," as "resources" to be cared for in much the same way as a rancher cares for his cattle. Problems that arise within the herd will be dealt with mechanistically and collectively: anthrax vaccinations and uniform diets for all; individual tastes and preferences being irrelevant to the "greater good."

I also heard no mention made of what, I suspect, is the principal contributor to the escalating rates of suicide: the insanity of the war system itself, its moral and spiritual bankruptcy. In the time that I watched these hearings, I heard not even an oblique reference to the spiritual costs of persons having their lives robotized and directed by the state for no other purpose than to kill men, women, and children who have been selected as targets. What does it do to an otherwise psychologically and emotionally centered person to have one's training as a systematic killer of strangers become the highlight of his or her life?

It is the war system, itself, that must be confronted and ended, lest it destroy all semblance of humanity. Those who have chosen to devote themselves to the planning and carrying out of programs designed for no other purpose than the mass slaughter of millions of fellow humans experience psychic costs that no amount of militaristic strutting or patriotic blather can suppress. It is not in the nature of any species to consciously destroy itself.

---

1   *A Clockwork Orange* (Warner Brothers, 1971).

Individuals have a spiritual and emotional nature that is absent from institutions. Institutions are, at best, tools driven entirely by linear, mechanistic, and materialistic considerations. They are *abstractions* which, like computer games, are purely the product of thought. They operate on the basis of compulsion, not compassion; what is *non*material is *im*material to such entities; they have become ends in themselves, while individuals are but transient beings who can be conditioned into serving as fungible resources to be exploited for collective ends. "Liberty" is a condition valued by individuals, but it is a form of entropy—energy that cannot be put to use for the purposes of the institutional order.

There is nothing more contemptible, in my mind, than the spectacle of school systems training impressionable children in the evil doctrine that their lives exist to serve alleged "greater interests" than their own. Whenever I am asked to identify the one governmental program I would most like to see disappear, my answer has always been: the government school system. This institutionalized form of child abuse has generated far more destructiveness than even the war system, for its pernicious conditioning is what makes possible our identification with the state as well as our willingness to give up our lives for it. Schools have trained us to see the necessity and desirability of the institutional scheme of things. Through the use of standardized teaching and standardized testing, they have taken standardized categories of children and trained their minds in the virtues of standardized thinking for a standardized world. In the words of Ivan Illich, "[s]chool is the advertising agency which makes you believe that you need the society as it is."[2]

Many parents—having been previously conditioned to become state servo-mechanisms—are unavailable to their children at a time when most needed to help question any of this organized insanity. Far too many mothers and fathers, I am sorry to say, end up loving the state more than they do their own children, and content themselves with a folded flag—handed to them by a uniformed officer—as a substitute.

It is not just the soldiers who commit suicide that provide evidence for the pathology of war. Those who die, or end up as cripples, or who desert, or who survive war physically unscathed but remain silently torn up inside, are all victims of this depraved system. I can only imagine the turmoil a

---

2   Ivan Illich, *Deschooling Society* (New York: Harper & Row, 1972), p. 163.

young soldier must go through before, as an act of utter despair, deciding to take his or her own life.

It is sad that adults—who express concern when an "Amber Alert" informs them of a missing child—will turn their backs on grown children who need support to help them through their spiritual crises. Of course, when "support the troops" really means "support the war," persons conditioned in the virtues of war and statism will provide no genuine help for the potential suicide. They will respond like the man who, upon witnessing a child drowning in a lake, can do no more than offer swimming lessons!

What will come from all of this superficial institutional hand-wringing will be but another interventionist behavior-modification program to help the soldiers overcome their failures to better adapt themselves to the needs of the military. Suicidal soldiers are an embarrassment to the state, making it difficult to enlist new recruits with promises to "be all you can be." Such disrespect to the system must be confronted! Perhaps within the Pentagon, military officials are even now watching re-runs of *A Clockwork Orange*.

The state—like so much of medical practice—profits by focusing on *symptoms*, while carefully avoiding attention to the underlying *disease*. Raising more fundamental inquiries might produce doubts about the central role to be played by institutions. It is the *soldiers* who are in need of reformation. As long as they are looked upon as the source of the suicide problem—to be rectified by additional conditioning—we can expect the self-destruction to continue. It is sad to think that an awareness of the moral and spiritual bankruptcy of the war system might be grasped most strongly by young people caught up in the middle of its destructiveness without what Joseph Campbell called "invisible means of support." Paradoxically, their acts of desperation may reflect a sanity that will be lost to a world wrapped in flags. Their suicides may be a harbinger of the fate of civilization itself.

CHAPTER 15

Vonnegut on War

I am reminded of a television interview I saw with Kurt Vonnegut and Joseph Heller, reliving their war experiences and how these had influenced their writings. Toward the end of the interview, Vonnegut told of coming back to America on a troop ship and asking a friend of his what the most important thing was that he learned from the war. "Never to believe your own government," was his friend's reply.

CHAPTER 16

How We Lost Our Souls

Attachment is the great fabricator of illusions; reality can be attained only by someone who is detached.

—Simone Weil

Anyone who has not seen the videotape of the July 12, 2007, helicopter attack by American soldiers that resulted in the deaths of unarmed Iraqi civilians and two Reuters news employees, can view it on YouTube.[1] After months of requests, by Reuters, for this video—followed by refusals from the military—WikiLeaks received a copy from an unknown source. The revelation of this atrocity quickly raised criticisms not just of the practice, but of the mindsets of soldiers who could so eagerly and gleefully carry out this slaughter of innocents. Even the shooting of children at the scene produced no apparent sense of wrongdoing on the part of the soldiers.

How does such moral depravity not just occur, but become so pervasive in our world? The occasional recordings of such behavior touch only the surface of institutionalized viciousness. Was Rodney King the first person to be brutalized by police officers? Were civilians shielded from

---

1   www.youtube.com/watch?v=c107jl_hKXQ&oref=http%3A%2F%2F; www.google.com%2Furl%3Fs

execution-style murder prior to the My Lai massacre? Did the revelations at Abu Ghraib constitute the first acts of torture practiced by American soldiers upon captive civilians? In each of these occurrences—a precedent no doubt to be followed in the current criminal machine-gunning of Iraqis—one or more scapegoats were selected for punishment, so as to distance the brutality of their actions from the more pervasive inhumanity that inheres in the institutions for which they acted.

The central theme of my writing has been to demonstrate that allowing institutional purposes to pre-empt our own has been destructive of life, liberty, peace and, ultimately, of civilizations. We have long walked a line between our need for social organization—as a way of satisfying various mutual needs—and becoming so attracted to the systems that serve our interests that we want to make them permanent. We move imperceptibly from associations that we control in pursuit of our ends, to organizations that become ends in themselves, and that control us in order to foster their interests. When this occurs, the informal organization has metamorphosed into an *institution*. I have developed this process more fully in my book, *Calculated Chaos*.[2]

When we *identify* ourselves with, and *attach* ourselves to these institutional entities, we absorb their values; their purposes; their modus operandi. Such practices of attachment can be analogized to a cancer that metastasizes our inner sense of being. In the process, we become dehumanized, for institutions have no souls; no emotions; no spiritual, moral, or intuitive sense. They neither cry, bleed, love, or experience elation. They are *machines* and, like other machines, operate solely on the basis of mechanics, linear processes, and material ends. When we become institutionalized, we become little more than robots—servo-mechanisms—functioning in response to how we have been programmed to perform.

The emotional and spiritual dimensions that make us human are of no value to institutions which, in times of political wrong-doing, urge us to suppress such sentiments. In so complying, we replace the spiritual core of our being with commitments to the lifeless and dispirited interests of organizations. In place of deeply-held philosophic *principles*, institutions have *policies*; their sense of "meaning" consists only of *perpetuating* themselves by maximizing their power and material wealth. To such entities,

---

2   Shaffer, *Calculated Chaos*.

human beings have value only as fungible resources to exploit on behalf of institutional ends.

It would be easy to condemn the soldiers who engaged in this slaughter as "evil" or "depraved" or "insane" beings. Such is the manner in which we have long accustomed ourselves to blanking out any awareness of the "dark side" of our own unconscious. In such ways have we isolated ourselves from the Hitlers, Stalins, Mao Tse-Tungs, Pol Pots, and other tyrants, leaving us with the comforting feeling that we shared nothing in common with them. But history informs us—if we will only look—that, once we have identified ourselves with any purpose beyond ourselves, we can become capable of the most vicious forms of wrongdoing. How do otherwise decent men participate in a lynch-mob?

The state—with its lawful powers of compulsion—is particularly attractive to men and women whose "dark sides" are closer to the surface than those of more tolerant and peaceful persons. When the state energizes this "dark side"—which it does particularly in wartime—otherwise decent men and women can turn themselves into agents of savage brutality. When their murderous acts are conducted on behalf of the state—with which most people identify themselves—their actions acquire an aura of legitimacy that would not have obtained under other circumstances; a distinction that would prevent them from becoming serial killers upon their return home.

Identifying ourselves with the state, in other words, has a way of turning us into sociopaths. It is not that the *state* does this to *us,* but that our willingness to attach ourselves to external entities—and the values upon which they are grounded—separates us from our focused inner sense of being. This applies not just to the pilots of helicopter gun-ships over Baghdad, but to more visible political figures such as Madeleine Albright—who defended her Clinton-era policies that led to the deaths of 500,000 Iraqi children—and Janet Reno, who defended her massacre of Branch Davidian men, women, and children at Waco. More recent application of these dynamics are found in George W. Bush's fascination with starting pre-emptive wars against the rest of the world, and Barack Obama's apparent willingness to use nuclear weapons in future pre-emptive attacks, as well as to assassinate Americans.

People who are willing to embrace—or even to tolerate—such sociopathic conduct, have lost all touch with what it means to be human; have lost their souls. No federal bailouts; no increase in the Dow Jones Industrial Average, or decrease in unemployment levels, will overcome this loss.

Nor can any "stimulus package" be enacted—with or without bipartisan support—to restore the personal integrity long since lost.

There was a time, not so many decades ago, when brute force—particularly when engaged in by police and military agents of the state—was at least frowned upon, if not condemned, by decent men and women. The threshold level for such practices continues to get progressively lower. A major contribution to Barry Goldwater's defeat in the 1964 presidential campaign, was the unfounded fear that he might be willing to use nuclear weapons in the war in Vietnam. Modernly, Bush's and Obama's willingness to *initiate* a nuclear war have raised no major outcries from most Americans, who seem to prefer "hope" (i.e., wishful thinking) over intelligent "understanding" as a way of making the world free, peaceful, and productive.

When the 2008 GOP presidential candidate, John McCain, can garner nearly 60,000,000 votes with his sociopathic dance of "bomb, bomb, bomb Iran,"[3] should we be shocked by the butcherous conduct of some American helicopter pilots?

---

3   Wikipedia.org/wiki/Bomb_Iran

CHAPTER 17

The Wee Ones Revisited

On April 20, 2010, a major oil spill occurred at a British Petroleum facility in the Gulf of Mexico, causing severe damage along the coastlines. On June 16, 2010, the company's chairman, Carl-Henric Svanberg, responded to the problems caused to people along the Gulf Coast by publicly declaring "we care about the small people."[1]

Corporate-state systems have long employed the mantra "do it for the children" to propagandize on behalf of public acceptance of increased politicization of their lives. The chairman of BP may have expanded on this idea in asserting that "we care about the small people" in their corporate policies. When I first saw this report, I thought that the chairman might have just seen *The Wizard of Oz*, and was commenting on the Munchkins!

While a BP official tried to pass off the remark as only "a slip in translation," the "slip" may have been more *Freudian* than purely *linguistic*. Perhaps his comment reflected—at an unconscious level—the innate division that separates *institutional* from *human* purposes. That distinction was not lost on some Gulf area residents, one of whom stated "BP does not care

---

1   *Daily Finance*, June 15, 2010.

about us . . . . We are the nickel-and-dime folks of this world." Another commented "We are not small people. We're human beings. They're no greater than us. We don't bow down to them. We don't pray to them."[2]

By their very nature, institutions have always regarded those subject to their will as "small people," as "children" whose interests are to be looked after by more dominant systems. Members of the aristocracy used to toss "nickels-and-dimes" to the common folk, as their carriages rolled through the streets. The means of transportation have greatly changed, but the same hierarchical mindset remains.

---

2   www.msnbc.com/id/37739658/ns/disaster_in_the_gulf/t/bp-boss-sorry-about-small-people-remark/

CHAPTER 18

Resisting the Deadly Virus

It matters little which system I join; they all have the same character.

—Jacques Ellul

I ran into one of my former students the other day. He declared: "you were right; you said the entire institutional system is coming apart, and you were right." "And I'll bet," I replied, "that, at the time I said this, you giggled and guffawed along with your classmates." "I'll admit that I did," he said, "but I'm also admitting that you were right." I then told him that one didn't have to be clairvoyant to see what was coming; that the self-destructive nature of institutionalism is implicit in the premises by which modern society is organized.

When asked by a reporter, "what do you think about Western Civilization," Mahatma Gandhi is said to have replied: "I think it would be a good idea!"[1] Gandhi's words reflect the historic—but too often unacknowledged—struggle between the creative, peaceful, and life-enhancing forces of civilization, and the violent and destructive character of institutionally-centered systems, particularly those organized around the state. Based

---

1   www.anvari.org/fortune/Quotations_-_Random/1320_quote-135-reporter-mr-gandhi-what-do-you

upon the study of past civilizations, there is an almost deterministic sense that Western Civilization has been destined to collapse, as though cultures go through comparable birth-life-death cycles as organic systems.

Part of the dilemma in which mankind has long found itself arises from our dualistic nature: we are not only unique *individuals*—each with a DNA unmatched by any other—but also *social* beings who require the cooperation and companionship of others. None of us would have survived for more than a few hours had our mothers, following our births, tossed us beside the road and continued along their way. We require the constant, loving assistance of adults to get us to a point where we can sustain ourselves. As adults, we discover the advantages of a specialization of labor that permits us to exchange our work efforts with others and, in the process, to live well, not only materially but psychologically.

There are implications to such fundamental truths that have proven destructive to our capacities for living both productive and personally satisfying lives. If social cooperation is essential to our very existence both as individuals and civilizations, what organizational forms are *supportive* of and, alternately, *detrimental* to, such ends?

Such a question is crucial to the long-term well-being of a society due to the record of past civilizations' respective declines and falls. For all of the creative, life-sustaining benefits that have arisen within civilizations, there are internal forces that contradict such advantageous interests. These destructive influences can be analogized to a *virus* which, if left unchecked by inattentiveness, can metastasize and overwhelm immune systems. This virus is *institutionalism*, or the transformation of organizational systems from convenient *tools*, into their own purposes for being.

Returning to the metaphor of the cutting-and-filling nature of a river, the course of the river—when its cutting and filling functions complement each other—expresses the processes of continuing change that are essential to the health of any living system. Our economic life, for instance, has been characterized by Joseph Schumpeter as one of "creative destruction," wherein the established gets altered or replaced by the new. Schumpeter saw this as a "process of industrial mutation . . . that incessantly revolutionizes the economic structures *from within*, incessantly destroying the old one, incessantly creating a new one."[2]

The problem is that many of those who have been able to establish their positions on the banks become uncomfortable with this incessant

---

2   Schumpeter, *Capitalism, Socialism, and Democracy*, p. 83 (emphasis in original).

interplay between the destruction and creativity that is the productive process. They may then undertake efforts to restrain such changefulness, a topic I explored more fully in my book *In Restraint of Trade.*[3] They usually begin with voluntary efforts to restrain the pace of competition. But, being unable to keep up with the dynamics they face, they turn to the state, whose tools of coercion enable them to forcibly constrain such creative threats to the status quo. Without the state—or other violent means—organizational size would be restrained by the internal pressures that oppose resiliency.

Herein are found early symptoms of the virus that can attack and destroy an otherwise healthy society. Because of its powerful energies, the river may cut into the banks upon which established interests have set their foundations in the expectation that they will enjoy permanency.

When dealing with diseases to our bodies, we are accustomed to focus our attentions on *symptoms*, and imagine that *they* are what ail us. We too often assume that, if we can suppress the symptoms we can restore our health. We apply such thinking not only to personal health concerns, but to *political* matters. Thus, as we encounter increasing social violence, many find it easy to imagine that *guns* are the cause of our difficulties, and promote legislation to criminalize gun ownership. If children—failing to find inspiration in the mechanistic and regimented teaching methods of formal education—pursue their own interests, they may be singled out for drugging or other behavior modification practices. As the American corporate-state expands its militarization throughout the world, many explain away the reactive anger of foreigners as the "terrorism" inhering in non-Western cultures.

Just as a competent physician will look beyond the manifestations of a disease in search of its root causes, we—as members of a civilization—must learn how to discover deeper causes for the terminal state of our culture than those superficial explanations that entertain more than they inform. My reading of history points to *institutionalism* as the deadly virus. The infection seems to take hold at the point when an organization becomes repeatedly effective, such that its members want to make it permanent. In the minds of its supporters, the system is transformed from being a convenient tool for the accomplishment of mutual objectives, and becomes an *abstraction;* an end-in-itself.

---

3   Shaffer, *In Restraint of Trade.*

The health of a system depends upon its capacity for resiliency and adaptability to changing conditions. A business organization facing a new source of competition must, in a free market, either make an effective response to the price and/or quality of a competitor's product, or suffer income losses that may eventually force them out of business. Accepting the institutionalist premise that having become established entitles one to a permanent status is, as the historians advise us, an invitation to the collapse of a productive civilization.

It is not inevitable that institutionalism, alone, will produce harmful consequences, any more than being a drunken driver will necessarily result in an accident. But each such condition increases the likelihood of adverse effects. As long as we continue to believe in state coercion as a necessary means for social order, those who regard their interests as being best served through violence, will have recourse to the state, and to the detriment of the rest of us.

As the belief in institutionalism fully infects the mind, many regard the preservation of established systems as more important than maintaining the conditions that led to the creation of such organizations in the first place. Liberty and spontaneity come to be regarded as threats to a status quo that must be maintained at all costs. Evidence for this paralyzed mindset is found in the current practice now being engaged in with the federal government bestowing untold hundreds of billions of dollars upon banks, insurance companies, automobile manufacturers, and other major corporate interests that have been labeled—in words reflective of institutionalism—"too big to fail."

Microsoft and "Time" magazine—whose established economic interests are challenged by the Internet—have recently proposed that the government license access to the Internet.[4] This is the same proposal Hillary Clinton made, a number of years ago, in proposing a government "gatekeeper" that would keep just *anyone* from putting their opinions out into the world.[5] The free flow of information is not only quite liberating—as the consequences of Gutenberg's fifteenth century invention made clear—but also increases complexity within society, to which individuals and organizations must respond. The more complex a society becomes, the greater the

---

4   Paul Joseph Watson, Infowars.com, October 7, 2010.

5   Rebecca Eisenberg, "First Lady Just Doesn't Get It," *sfgate*, February 22, 1998 (sfgate.com).

need for more informal, decentralized systems to provide order; complexity is a destabilizing influence to an institutionalized world that requires standardization and uniformity to maintain the status quo.

Licensing has replaced Inquisitions as the principal means for protecting established institutional interests from the specter of unbridled competition. Physicians, lawyers, dentists, accountants, and numerous other trades and professions have used this self-protective device. The logic remains the same in each case: a state licensing board will be set up—comprised of persons already in the business—to decide who will and will not be permitted to compete with them!

Whether we are considering licensing, the establishment of tariffs, or the opening of the federal treasury for wholesale looting to benefit the friends of those holding the keys to the treasury, it is always governmental *force* that is called upon to transmit the virus of institutionalism. The nation-state—which has become the *"typhoid Mary"* in all of this—continues to expose otherwise healthy tissue to the disease-ridden influence that has reduced Western Civilization to a terminal state.

CHAPTER 19

Structuring the Instruments of Expansion

The goal is to restrain disturbing influences, to stabilize prices, and to assure those in the business the comfortable feeling that their position is secure.

—Harold Fleming

A n illustration of how political and corporate institutions have generated a symbiotic relationship to restrain the processes of creativity and change that keep a civilization vibrant, can be found in the history of government regulation of business. In one form or another in America, modern government economic policies are centered on forcibly preserving the interests—including the existence—of large corporate enterprises from the turbulence and uncertainties that are so much a part of a flourishing culture. Free and unrestrained competition demanded a continuing resiliency in responding to market changes. The innovation in products, services, and business methods that made economic life creative and vibrant came to be seen as a threat to the survival of firms unable or unwilling to respond. Concerns for *security* and *stability* began to take priority over *autonomy* and *spontaneity* in the thinking of most business leaders.

In the volatile climate of a creative culture, change is one of the few constants upon which businessmen could rely. Economic survival often depends upon innovative adaptability; firms with higher unit costs and prices must either become more efficient, or drop out of the race. Instability and turnover have been continuing threats with which firms have had to contend. The severity of the competitive struggle has been no better reflected than in the automobile industry: of the 181 firms manufacturing cars at some time during the years 1903 to 1926, 83 remained in business as of 1922, while 20 managed to survive through 1938.[1]

Economist Joseph Schumpeter has observed that *price* competition is not the most significant factor to which firms have to respond. In his view—and particularly relevant to the theme of this book—it is not that kind of competition that matters, but the competition provided by "the new commodity, the new technology, the new source of supply, the new type of organization, . . . competition which commands a decisive cost or quality advantage and which strikes not at the margins of the profits and the outputs of the existing firms, but at their foundations and very lives." Citing retailing as an example, Schumpeter declared that the competition that was most critical arose "not from additional shops of the same type, but from the department store, the chain store, the mail-order house, and the supermarket."[2] Schumpeter's analysis may provide insight into how technology-driven innovations—including the Internet—are forcing the institutional order to respond.

With an ever-increasing frequency, the state has imposed upon the marketplace controls to regulate such matters as trade practices, pricing policies, and the size and entry of business firms. Government contracting and research and development funding, along with outright subsidies, have become so much a part of corporate life as to cause many people to regard such practices as synonymous with a "free market" system. The benefits of maintaining openness in competition—with no legal restrictions on freedom of entry, product design, or on the terms and conditions for which parties could contract with one another—have long been rejected by major business organizations more concerned with the survival of

---

1   Taken from Ralph C. Epstein, *The Automobile Industry* (Chicago: A.W. Shaw Company, 1928), pp. 164ff., and other sources cited in Donald A. Moore, "The Automobile Industry," in Walter Adams, ed., *The Structure of American Industry*, rev. 2nd ed. (New York: Macmillan, 1954), pp. 274 ff.

2   Schumpeter, *Capitalism, Socialism, and Democracy*, pp. 84, 85.

individual firms and industries. The phrases "laissez-faire" and "invisible hand" that once articulated an awareness of the conditions under which prosperity might prevail, have been replaced by the dogma "too big to fail," that have allowed modern governments to "bail out" failing firms with gifts of hundreds of billions of dollars!

The conversion from a more openly competitive to a protected security environment for American businesses was focused on the period from World War I to the start of World War II. During these years, a broad range of turbulent social and economic conditions existed: a war, an era of seemingly endless prosperity, the "Great Depression," and the New Deal with its promises of a politically engineered recovery.[3] Continuing throughout this period was an organizational transformation that had begun long before World War I: the "collectivization" of human society. The principle of "collective organization," postulating the superior interests of the *group* over those of its *individual members*, was emerging within the business system as well as within other sectors of society.

It must be recalled that the 1930s was a period of intense interest throughout much of the Western world in the collectivization of economies. The Soviet Union, Mussolini's Italy, Hitler's National Socialism in Germany, and the New Deal in America had in common the premise that economic life should be centralized under the strict authority of a bureaucratic state. Franco's coming to power in Spain in 1939 added to the phenomenon. The experience in America demonstrates that the driving force for such a system came from members of the business community desirous of controlling the inconstancy of a free market—wherein the self-interested actions of individual firms generated destabilizing competitive conditions—in order to moderate the pace of competition. The collectivism implicit in the New Deal came from within the business system, with the dominant firms working to restrain the "instruments of expansion" of which Quigley has written. Here is to be found one of the clearest examples of how collectivist thinking and practices have thwarted the productive efforts of individuals and, in the process, contributed to the enfeeblement of the civilization itself.

Because "collectivism" reflects conservative, status quo sentiments, its underlying premises were consistent with business efforts to resist change. Under the National Recovery Administration (NRA), industries organized

---

3   I have written more extensively on this period in *In Restraint of Trade*.

themselves through the machinery of the trade associations and began the task of altering the attitudes, belief systems, and practices that represented the old order. Business decision making that emphasized the well-being of the *individual firm* was to be eschewed in favor of attitudes that stressed the *collective* interests of the *industry* itself. Individual profit maximizing was to be de-emphasized when confronted by the "greater interests of the group"; independence and self-centeredness were to be put aside in favor of a more "cooperative" form of "friendly competition;" "standardization" and "uniformity" were to help define trade practices.

Nothing so threatened the interests of this emerging industrial order as the free play of market forces at work in an environment of legally unrestrained competition. Nothing so preoccupied industry-oriented business leaders in the post–World War I years as the effort to structure this environment so as to keep the conduct of trade within limits that posed no threat to their collective interests. The interplay between the creative influences of inconstancy, and the forces of stabilization that restrained change, became dominated by corporate interests that were more readily satisfied through state power than through the marketplace. The resulting transformations reflect a continuing institutionalization of economic life, contributing to the conditions various historians have identified as bringing about the demise of civilizations.

CHAPTER 20

Why TSA, Wars, State Defined Diets, Seat-Belt Laws, the War on Drugs, Police Brutality, and Efforts to Control the Internet, are Essential to the State

Whenever justice is uncertain and police spying and terror are at work, human beings fall into isolation, which, of course, is the aim and purpose of the dictator state, since it is based on the greatest accumulation of depotentiated social units.

—Carl Jung

The title of this article encompasses topics that arouse attention and criticism among persons of libertarian persuasion. The discussion of such matters usually treats each issue as though it were sui generis, independent of one another. Most of us respond as though the woman who is groped at the airport has no connection with the man who is tasered by a police officer; that the person serving time in prison for selling marijuana is unrelated to the men being held at Guantanamo.

The belief that one person's maltreatment is isolated from the rest of us, is essential to the maintenance of state power.

What we have in common is *the need to protect one another's inviolability from governmental force.* When we understand that the woman being groped by a TSA agent stands in the same shoes as our wife, mother, or grandmother; when the man being beaten by a sadist cop is seen, by us, as our father or grandfather, we become less willing to evade the nature of the wrongdoing by invoking the coward's plea: "better him than me." The state owes its very existence to the success it has had in fostering division among us. Divide-and-conquer has long been the mainstay in political strategy. If blacks and whites; or Christians and Muslims; or employees and employers; or "straights" and "gays"; or men and women; or any of seemingly endless abstractions, learn to identify and separate themselves from one another, the state has established its base of power. From such mutually-exclusive categories do we draw the endless "enemies" (e.g., communists, drug-dealers, terrorists, tobacco companies) we are to fear, and against whom the state promises its protection. By becoming fearful, we become existentially disabled, and readily accept whatever safeguards the institutional fear-mongers impose, . . . all for our "benefit," of course!

Look at the title of this article: do you find any governmental program or practice therein that is not grounded in state-generated fear? "Fear," as Spencer MacCallum has so well-stated, "is the coin of the realm of politics."[1] Each program—and the numerous others not mentioned—presumes a threat to your well-being against which the state must take restrictive and intrusive action. Terrorists might threaten the flight you are about to take; terrorist nations might have "weapons of mass destruction" and the intention to use them against you; your children might be at risk from drug dealers or from sex perverts using the Internet; driving without a seat-belt, or eating "junk" foods might endanger you: the list goes on and on, changing as the fear-peddlers dream up another dreaded condition in life.

It is not sufficient to the interests of the state that you fear other groups; it is becoming increasingly evident that you must also fear *the state itself!* Implicit in its legal monopoly on the power to coerce is the recognition that is the recognition that there be no limitations on its exercise, other than what serve the power interests of the state. In relatively quiet and stable periods (e.g., 1950s) the state can afford to give respect to notions of

---

1   From a personal communication with Spencer MacCallum.

individual privacy, free speech, and limitations on the powers of the police. In such ways, the state gives the appearance of reasonableness and respect for people. But when times become more tumultuous—as they are now— the very survival of the state depends upon a continuing assertion of the coercive powers that define its very being.

For a number of reasons—some of it technological—our social world is rapidly becoming decentralized. The highly-structured, centrally-directed institutions through which so much of our lives have been organized (e.g., schools, health-care, government, communications, etc.) no longer meet the expectations of many—perhaps most—men and women. Alternative systems, the control of which has become decentralized into individual hands, challenge the traditional institutional order. Private schools and home-schooling; alternative health practices; the Internet, cell-phones, and what is now known as the "social media," are in the ascendancy. With the state becoming increasingly expensive, destructive, economically disruptive, oppressive, and blatantly anti-life, secession and nullification movements have become quite popular.

Of course, such transformations are contrary to the established institutional interests that have, for many decades, controlled the state, and with it the coercive power that is its principal asset. Having long enjoyed the power to advance their interests *not* through the peaceful, voluntary methods of the *marketplace*, but through such *coercive* means as governmental regulation, taxation, wars, and other violent means, the established order is not about to allow the changing preferences of hundreds of millions of individuals to disrupt its traditional cozy racket.

Because the institutional order has become inseparable from the coercive nature of the state, any popular movement toward non-political systems is, in effect, a movement *away* from the violent structuring of society. The corporate interests that control the machinery of the state may try to convince people that government does protect their interests vis-à-vis the various fear-objects. Failing in this, the statists must resort to the tactic that sustains the playground bully: to reinforce fear of the bully, who controls his victims through a mixture of violence and degradation.

Neither the TSA nor the alleged "war on terror" have *anything* to do with terrorism. The idea that the TSA came about as a consequence of 9/11 ignores the fact that the state's practice of prowling through the personal belongings of airline passengers goes back many decades. I recall how upset a friend of mine was—in the early 1970s—when government officials went through his hand-luggage, and ordered him to unwrap a birthday gift he was carrying home to a relative. The purpose of such a search then, as now, was to remind passengers of the bully's basic premise: "I can do anything I want to you whenever I choose to do so." It is for the purpose of keeping us docile—an objective furthered by degrading and dehumanizing us—that underlies such state practices. The groping of people's genitals and breasts is but an escalation of this premise, and should the TSA later decide that all passengers must strip naked for inspection, such a practice will go unquestioned not only by the courts, but by the mainstream media who will ask ". . . but if you don't have anything to hide . . ." Those who cannot imagine state power going to such extremes to humiliate people into submission, are invited to revisit the many photographs of German army officers at such places as Auschwitz, who watched—as "full body scanners"—naked women being forced to run by them.

The extension of wars—against any enemy that any president chooses as a target—serves the same purpose. It is not necessary that there be any plausible rationale for the bombing and invading of other countries: it is sufficient that Americans and foreigners alike be reminded of the violence principle upon which government rests. "I will go to war against you if it serves my interests to do so, and any resistance on your part will only confirm what a threat you are to America!" The state directs its wars not so much against foreign populations, as against its own. War rallies people into the mindset of unquestioning obedience because, by engaging in such deadly conduct, the state reminds us of its capacities to destroy us at its will.

You can apply this logic to any of the aforementioned government programs. The state—and the corporate order that depends upon the exercise of state power—is fighting for its survival. Rather than treating this as a "war against terrorism," it is more accurate to consider it as a "war to preserve the institutional order." There are too many trillions of dollars and too much arbitrary power at stake for those who benefit from controlling the state's instruments of violence to await the outcome of ordinary people's thinking. If the survival of the corporate-state power structure required the extermination of *two billion* people, such a program would be undertaken with little hesitation. Destructive violence becomes an end-in-itself to an organization that is defined in terms of its monopoly on such means.

On the other hand, I continue to remain optimistic that these institutional wars against life will come to an end. I believe that the United States of America is in a terminal condition; its fate already determined. But *America*—whose existence predates the United States—may very well survive in a fundamentally changed form. What is helping this transformation process are innovative technological tools for the decentralized exchange of information; mankind is rapidly becoming capable of communicating with one another in the most direct ways, methods that make traditional top-down forms less and less relevant. The Internet is one system that is the tip of an iceberg whose deeper challenges have thus far not captured the attention of crew members of the ship-of-state. *Wikileaks* is another step in the evolution of decentralized information systems that will bring greater transparency to the activities of the ruling classes. In the process, men and women will discover just how liberating the free flow of information can be. When the rest of the world has access to the same information that political systems try to keep secret, the games played at the expense of people begin to fall apart.

An awareness of the dynamics of change being brought about through decentralizing forces has not, however, managed to inform members of the established order. For all of their pretended knowledge and expertise about the world, they just don't get it. They seem to imagine that their decline-and-fall can be prevented by keeping the Bradley Mannings and Julian Assanges locked up; and that the political ramifications can be deterred by distracting attention away from a Ron Paul—who *does* understand the nature and direction of these changes—and toward a comic-opera Sarah Palin.

In the meantime, in an effort to keep Boobus and other members of the herd within their assigned stalls, the ever-present threat of force and its consequent degradation of the individual will be invoked as the state works feverishly—and futilely—to shore up its collapsing foundations.

CHAPTER 21

Saving Our Brave, New World

The symptoms of our decline-and-fall are becoming increasingly evident even to those who, not so many years ago, regarded the outcome of an *American Idol* contest as their most pressing concern. A public-opinion-poll mentality substitutes for thinking in our modern world, creating a collective mindset that insists upon instantaneous answers to questions that few people are capable of asking. As the processes of causation play out the inexorable consequences of premises grounded in utter stupidity, a holiday for the expression of socio-economic fantasies has beset us. Hardly a week goes by without some twit—whether in or out of office—upping the ante in a bull market for runaway imbecility. Such efforts continue to produce an upswing in GDP ("Grotesquely Delusional Programs"), with politicians, academicians, and media hacks jostling one another—like San Francisco cable-car passengers—to be first aboard.

Murray Rothbard said, more than once, that there was nothing wrong about a person not fully understanding economics; but that those ignorant of economic principles ought not to be proposing governmental policies to govern economic activity. I have a hard time imagining Murray remaining calm as multitudes of men and women—with nary an understanding of economics—consult their Ouija boards for additional "solutions" to the calculated chaos generated by earlier practitioners of political mysticism.

Unable to engage in the economic analysis that would both explain and provide a basis for resolving current crises—an approach that would call into question the entire logic of statism—the established order has been forced to seek other rationales for its authority. The New Deal gave us a proliferation of alphabetized federal agencies to do what Plato envisioned could be done, namely to plan for and direct the course of economic systems. But the study of chaos and complexity—along with the failed histories of state planning—have shown the fallacy of such thinking. As but one glaring example, ordinary people are discovering what Ron Paul and others have long observed: the vaunted, "independent" Federal Reserve system is not only incapable of regularizing the marketplace, but has been a principal agency for sowing confusion into our economic life.

The Platonic image of "philosopher kings" sitting atop pyramids of power and directing the lives of hundreds of millions of people to ill-defined ends, is increasingly questioned by those who produce the genuine order in society. Contrary to the basic tenets of all forms of statism, it is the spontaneous order generated by the individual pursuit of self-interests in a marketplace that accounts for both our liberty and material well-being. But in the marbled halls of state, as well as the sycophantic media and academic institutions that are well-paid to propagate a continuing faith in the cult of centralized power, the mantra is still heard, with only the content of the litanies modified to fit new situations. "Save the planet" now substitutes for "save democracy," but the premise of state power structures remains intact.

For a culture fast descending into history's memory hole, and with the illusion of central planning no longer enjoying the intellectual support it once did, the established order has turned to the most desperate of measures: *magical* thinking enforced by undiluted, unprincipled *coercion*. No longer does the pretense of a scientific, rational basis for state planning prevail. Instead, resort is had to a kind of political *sorcery*—wrapped in the behavior-modification terminology of "stimulus." Trillions of dollars are given away to the corporate friends of those in power, and the system waits to see what happens. When vice-president Joe Biden admitted, on a *Meet the Press* program, that "everyone guessed wrong" on the government's stimulus program[1], the state has revealed its underlying sophistry.

In a society as thoroughly politicized as ours, the booboisie will always react with demands for the state to "do something," a mindset that

---

1   www.freerepublic.com/focus/f-bloggers/2272088/posts

gives the statists a continuing incentive to identify—or concoct, if necessary—fears that can be used to increase state power. When the civilization, itself, is in collapse, Boobus will insist that *something—anything*—be done, if for no other reason than to keep alive the illusion that the state is still in charge of events in the world, and can act to bring about desired results. An awareness that there is nothing the state *can* do to reverse the fate it has unleashed is as unavailable to most people as would be a physician's assurances, to family members, that Uncle Willie's terminal condition cannot be overcome with Dr. Quack's Cancer Salve!

What else could be expected from political systems, whose only distinguishing characteristic is an enjoyment of a monopoly on the use of violence? "Reason" in the mouths of government officials, always reduces to no more than rationalizations to justify whatever it is the statists want to do. When the promised results of economic planning are not forthcoming, the troops—with their tanks, armored personnel carriers, attack helicopters, and machine guns— will be sent in to enforce the state's will. At that point, Boobus may begin to learn what the German and Russian people learned, namely, that the alleged distinction between "law enforcement" and "national defense" has been but another deception employed to protect the establishment from its own people.

And so, we seem to have reached that stage where state violence has become its own raison d'etre. Social and economic problems are no longer considered within the sphere of authority of legislative bodies; Congress is too slow to act when "we need action, now!," and so the president or governor takes over and appoints—without anyone else's approval—"czars" to rule over various realms of human activity. My thesaurus advises me that synonyms for "czar" include "despot," "tyrant," "dictator," "slave driver," "duce," "oppressor," and "fuhrer." One source informs us that some thirty-three "czars" have been appointed by President Obama.[2]

This is what we have become, a consequence that should reveal to all that scribbling words on parchment and calling them a "constitution" is ineffective to prevent any significant number of people from doing whatever they want to do. The response of some mainstream media's "talking heads" to America's embrace of "czars" has been *not* to question the statist power implications, but only to suggest calling such officials by a different name! As has become the norm in our world, if we use an alternative word to

---

2   en.wikipedia.org/wiki/List_of_U.S._executive_branch_czars

describe something (e.g., "waterboarding" instead of "torture") it becomes a different act.

With Boobus having learned his catechisms about health-care costs, and the terrible-of-terribles attending "climate change," might we expect some of these "czars" to get together and plan a solution to both? Perhaps we shall soon be informed that each person produces approximately 2.3 pounds of carbon dioxide per day, an amount that translates into 2.5 *billion* tons of carbon dioxide per year for all six billion humans. Perhaps people could be euthanized at age 65—when most have become economically nonproductive, and increasingly costly drains upon Social Security and the health-care system—a result that would greatly reduce their production of carbon dioxide. While such a program would exempt the philosopher-kings from its operation, the next generation of Boobus—unfamiliar with both the philosophically-principled and spiritual nature of what it means to be human—could probably be counted upon to embrace it. All it would take to reinforce a popular commitment to ridding the planet of us pesky humans would be an occasional showing of the picture of a polar bear clinging to its melting patch of ice.

CHAPTER 22

"Klaatu barada nikto!"

I f you want to protect your life—and those of your children and grand-children—you'd better memorize this phrase. It may save you from a threat apparently being voiced at NASA: an attack from another planet somewhere in the vastness of our universe.[1] Why might such an assault be forthcoming? Because we humans have not heeded the warnings of Al Gore! Our carbon-based activities could spread their deadly influence to *other* planets which, for the sake of their own survival, might lead them to decide to destroy our planet. This would be done, of course, as an act of "preventive war," a proposition that has caused *Boobus Americanus* to embrace the Bush-Obama doctrine of declaring war against anyone on the planet. If such a notion provides sufficient cause for Americans to unfurl their flags against the rest of the earth, why wouldn't it equally justify an at-tack by the forces of the planet Zanyptikon? We might even find ourselves targeted by an alliance of *other* planets! At this point, there may be those who will argue that having the earth obliterated as an act of self-defense by other worlds is less objectionable than having it destroyed in order to make way for a planned intergalactic highway.

I know what you're thinking: Shaffer is just rattling our cage; not only is there no factual basis for supposing such an attack, there is no evidence—

---

1   See guardian.co.uk, August 18, 2011.

not even among the Cassandras at NASA—of any life existing beyond the planet Earth. After the absurdity of this claim became evident to intelligent minds, its apparent author—describing himself as a post-doctoral employee of NASA—admitted that it had been "a horrible mistake" to "have listed my affiliation as 'NASA headquarters.'" This is the sort of mea culpa often heard from members of the political classes whose peccadilloes have been made public. Perhaps this man—having seen how much mileage had been obtained by those who triggered intra-planetary wars with lies, forged documents, and visions of mushroom clouds over American cities—decided to get in on the game. After all, if Al Gore could make so much headway with the chattering classes with his scientifically unfounded allegations of global warming having been caused by SUVs, why not take the charade to the next level?

But in a world in which truth is a negotiable commodity; in which reality and fantasy have become interchangeable qualities, our NASA muse may have a fallback position. To those with a spirited imagination, there *is* empirical evidence of just such an impending attack; evidence clearly available to anyone whose epistemological skills have been honed by Hollywood films. The 1951 motion picture, *The Day the Earth Stood Still*[2], remains one of the better sci-fi efforts. In it, an interplanetary visitor, Klaatu—played by Michael Rennie—is sent to earth to warn humans that the continued proliferation of atomic weaponry will threaten the existence of life on other planets. In response to such a danger, Klaatu intones, the planets he purports to represent will have no choice but to destroy the earth. Klaatu is accompanied on his journey by a robot, Gort—who has the physique and disposition of ten combined NFL linebackers on steroids—along with great powers of destruction. Should Klaatu be captured—which he is—he tells the earthly heroine—played by Patricia Neal—that she can restrain Gort's violent powers by saying to it: "Klaatu barada nikto." She does so, Gort returns to the spacecraft—along with Klaatu—and earthlings are left to contemplate Klaatu's warning.

Is this what passes for scientific inquiry and research at NASA these days, or is someone generating a hoax at NASA's expense? Considering that so much of what the institutional order regards as "evidence" has the solidity of grape jelly left out in the sun all day, one must confront such reports—whether coming from the state or from its critics—with an abundance of

---

2   *The Day the Earth Stood Still* (Twentieth Century Fox, 1951).

skepticism. The environmental movement is little more than a secular religion made up of members of the faith I described as "Gang-Green." Complete with its version of "original sin" (i.e., being human), an assortment of saints (e.g., Rachel Carson, Al Gore, et al.), a multitude of sins (virtually anything associated with the processes of living), and an apocalypse, it has all the fervor of a tent-revival show. Whenever I see news coverage of an Al Gore speech, I half-expect to see mothers rushing to the stage screaming "bless my baby!, bless my baby!"

I wrote, as well, of the satirical book, *Report From Iron Mountain*[3] which purported to be the product of a lengthy study, begun under the Kennedy administration, to determine the consequences to political systems should universal peace suddenly break out in the world. The alleged study took place over a period of some three years, with academicians from various fields of study as well as non-academicians. Understanding that war "is the basic social system" for the organization of nations, and that "the end of war means the end of national sovereignty," the participants explored the question of how "alternate enemies" might be developed to serve the herding function brought about through fear. Possible substitute threats included environmental pollution, attacks from other planets, and ethnic minorities, among others. "Selective population control," and the "reintroduction of slavery" through "'universal' military service," were offered as means to such ends. If an existing "enemy" could not be found, the report stated, "*such a threat will have to be invented.*"[4] Shortly after Barack Obama's election to the presidency, his chief of staff—and now Chicago mayor—Rahm Emanuel told a *Wall Street Journal* conference: "you never want a serious crisis to go to waste. And what I mean by that is an opportunity to do things you think you could not do before."[5] These words echo the Iron Mountain mindset; they may even have inspired NASA's fabulist.

One can obtain insight from the creative use of parodies. Humor allows us to see beyond the boundaries of our limited understanding, and allows a sense of humility to overcome any tendencies for self-righteousness. This explains why bureaucrats, clinging to the absoluteness of their ordained rules, are such a humorless lot. Their lives would be stripped of all meaning were they to grasp the farcical nature of their work. But what

---

3   *Report From Iron Mountain On the Possibility and Desirability of Peace* (New York: Dell Publishing, 1967).

4   Ibid., pp. 29–30, 34, 44, 57ff., 64, 67 (emphasis added).

5   Online.wsj.com/article/SB122721278056345271.html

are the consequences for sane living when people take the parody as literal fact? How does one satirize absurdity? Jon Stewart has provided one effective method: give politicians and government officials a platform upon which to play out the burlesque character of their thinking.

It is in times of social turbulence—such as we are now experiencing— that "dark side" forces often get loosed upon the world. The Reformation and the emerging scientific revolution were destabilizing influences to the established order of the Middle Ages, leading to the prosecution of heretics and witches. It has been estimated that, between the years 1500 and 1660, some 50,000 to 80,000 witches were executed in Europe.[6] The witch trials at Salem, Massachusetts in 1692 arose during a period in which political turmoil in England threatened the existence of the colony through the revocation of the Charter that had created it. The reign of terror that helped to define eighteenth century France arose during the frenzy of the French Revolution. The nineteenth century Luddite machine-breaking riots were the violent reactions of many artisans to the major economic transformations occurring during the Industrial Revolution, a reflex action that continues to find expression among critics of capitalism. The collective insanity of Nazi Germany arose from the post-World War I excessive burdens imposed upon Germany by the Versailles Treaty. The collapse of the Soviet Union discommoded the established order in America by eliminating the need for an enemy powerful enough to cause Boobus to prostrate himself before the state. The resulting stress upon the system led to a search for "alternate enemies." Child abductors were offered as a possible threat, with childrens' pictures appearing on milk cartons until the FBI advised that almost all such abductions arose out of parental custody battles. Satan— having served the institutional order so well during the earlier persecution of witches—was then auditioned for the role, with Tipper Gore seeking his presence in rock music, while others tried exploiting his influence in preschools. But "Old Scratch" didn't have sufficient staying power, leaving the system in limbo until the ubiquitous and amorphous threat of the "terrorist" was concocted. Al Gore added "global warming" to the mix, giving the state a base from which it could conduct its endless wars against endless enemies.

With Boobus under the spell of "dark side" forces, is it so remarkable that the Iron Mountain mandate to invent threats might have inspired a

---

6   www.timelessspirit.com/MAR08/marlene.shtml

NASA post-doc to dream up his own contribution to the effort? Perhaps he had seen *The Day the Earth Stood Still* and thought substituting "global warming" for "atomic warfare" would provide a plausible threat for an alien attack! Nobel laureate Paul Krugman's allusion to such an interplanetary invasion—in order to illustrate Keynesian stimulus policies[7]—must have added encouragement to the fantasy.

As Carl Jung and others have observed, the "dark side" resides within each of us, ready to be mobilized when we are adequately provoked. Periods of great turbulence are often the breeding ground for the proliferation of enemies and other threats upon whom can be directed our latent fears, anger, and uncertainties. Nor can we take comfort in pretending that such eruptions are generated only by the ignorant among us: neither intelligence nor formal education has any inverse correlation with such behavior. Inquisitors and Robespierre alike were intelligent, educated men. The person most associated with the Salem witch trials was Cotton Mather, a Harvard grad whose father was president of that university. Paul Krugman is an alum of both Yale and M.I.T., while the aforesaid NASA visionary reportedly holds a doctorate degree. Nor are the rest of us immune to such fanciful thinking. Our ancestors who cheered the burning of witches, or rubbed elbows with the likes of Madame Defarge, are not as far removed from us as we like to imagine. We laugh at the mass-suicidal runs of the lemmings, even as we march off to self-destructive wars which, to many, provide the highest meaning to their lives.

As our civilization continues its entropic collapse—with our resistance to goofy thinking being tested in the process—it is timely to review some of the better contributions to the study of mass-mindedness. One should start with the works of Carl Jung, and revisit such classic writings as Gustave Le Bon's *The Crowd,*[8] Elias Canetti's *Crowds and Power,*[9] Stanley Milgram's *Obedience to Authority,*[10] Otto Friedrich's more recent *The End of the World: A History,*[11] as well as Philip Zimbardo's *The Lucifer Effect: Understanding*

---

7   www.huffingtonpost.com/2011/08/15/paul-krugman-fake-alien

8   Gustave Le Bon, *The Crowd: a Study of the Popular Mind* (New York: The Macmillan Co., 1896).

9   Elias Canetti, *Crowds and Power* (New York: Continuum Publishing Corporation, 1973); originally published as *Masse und Macht* (Hamburg: Claassen Verlag, 1960).

10   Stanley Milgram, *Obedience to Authority* (New York: Harper & Row, 1974).

11   Otto Friedrich, *The End of the World: A History* (New York: Fromm International Publishing Corporation, 1986).

How Good People Turn Evil.[12] Perhaps some ambitious soul might want to update Charles Mackay's nineteenth century classic *Extraordinary Popular Delusions and the Madness of Crowds.*[13]

In the meantime—and to play it safe, lest the Al Gore Brigade is now being mobilized against us somewhere in the constellation Andromeda— we might heed the words of Klaatu. Perhaps some of the expeditionary forces from Zanyptikon are already in our presence. Should you be confronted by a menacing Gort-like humanoid, just say to it "Klaatu barada nikto." At the very least, it may find your words confusing and disarming; at best, it may cause the creature to get into its vehicle and depart!

---

12   Philip Zimbardo, *The Lucifer Effect: Understanding How Good People Turn Evil* (New York: Random House, 2007).

13   Charles Mackay, *Extraordinary Popular Delusions and the Madness of Crowds* (New York: Farrar, Straus and Giroux, 1932; originally published, 1841).

CHAPTER 23

"Support the Shopping Mall Killers"

On December 5, 2007, nineteen year-old Robert Hawkins went on a shooting spree at a shopping mall in Omaha, Nebraska, killing eight persons plus himself, and wounding four others.

Now that I have your attention, did you find yourself offended by the title of this piece? Good! It was intended to be offensive, not because I derive any pleasure from the angry reaction of others, but to make a point as bluntly and as poignantly as I can.

What if I had created a bumper-sticker with such a message on it, attached it to my car, which I then drove around Omaha—a city in which I lived for some nine years. Would you—or my fellow Omahans—be rightfully angered by my actions? My message would be clear enough: urging others to heap praise and support upon those who go about killing innocent men and women. The "bad-taste police" might be the least of my worries from such an action: I might even find myself criminally charged with aiding and abetting the crime of murder!

What kind of twisted mind could concoct such a message, you may wonder? When a mass-killing is followed by a similar atrocity elsewhere, many are quick to label the latter the work of a "copy-cat" killer. I shall fall back on the same explanation: my proposed bumper-sticker is "copy-catted" from the works of others, as we shall see.

While young Robert Hawkins was carrying out his mayhem, there were doubtless many cars in the shopping center parking lot with bumper-stickers reading "support the troops." What does this message mean if not for us to offer comfort and encouragement to American soldiers in Iraq and Afghanistan; to provide our confirmation of the validity of what they are doing in those countries? And what *are* they doing, if not killing thousands of men, women, and children? How have Iraqi civilians been any more deserving of the death and suffering visited upon them than were the customers and workers at a shopping mall? Whose innocence is entitled to greater respect or protection in either battle zone?

Most of us—in whatever nation, religion, or culture we were raised—are uncomfortable exploring the dysfunctional and destructive nature of our thinking. Our identities are so wrapped up in such collective abstractions that we regard any critical examination of them as a challenge to our personal worthiness. It is far more comforting to take the easy route of casting the world into camps of the "good" and the "bad," and to follow leaders who reassure us of the school-playground principle that "if you're not with us, you're against us."

Our institutionalized thinking—which you and I, alone, have produced and are capable of changing—has turned us into the reactive beings eager to man the barricades of whatever conflicts the established order chooses for us. I suspect that if the present administration were to declare Lapland part of the "axis of evil," most Americans would accept such a characterization, and turn upon neighbors who displayed reindeer Christmas decorations as "terrorist-sympathizers." To voice any doubts to the contrary would be to entertain the possibility that the very core of their identities is grounded in lies.

In this way, faceless "others" become the shadow forces against whom we fight in a vain effort to find peace within ourselves. Randolph Bourne's "war is the health of the state," and Charles Beard's "perpetual war for perpetual peace,"[1] reveal far more than the destructive foundations of every political system. Worse yet—and what we choose not to know—they reveal who and what we have made of ourselves. So much of the content of motion pictures, television, video games, and the lyrics of popular music, are awash in themes of violence. But these expressions of our culture are

---

1   This phrase became the title of a book by Harry Elmer Barnes, ed., *Perpetual War for Perpetual Peace* (Caldwell, Idaho: Caxton Printers, 1953). Barnes attributed the words to Beard.

not the *causes* of our difficulties, but only a *reflection* of who we are. Not wanting to endure the pain of self-examination, we focus on Hollywood, or drugs, or the availability of guns, to explain what we have made of ourselves and, derivatively, the society in which we live. We will put a "support the troops" bumper-sticker on our cars as a way of disguising our refusal to challenge our own thinking.

In his despairing suicide note, Robert Hawkins lamented the "meaningless existence" of his life. But where, within the families or the cultures in which they are raised, are children encouraged to find a sense of "meaning?" For most, any existential purpose usually amounts to little more than an attachment to some external agency—an institution—that offers but a superficial, ersatz significance. What school system, for instance, spends *any* amount of time helping a child develop his or her own sense of being if it does not serve institutional interests? Behavior-modifying drugs await the child who insists upon pursuing his or her own interests in most school systems, prescriptions that have almost always been found in the case histories of young mass-murderers. At their worst, government schools are breeding farms for the domesticated humanoids who provide the energy to operate and sustain institutional machinery. At their best, they help children discover and get trained for their assigned stall in the organizational hierarchy.

I recently saw a couple getting out of their car in a parking lot. Their auto was a bandwagon of slogans for the war system: "proud parents of a sailor," "support the troops," and other patriotic messages adorned with flags. The man also wore a very noisy T-shirt that proclaimed his commitment to the war effort. I thought to myself what terrible parents these people must have been, to not only fail to *protect* their child from the war system that wants to consume him or her, but to brazenly *celebrate* it! If their child should die in battle in furtherance of the state's political and economic ambitions, will they regard the death as the fulfillment of a "meaningful existence?"

Before answering such a question, every parent should think back to the sense of "meaningless existence" that preceded Robert Hawkins' suicide attack in Omaha. One of the stories unreported from most of the mainstream media relates to the high suicide rates among soldiers. In one investigation, CBS discovered that, in the year 2005 alone, at least 6,256 suicides were reported among those who had served in the military,[2] while another study revealed that, during the period 2005-2010, members of the military committed suicide at a rate of once every 36 hours.[3] Apparently, a chestful of medals was not sufficient to remove the sense of "meaningless-ness" experienced by so many young people who directed their violence against foreigners; there was no felt transcendence associated with being a fusilier in an invading imperial horde.

Within a handful of years, we shall begin to glimpse an answer to whether America will remain in its present state of free-fall, or whether individual intelligence will overcome mass-mindedness in informing so-cial behavior. The decentralizing role of the Internet and other personal-ized technologies provide encouragement for the future, as do the efforts of Ron Paul and his spontaneous network of individualized supporters to extend such peaceful, creative, and orderly transformations. This continu-ing movement away from the vertically-structured power systems that destroy humanity is what, above all else, terrifies the stockholders of the established order. The early confrontation between Ron Paul and the dis-ingenuous Rudy Giuliani concerning the explanations for 9/11 raised the kinds of inquiries the rulers do not want considered.

What established authorities fear the most is an answer to the question raised by the bumper-sticker from the 1960s: "what if they gave a war and nobody came?"

---

2   www.cbsnews.com/stories/2007/11/13/cbsnews_investigates/main349671.shtml

3   Report, *Losing the Battle: The Challenge of Military Suicides* (Center for a New American Security, October, 2011). www.cnas.org/files/documents/publications/CNAS_LosingTheBattle_HarrellBerglass.pdf

Politics and War
as Entertainment

I f I were to offer a seminar on the nature of war, I believe the first class
session would include a showing of the film *Wag the Dog.*[1] Those who
wish to justify the obliteration of hundreds of thousands of total strangers in the name of "good" versus "evil," or "national honor," will likely
find the movie discomforting. As the governments of India and Pakistan
self-righteously, and in the name of "God," threaten one another with a
nuclear war that could instantly kill anywhere from ten to twenty million
people, it is time for decent, intelligent people to put down their flags and
begin to see war for what the late General Smedley Butler rightly termed it:
"a racket."[2] This film offers a quick reality fix.

Randolph Bourne's observations about the nature of the state are familiar to most critics of militarism, but few have delved into why this is
so. Statism is dependent upon mass thinking which, in turn, is essential to
the creation of a collective, herd-oriented society. Such pack-like behavior is reflected in the intellectual and spiritual passivity of people whose
mindsets are wrapped up more in *images* and *appearances* than in concrete
reality.

---

1   *Wag the Dog* (New Line Productions, 1997).

2   Smedley Butler, *War Is a Racket* (New York: Round Table Press, 1935).

Such a collapse of the mind produces a society dominated by *entertainment*—which places little burden on thinking—rather than critical inquiry, which helps to explain why there has long been a symbiotic relationship between the entertainment industry and political systems. Entertainment fosters a passive consciousness, a willingness to "suspend our disbelief." Its purpose is to generate *amusement*, a word that is synonymous with "diversion," meaning "to distract the attention of." As the word "muse" reflects "a state of deep thought,"[3] "amuse" means *without* such a state. The common reference to movies as a form of "escape" from reality, reflects this function. Government officials know what every magician knows, namely, that to carry out their illusions, they must divert the audience's attention from their hidden purposes.

Michel Foucault has shown how the state's efforts to regulate sexual behavior—whether through *repressive* or *"liberating"* legislation—serves as such a distraction, making it easier for the state to extend its control over our lives.[4] It is instructive that, in the months preceding the World Trade Center attacks which, in turn, ushered in the greatest expansion of police powers in America since the Civil War, the news stories that dominated the media had to do with allegations of adulterous affairs by a sitting president and a congressman. It is not coincidence that both the entertainment industry and the government school systems have helped to foster preoccupations with sex.

The authority of the state is grounded in consensus-based definitions of reality, whose content the state insists on controlling. This is why so-called "public opinion polls," rather than factual analysis and reason, have become the modern epistemological standard, and why imagery—which the entertainment industry helps to foster—now takes priority over the substance of things. That the government's interest in expanding its control over human activity under the guise of "global warming" was helped along by Al Gore receiving an Academy Awards "Oscar" for leading this campaign, reinforces the point.

Politics and entertainment each feed upon—and help to foster—public appetites for illusions and fantastic thinking. The success of such

---

3   *Webster's New Collegiate Dictionary* (Springfield, Mass.: G. & C. Merriam Company, 1973), p. 758.

4   Michel Foucault, *The History of Sexuality: An Introduction,* trans. by Robert Hurley (New York: Vintage Books, 1990; originally published as *La Volente de savoir* [Paris: Editions Gallimard, 1976]).

undertakings, in turn, depends upon unfocused and enervated minds, which helps to explain why motion picture and television performers, popular musicians, and athletes—whose efforts require little participation on the part of the viewer—have become the dominant voices in our politicized culture. It also helps to account for the attraction of so many entertainers throughout the world to visionary schemes such as state socialism, as well as the increasing significance of entertainment industry gossip and box-office revenues as major news stories.

The entertainment industry helps shape the content of our consciousness by generating institutionally desired moods, fears, and reactions, a role played throughout human history. Ancient Greek history is tied up in myths, fables, and other fictions, passed on by the entertainers of their day, the minstrels. In the *Iliad* and the *Odyssey*, was Homer relating a war that actually occurred, or was he only engaged in early poetry? This is a question modern historians continue to debate. We need to ask ourselves about the extent to which our understanding of American history and other human behavior has been fashioned by motion pictures, novels, and television drama. Regular gun-fights at high noon in nineteenth century western towns may make for exciting films, but don't seem to reflect the historic record.[5] Through carefully scripted fictions and fantasies, *others* direct our experiences, channel our emotions, and shape our views of reality. The fantasies depicted are more often of *conflict*, not cooperation; of *violence*, not peace; of *death*, not the importance of life.

Nowhere is the interdependency of the political and entertainment worlds better demonstrated than in the *war system*, which speaks of "theaters" of operation, "acts" of war with battle "scenes," "staging" areas, and "dress rehearsals" for invasions. Modern war-planning carries with it an "exit" strategy. Fighter planes at an air-base are often parked on "aprons" which, in theater, refers to the front area of a stage. The pomp and circumstance of war is reflected in military uniforms that mimic stage costumes, all to the accompaniment of martial music that can rival grand opera. Powerful pyrotechnics have been used to create battlefield-like settings for many rock concerts.

A Broadway play can become either a "bomb" or a "hit;" troops are "billeted" (a word derived from the French meaning of a "ticket"); while the premiere of a movie is often accompanied, like a World War II bombing

---

5   Terry L. Anderson and P.J. Hill, *An American Experiment in Anarcho-Capitalism: The* Not So Wild, Wild West. http://mises.org/journals/jls/3_1/3_1_2.pdf

raid, by searchlights that scan the skies for enemy planes. Even the Cold War was framed by an "iron curtain." Is it only coincidence, devoid of any symbolic meaning, that at the end of the American Civil War—one of the bloodiest wars in human history—its chief "protagonist" (another theater term) was shot while attending the theater, and that his killer was an actor who, upon completing his deed, descended to the stage, pausing at center stage where he uttered his line "Sic Temper Tyrannis," and then "exited"?

Adolf Hitler understood, quite well, the interplay between political power and theater, making use of the filmmaker, Leni Riefenstahl, to advance his ideology. This symbiosis continues to reveal itself in entertainers involving themselves so heavily in political campaigns, some even managing to get themselves elected to Congress or the presidency! Nor was it surprising that one of the first acts of the Bush Administration, following the announced "War on Terrorism," was to send a group of presidential advisers to Hollywood to enlist the entertainment industry's efforts to portray the war as desired by Washington! Frank Capra's World War II government-commissioned film series, "Why We Fight," was not the last insistence by the "military/entertainment complex" to write the scripts and define the characters required to assure the support of passive minds in the conduct of war. George M. Cohan used his stage musicals to help reinforce a militaristic fervor. Even Walt Disney enlisted some of his cartoon characters in the war effort. In June, 2011, First Lady Michelle Obama and Jill Biden—the vice-president's wife—came to Hollywood to encourage the creation of films that "inform and inspire" a more positive presentation of the military.[6]

Furthermore, because entertainment is often conducted in crowded settings (e.g., theaters, stadiums, auditoriums) there is a dynamic conducive to the generation of mass-mindedness. One need only recall the powerful harangues of Adolf Hitler that coalesced tens of thousands of individuals into a controllable mob, to understand the symbiotic relationship between entertainment and politics. On a much subtler level, one sees the exploitation of such energies in modern sporting events that seem to have taken on increasing military and patriotic expressions.

Entertainment is a part of what we call "recreation," which means to "re-create," in this case to give interpretations to events that are most favorable to one's national identity and critical of an opponent. In this connection,

---

6   *The New York Times*, June 13, 2011.

entertainers help to manipulate the "dark side" of our being which, once mobilized, can help to generate the most destructive and inhumane consequences. World War II movies portrayed Japanese kamikaze pilots who crashed their planes into U.S. Navy ships as "crazed zealots," while American pilots who did the same thing to Japanese ships or trains were represented as "brave heroes," willing to die to save their comrades. German and Japanese soldiers were presented as sneering sadists who delighted in the torture of the innocents, while the American soldiers only wanted to get the war over with so they could get back home to mom and her apple pie and the girl next door! How many of us, today, think of nineteenth century U.S. cavalrymen—as portrayed by the likes of John Wayne and Randolph Scott—as brave soldiers, while Indian warriors are considered "savages" for having forcibly resisted their own annihilation?

The motion picture industry provides a further example of how politics and entertainment feed upon psychological forces. The images with which we are induced to identify ourselves—whether on stage, screen, or the battlefield—are often *projections* of unconscious inner voices. (Why, for example, do the "bad guys" always have to lose?) These images, in turn, are made conscious through acts of "projection": getting the motion picture images to the front of the theater, a stage actor's voice to the back of the theater, and maintaining an enthusiastic audience for the theater of war, all depend upon *projection.*

All of this leads me to ask whether the *entertainment* industry is an extension of the *war* system, or whether *war* is simply an extension of our need for *entertainment*? What should be clear to us is that entertainment is one of the principal means by which our thinking can be taken over and directed by others once we have chosen to make our minds *passive*, which we do when we are asked—whether by actors or politicians—to suspend our judgment about the reality of events we are witnessing. When we are content to be *amused* (i.e., to have our attention diverted from reality to fantasy), and to have our emotions exploited by those skilled in triggering unconscious forces, we set ourselves up to be manipulated by those producing the show.

Politics differs from traditional theater in one important respect, however: in the political arena, we do not call for the "author" at the end of a war. Most of us prefer *not* to know, for to discover the identities of those who have scripted such events might call into question our own gullibility.

CHAPTER **25**

Can Liberty be Advanced Through Violence?

We cannot solve our problems with the same thinking we used when we created them.

—Albert Einstein

A Republican candidate running for Congress in Texas set many minds and mouths atwitter with his suggestion that, should state tyranny ever become a problem in America that could not be resolved by political means, the use of violence, while "not the first option," would be "on the table."[1] There is a deep-rooted frustration and anger among millions of Americans directed at the entirety of a political establishment that is forever employing lies, deceit, contradictory reasoning, violence, increased regulatory and taxation schemes, Federal Reserve monetary policies, wars, expanded police and surveillance powers, and other practices that advance corporate-state interests at the expense of ordinary people. Those upset with such behavior have tried resorting to the politically-acceptable means of bringing about change. They have gone to voting booths to support candidates who promise to "get the government off your backs," or "no more taxes," or to not engage in "nation-building." With but a handful of exceptions, those elected turn around and violate

---

1   See *The Dallas Morning News,* October 22, 2010.

such promises, leaving the disenchanted voters to seek out other political saviours at the next election.

The current "Tea-Party" movement began as yet another expression of popular disaffection with our politicized society. It was, however, quickly co-opted by the same right-wing franchise of the political establishment that participated—in bipartisan efforts with its left-wing branch—in the construction of the modern empire. Just as in the 1994 Republican Party's congressional victories, persons of libertarian sentiments will discover that dressing a Tea-Party candidate in a three-cornered hat will not change his fundamental character as a pimp for the prevailing order.

When the futility of using institutionally-approved methods for making change becomes increasingly evident to people, it is not surprising that many might look to violence as the only effective solution. Students of social psychology often speak of the "frustration/aggression" hypothesis, wherein a repeated interference with goal-directed activity may result in a resort to violence. As Fred Berger expressed it, where

> certain segments or groups within the population are systematically exposed to these weaknesses in the ability of the legal system to provide or protect security, those subjected to such treatment come to feel "left out" of the social process, come to regard themselves as the "victims" of the social and political scheme, rather than full participants in it. . . . Such conditions tend to foster counter-violence and retaliatory disorder. . . .[2]

In a world in which it has become evident to so many that the institutional order exists to promote the interests of the few at the expense of the more numerous, is it so remarkable that such an awareness would be responded to with anger and violence? To regard oneself as being endlessly at the mercy of increasingly malevolent forces that one is otherwise unable to control or resist, can produce a sense of hopelessness that may lead to violence directed against its perceived source.

How is one to respond to the systemic violence that is the lifeblood, the very essence, of the state? Society has always been a struggle between the "invisible hand" of a peaceful and productive order that arises, without direction, as the unintended consequence of people pursuing their own interests; and the "iron fist" of institutionally structured violence we have

---

2   Fred R. Berger, "'Law and Order' and Civil Disobedience," 13 *Inquiry* 254, at 262-63 (1970).

been conditioned to equate with "social order." I have defined "government" as "an institution of theft, predation, rape, destruction, and mass murder, the absence of which, it is said, would lead to disorder."

To understand political systems, and to learn how to protect oneself when dealing with them, one must cast aside all of the illusions and lies in which we have been trained to see them. Even their defenders understand the essence of government to consist of the lawful exercise of unrestrained power. There is nothing, *nothing*, that the state ever does that does not derive from a presumed authority to employ whatever amount of deadly force its officials deem necessary—or just convenient—to achieve its ends. Contrary to the mantle of "public servant" in which they like to cloak themselves, government employees—from the president on down to janitors—insist upon their power to compel obedience by force.

The mainstream media and high-ranking government officials feigned righteous indignation over city officials in Bell, California, who paid themselves gargantuan salaries—one as high as $800,000 per year, and with retirement pay nearing $1,000,000 annually.[3] What is most upsetting to such critics, however, is not the enormity of their racket, but that these local officials failed to conform themselves to established methods for the looting of taxpayers. Like Captain Renault in the movie, *Casablanca*[4], who informs Rick that he is "shocked, shocked to find that gambling is going on" in his business—as he receives his gambling payoff from the croupier—the town government of Bell will receive a selective criticism of its behavior. Government defense contracts; hundreds of billions of dollars in "stimulus" gifts to favored business interests; the refusal of the Federal Reserve system—or of Congress—to reveal the beneficiaries of its monetary policies, these and other politically-correct forms of looting will pass without significant comment from right-thinking people. Nor, in contrast with the Bell racket, will much be made of the fact that a candidate for governor in California spent $141.5 *million* of her own money in an effort to get elected. Why? As one who understands that people act in order to be better off *after* acting than they would have been otherwise, what returns does this woman expect from her investment? Who is insisting upon an explanation from her?

---

3   Foxnews.com, September 21, 2010.

4   *Casablanca* (Warner Brothers, 1942).

I have long been of the view that parents have a moral obligation to keep their children from living under tyranny. As such, how do I go about the task of helping to make their world one in which they may enjoy the conditions of peace and liberty? My experience convinces me that participation in electoral politics is more than *futile*: it only adds energy to the system; it confirms the central premise of all political thinking, namely: important change can occur only within the halls of government. Besides the fact that the electoral process is unavoidably rigged in favor of the status quo, it also assures that, no matter who you vote for, the *government* always gets elected. Voting is designed to give people the false sense that *they* are in control of the machinery and the policies of the state. Emma Goldman got it right when she said that "if voting changed anything, they'd make it illegal."[5]

My opposition to voting arises from the same sense as my opposition to other forms of violence. Implicit in efforts to persuade the state to act according to your preferences—whether through voting, lobbying, or threats of force—is the idea that, should you prevail, others will be compelled to abide by what you have chosen for them. Voting is anything but the peaceful alternative to violence: it is premised on the coercive machinery of the state being employed on your behalf should you prevail in amassing a greater number of people on your side than do others.

More direct forms of violence—as some suggest to be the ultimate solution to statism—are likewise inconsistent with a condition of liberty. Violence is an expression of reactive anger, born of unrequited frustration. Violence is the nature of the state: can one expect mankind to free itself of political destructiveness by adopting its very essence?

We will not become free when the state goes away. Rather, the state will go away once we are free. "Freedom" is a very personal quality, wherein the individual enjoys a centered, integrated life, unburdened by the conflicts and contradictions that make up our normally neurotic lives. We must learn to respect the inviolability of one another's lives and other property interests if we are to enjoy this inner sense of being free. A need for *liberty* is what we have in common with one another; it is the condition in which *free* men and women live together in society. We will experience *liberty* only when each of us is *free* of the inner forces that keep us divided and in conflict.

---

5   www.counterpunch.org/2004/03/20/emma-goldman-for-president/

The *desire* for liberty is not rational. It is not a logical extension of certain abstract philosophical premises, but a right-brained expression of our spiritual and emotional character. *How* we define and manifest liberty in society is a left-brained, rational process, its substance determined by whether we have developed a personal, inner sense of being free. How many people have been attracted to the novels of Ayn Rand, for instance, because of her facility in logically playing out the premise of rejecting the initiation of force? By contrast, how many were moved by her passion for liberty and the inviolability of the individual?

We have conditioned our minds to think of ourselves in conflict-laden ways, be they nationalistic, religious, racial, gender, or other forms of separation. Our political masters have trained us to think of one another in "we/they," "us" against "them" categories, divisions that are—like the scapegoats upon whom we play out our conflicts—changeable to suit the political needs of the moment. The fear of unseen "communists" that helped fuel the Cold War, has morphed into the concealed "terrorists," with each serving the same purpose: to expand the power and plundering of the state. Only by our individual ending of such divisive thinking and discovering the inner sense of non-contradictory wholeness that respects the inviolability of our neighbors' lives and interests, can we become free.

"Liberty," on the other hand, is the condition in which free men and women can live together in society. Trying to twist or manipulate *unfree* people into social systems—even those grounded in a *verbal* support of liberty—will never foster liberty. This is why the Constitution was doomed from the start: there was too much conflict and contradiction in the minds of most people to allow for the assemblage of free men and women. It is also why, once we have discovered the inner meaning of freedom, constitutions—and the governments they create—will be wholly unnecessary for a condition of liberty. This is part of the meaning of F.A. Harper's observation that "the man who knows what freedom means will find a way to be free."

How can a person whose mind and conduct is grounded in divisive thinking that considers violence as a means to wholeness, be regarded as "free"? Free of *what*? Is it not evident that resort to violence can never be a means to liberty; that such methods presume a fundamental separation of interests that would reduce society to the Hobbesian dystopia of "all against all"? If a group sought to dismantle the state by violent means, is it not clear that it could accomplish such ends only by amassing coercive powers superior to the state itself; that it would have to become a *super*-state? And if this group were to be successful, it would dare not dismantle its *own* machinery, lest another group should seek to recreate the previous apparatus; it would have to remain diligent in policing the thinking and actions of others who might be inclined to favor a more structured society.

One can no more advance liberty through violence than he can regain sobriety by embracing an alternative brand of alcohol. The state is nothing more than a system of legally organized force. It is no answer to this destructive menace to introduce a competitor who employs the same means and seeks the same ends, namely, to construct society on the principle of the power to compel obedience to authority.

Albert Einstein got to the essence of the problem when he declared that "force always attracts men of low morality."[6] I understand how being frustrated by others as we pursue interests we are entitled to pursue can generate intense feelings of anger. But it is not out of reactive rage or desperation that we discover our individual freedom and the resultant liberty we can share with our neighbors. It is such divisiveness that keeps us enslaved to the state. We need to discover what we share with one another, namely, a respect for our *individuality* that can arise only from the integration of our *rational* and *emotional* energies into a focused intelligence. If mankind is to avoid the fate of being the first species to intentionally make itself extinct, we must transform our own *minds*, and abandon our ageless and contradictory efforts to force others to be free!

---

6   Alice Calaprice, ed, *The Expanded Quotable Einstein* (Princeton, N.J.: Princeton University Press, 2000), p. 284.

CHAPTER 26

When the
World Went Bankrupt

To understand the machinations of a complex world, one must become sensitive to how apparently separate phenomena interconnect to produce unexpected consequences. Otherwise intelligent men and women struggle to make sense of the destructive turbulence that is fast becoming the norm in modern society. Wars that fail to satisfy even the most meager of excuses for their prosecution; rapidly-expanding police states rationalized as necessary for the ferreting out of "terrorist" bogeymen; state-sponsored torture conducted for no more apparent purpose than an end in itself; the wholesale looting engaged in—with bipartisan support—for the purpose of creating trillions of dollars of booty to subsidize the corporate owners of American society for losses sustained through incompetent management; these are the major examples of the failure to see interrelated causes of social disorder.

Throughout all of this, we see exhibited by those who presume the powers of omniscience and rational planning, a thorough ignorance not only of the causal factors that continue to produce our horribly disrupted world, but of the propriety of statist actions that respond to such dislocations with the same mindset that produced the turmoil. One sees symptoms of this disconnectedness in such absurdities as Al Gore's receipt of the 2007 Nobel Peace Prize, or the 2008 Nobel Prize in Economics to Paul Krugman. It is as though the Nobel Prize judges wanted to go out of their

133

collective way to refute the proposition attributed to Einstein: "The significant problems we face cannot be solved at the same level of thinking we were at when we created them."[1]

Another example of ultra-myopic thinking is to be found in a recent editorial from the erstwhile free-market publication, *The Economist*. Focusing on the travails that beset economies throughout the world, the magazine advises: "This is a time to put dogma and politics to one side and concentrate on pragmatic answers. That means more government intervention and co-operation in the short term than taxpayers, politicians or indeed free-market newspapers would normally like."[2]

Whenever I hear or read such arrant nonsense, I am reminded of my law school jurisprudence professor, Karl Llewellyn's interchange with a classmate of mine who had challenged a statement of Llewellyn's by saying: "that may be good in theory, but it isn't practical." Llewellyn responded: "if it's not practical, it's not good theory."

Much of the explanation for this disconnected mindset can be found in the "specialized" ways in which we learn and work. Economists, lawyers, historians, scientists, et al., are to learn and to practice a presumed "expertise" in their chosen field. Each is to stick to his territory, and to defend the collective interests of his colleagues by attacking those who presume to speak or write in subject areas for which they do not hold graduate degrees. This is the ultimate form of reductionist thinking, a travesty which, fortunately, is openly confronted by the holistic premises of chaos theory. The world is simply too complex; subject to a myriad of interconnected influences that are both unidentifiable and not confined to the tenets of any academic discipline.

So many of our current difficulties are underlain by the kind of unfocused, fragmented thinking expressed in *The Economist* editorial. "Pragmatism" has no meaning in the absence of ends to be served, objectives that necessarily incorporate explicit or implicit values of the actor. One who seeks "pragmatic answers" to problems—without addressing the principles by which "answers" are to be evaluated—is engaged in the smuggling of hidden premises into the discussion. If people act to be better off afterwards than they were before, what criteria and purposes motivate their actions?

---

1   Calaprice, ed., *The Expanded Quotable Einstein*, p. 317.

2   Economist.com, October 9, 2008.

In our commercially-dominant culture, it is too often assumed that material values pre-empt all others, an assumption that seems to direct almost all of the proposals offered in response to the economic turbulence now besetting both America and the rest of the world. As one who regards the Industrial Revolution as the most humanizing period in history, I unequivocally acknowledge that material values *are* important to pursue. While such ends are *necessary* for living well, they are not *sufficient*. Let any who doubt this inform me of the value of a baby, or the costs associated with German National Socialist concentration camps or Soviet gulags!

Materialistic thinking that is separated from other values dominates proposals for dealing with the current economic collapse. Politicians and media voices speak in terms of *numbers*, but not much else. Congress' giving trillions of dollars to banks is defended on the grounds that "it will strengthen their balance sheets." Of course it will, just as a mugger will have more money in his pockets after a night of robbery. But at whose cost? "Will this work?" is another commonly-asked question, reflecting the same kind of morally bankrupt questioning with which most address the continuing wars in Iraq and Afghanistan, or the propriety of torture.

If, as seems to be the case, Western Civilization is in a state of collapse, we might have occasion to consider the causes so that we might rethink our assumptions—and behavior—for whatever is to follow. The well-being of any system depends upon more than just its material characteristics. A vibrant business organization, for instance, requires more than abundant investment capital. Whether the firm's decision-making is centralized in an individual who issues directives to underlings, or is decentralized among those who perform the work of the organization, will have much to do with determining how much creativity and job satisfaction will be fostered. Likewise, the well-being of a family depends on more than the principal wage-earner bringing money home for the purchase of goods and services.

In the same way, the prosperity of a society or a civilization requires much more than the generation of material wealth. All dynamic systems depend upon the importation and integration of life-sustaining influences to overcome—at least temporarily—the second law of thermodynamics. The failure to ingest such energies helps to bring about the demise of systems. These factors include peaceful relationships with one another (i.e., respect for the inviolability of the person and property interests of others, premised upon voluntary rather than violent relationships); and individual liberty (a condition necessary for the expression and production of the varied ends that enhance life). This is what is meant by living with *integrity*:

interacting with others, holistically, from within a non-contradictory center on the basis of values and principles that sustain one's well-being. But our institutionalized conditioning reminds us that living the integrated life in peace and liberty with one another in society is only an idealistic fantasy. How impractical, we tell ourselves, as we play out the violent, conflict-ridden premises in which our thinking has been carefully structured. What masses of contradiction have we become when we condemn young men who kill their classmates at school, while cheering those who kill strangers in foreign lands; when we are unable to see that "our representatives" in Washington, D.C. are treating us no differently than is the mugger we encounter in a dark alley?

It has become fashionable to speak of the impending *bankruptcy* of the American economic system. To so focus our attention, however, is to overlook the fragmented nature of what we have allowed ourselves to become. Economic bankruptcy does not arise independently of related factors. The seeds of such bankruptcy were planted long ago, and have been carefully tended to by subsequent generations. There is a more generalized bankruptcy whose disintegrative influences have combined to produce our impending collapse.

The first of such causal forces can be referred to as *moral bankruptcy*, a phrase intended to cut much deeper than the kinds of personal habits and lifestyle concerns that get conservatives agitated. I refer, instead, to the willingness of so many of us to rationalize the unearned taking of property from owners and bestowing it upon others, provided the process is stamped with the imprimatur of the state. This shortcoming also finds expression amongst those who sanction the conduct of wars, or who have no problem devoting their energies to designing or operating military weapons and other systems for monitoring or controlling the actions of people.

A most troubling expression of moral bankruptcy is reflected in the aforementioned editorial from *The Economist*; for the failure to live an integrated, centered life has detrimental consequences. Moral and other philosophic principles have the most practical implications for the very existence of our lives. Stated another way, the refusal to integrate moral and philosophic principles in one's life *is* the reflection of a principle, albeit one that is deftly smuggled into a discussion in service to unstated ends. Upon close examination, however, one discovers that the disguised principle is one that *fragments* rather than *integrates* one's life, producing destructive conflict rather than wholeness.

Intellectual bankruptcy has been another major contributor to our socially disordered world. The failure to understand the nature of economics, and the principles of causation and conservation of both mass and energy; the failure to respect the inviolability of property rights and contracts; as well as an ignorance of history, have been additional catalysts for our present disarray. Politicians who ought to have learned from recent history about the destructive effects of inflation and the stultifying nature of state socialism, responded to an immediate crisis by generating more than $1,000,000,000,000 of additional inflation and partially socializing banks! In so doing, Congress was unable to rise above the habit at which it has proven itself adept, namely, to print more debased currency and bestow it upon its corporate friends. As in the aftermath to 9/11, its reaction was one of reflexive desperation rather than considered analysis; like blind men throwing darts at a dart-board. As our entropic decline continues, the politicos generate no more intelligent purpose than to preach the need for "economic stabilization" (i.e., to maintain the status quo).

The intellectual insolvency of our culture has been demonstrated in the response of many politicians and news media people to the McCain/Palin charge that Obama is a "socialist." No doubt such allegations are correct—so, too, of course, does the accusation apply to McCain—but notice the response thereto. Were "socialism" to become an issue in this campaign, news reporters, commentators, and political hacks, would have to be prepared to analyze its philosophic, historic, and economic implications. One would have to have a mind versed in intellectual concepts, and such are not part of the curricula of journalism departments. The "debate" must thus be shifted to a safe topic about which no challenges to the mind can arise: Sarah Palin's wardrobe! One writer went so far as to try to equate criticism of "socialism" as an expression of racism![3]

The confusion about socialistic thinking and government regulation has been aided by the collapse of respect for the principle of privately-owned property. This, in turn, has been abetted by what we saw earlier in Joseph Schumpeter's analysis of the movement from *owner*-controlled to *manager*-controlled business firms, wherein non-owners become decision-makers over the property of others. We need to move beyond the kind of thinking that drives political systems. Governmental policies are like so much of traditional medicine that only covers up symptoms without treating the

---

3   Tim Wise, *Red-Baiting and Racism: Socialism as the New Black Bogeyman*. August 10, 2009, redroom.com.

underlying disease. If Americans have any hope of restoring a vibrant, productive economy, we need all the *de*stabilization we can muster. President George W. Bush babbled such incoherencies as how state socialism will preserve a free market—words that recall the Vietnam War illogic about "destroying a village in order to save it." With such thinking directing economic policies in Washington, you can be assured that institutionalized foolishness is what will end up being stabilized.

It is the *spiritual bankruptcy* of our culture that is most in need of recovery—a "bailout" that can be accomplished only by mobilizing the inner resources of individuals. The regeneration of the human spirit can arise only from a person's believing in his or her existential worthiness; to regard the individual, in Kant's words, "always as an end and never as a means only." It is only in the power of *individuals* to transcend their experiences and formal learning that a *society* can be rejuvenated. As we rediscover our individuality and withdraw our energies from the collective abstractions to which we have attached ourselves, our personal and social integrity will no longer be in destructive contradiction.

As institutional interests struggle to overcome their terminal fate, there is a wonderful opportunity for each of us to reinvest in ourselves and, in so doing, help our world to become human-centered. The corporate, political, academic, and media voices will continue to condemn our "selfishness" even as they insist upon satisfying their appetites for greed and power. But the creative and orderly forces of chaos will prevail—they always have. When former Federal Reserve chairman Alan Greenspan testified that he didn't see the housing bubble crisis coming, he was unwittingly admitting to the incapacity of anyone to do what he insisted was his power to do, namely, control and fine-tune a society of three-hundred million people to reach desired ends. "We all misjudged the risks involved. Everybody missed it—academia, the Federal Reserve, all regulators."[4] "Neither all the king's horses nor all the kings men"—with all of the violence, paper money, or prisons available to them—can achieve by indirection, political magic, or other quickie solutions to long-term problems, what you and I, alone, can accomplish by introspection.

Ralph Waldo Emerson expressed our present situation quite well: "This time, like all other times, is a very good one, if we but know what to do with it."[5]

---

4   *New York Times.com*, April 3, 2010; *bloomberg.com*, March 27, 2010.

5   Ralph Waldo Emerson, "The American Scholar," 1837. www.emersoncentral.

CHAPTER 27

Civilization in Free-Fall

This is the way the world ends
Not with a bang but a whimper.
—T.S Eliot

The news story and accompanying photo were quite startling. According to the report, Sony—a dominant firm in the electronic industry—held a party to announce a new computer game it was putting on the market. As part of this soiree, a goat was decapitated, with the photo showing its not fully severed head hanging over the table on which it lay, having been sacrificed to the gods of corporate sales. Party guests were even encouraged to reach inside the goat's body cavity to remove and eat the offal to be found therein.[1]

All around us can be found the evidence of a civilization in its death throes; a culture that has devolved from the creation of life-sustaining values to the ritualistic celebration of death. Dr. Pangloss' "best of all possible worlds" has backslid into an anti-life swamp. Sony's public relations stunt did not generate this collapse, but only reflects it.

---

1   *Mail Online.* www.dailymail.co.uk/news/article-451414/Slaughter-Horror-Sonys-depraved-promotion-stunt-decapitate

Upon reading this news report, my first response was to seek the confirmation of its validity elsewhere. Might this be nothing more than a dark side version of one of my favorite websites, *The Onion*? Jon Stewart, *The Onion*, and a few other sources have helped us to appreciate the difficulties associated with satirizing absurdity; only a faithful commitment to reciting the ludicrous details of what we now accept as "reality" will suffice.

Where does one begin to describe—much less analyze—our institutionalized commitment to death? The war system is certainly the most dramatic, having accounted for some 200,000,000 deaths in the twentieth century alone. So insistent is our culture on the perpetuation of this corporate-state slaughterhouse that those who sponsor debates among presidential aspirants have systematically excluded the two candidates—Democrat Mike Gravel and Republican Ron Paul—who have most consistently opposed continuation of the war in Iraq.

And what of the academic and corporate institutions that derive so much of their income from designing and producing "new and improved" weapons systems that reduce the unit costs of butchering others, thus fostering the values of "efficiency" by which the spiritually-bankrupt calculate their bottom-lines?

The state—with its recognized powers of deadly force—manifests this same hostility to life. Its very nature is to compel people to do what they do not otherwise choose to do. Life is a spontaneous, self-directed process; and to forcibly intervene in human action is to make life become or do what it does not choose to be or do. Because uncoerced people will always act for the purpose of achieving their desired outcomes, governmental action will, of necessity, produce lesser degrees of well-being.

And why does the state engage in such life-depleting behavior? Part of the explanation lies in the fact that there will always be some segment of humanity that enjoys the exercise of coercive power over others. As H.L. Mencken observed: "The urge to save humanity is almost always only a false-face for the urge to rule it."[2]

But there are others who find the use of force quite useful for their own ends: those with concentrated economic interests wanting to control political machinery in order to restrain the competitive behavior of others. Major business interests and labor unions have been the principal exam-

---

2   *Impact Press*, issue no. 29, table of contents (October-November 2000). impact-press.com

ples of such restrictive desires. My book, *In Restraint of Trade,* documented such efforts during the critical years in the development of government regulation of the marketplace. Such coercive efforts have both increased the costs and limited inventiveness in the production of goods and services upon which life depends.

This institutionalized war against life permeates our entire culture. Our world abounds with people-pushers who want to use state power to control the kinds and quantities of food we eat; how we raise our children; the language we can use with one another; the drugs we are both prohibited from and required to ingest; whether and where we can smoke; the weights, measures, and prices at which produce can be sold; and the health care services we may use. These are but a few examples of this mania, with additional proposals being offered on a regular basis.

The state insists upon its mechanisms of control, with expanded police powers, warrantless searches, the erosion of *habeas corpus,* increased government databases of people, an exponential increase in prison populations in America, and a greater domestic military presence. These are among the current practices that go largely unquestioned. In Great Britain, surveillance cameras and recording devices have become so widespread that it is estimated there is one such camera for every fourteen people! This has led at least one critic of the system to grasp the anti-life implications of such practices in saying that Britain risks "committing slow social suicide."[3]

At this point, in an effort to define the nature of our cultural collapse, one normally hears an indictment of television, motion pictures, rock music, video-games, or that all-encompassing demon: Hollywood. Such is an expression of the superficiality of our understanding. When Cho Seung-Hui shocked us, in 2007, with his slaughter of 32 fellow students at Virginia Tech, the shallow-minded reflexively blamed guns, computer games, violent films, or any other factor that would save them the trouble of looking more deeply. I was reminded of the vacuous responses to the Columbine massacre that sought an explanation in teenagers wearing long coats!

Institutions that either employ, or advocate, the use of coercion are, of course, responsible for the consequences of their actions. Furthermore, the butchery practiced by operatives of the state is quantitatively more destructive than that perpetrated upon a goat in order to kick off a sales

---

3   "Britain becoming a Big Brother Society, says data watchdog." *The Independent,* April 29, 2007. independent.co.uk

campaign. Having said that, I am obliged to look beyond institutions for the explanations of our anti-life, self-destructiveness. Even the state itself, for all its life-consuming viciousness, is of lesser significance in our plight than is the real culprit: *our thinking.*

Our conflict-ridden thinking has generated the institutions that mobilize our inner divisiveness. The state has expanded its powers over us by playing upon our fears: be it of "communists," "illegal immigrants," "drug dealers," "the Hun," or the now-fashionable "terrorists." This scapegoating practice was the critical means by which Hitler was able to exploit various groups of non-Aryans to expand his tyrannical regime. As "Muslims" and "Mexicans" are offered up as modern sacrificial lambs, it is well for us to observe the inner source of our conflicts: others are able to enjoy power over us only as we abandon both the authority and responsibility for our own lives. As Shakespeare expressed it: "The fault, dear Brutus, is not in our stars, But in ourselves, that we are underlings."[4]

Once we learn to look outside ourselves for meaning and direction in our lives, we set ourselves up to be exploited for whatever purposes our "authorities" have in mind for us. Having given up our own centeredness— our own integrity—we become as balls in a pin-ball machine, capable of being moved about by forces over which we have no control. Our conduct becomes guided by those who control the levers with which we come into contact. Over time, the logic of the machine defines our mindset and, like Pavlov's dogs, we learn to slobber on cue and press the levers that deliver our prearranged rewards.

When our minds become other-directed, we should not be shocked to find our actions reflecting the values and emulating the behavior of external forces. To what extent might Cho Seung-Hui have unconsciously identified the faceless bullies who had terrorized him in his youth, with the faceless schoolmates he ritualistically slaughtered? To what extent might his rage against his innocent victims have found rationalization within a nation that continues to wave the flag against innocent Iraqis made to serve as surrogates for the faceless wrongdoers of 9/11?

Why did Sony undertake its tasteless and grotesque action? Probably for the same reason that it sells video games that appeal to appetites for computerized violence: because there are enough people whose thinking attracts them to such products. That there is a demand for such merchan-

---

4   William Shakespeare, *Julius Caesar* (1599), Act I, Scene ii, ll. 134.

dise provides no more justification for criticizing the marketplace than attends the sale of anything else. Animal-rights advocates who would turn to the state to prohibit such conduct unwittingly contribute their energies to a disrespect for life that generates the wrongs they seek to prevent.

Our civilization is experiencing more than a "slow social suicide." It is more in a state of free-fall. A vibrant society is one that encourages the production of life-sustaining values—which include a respect for the inviolability of the lives and property interests of one another, a condition that becomes synonymous with peace. America, however, is a nation in a constant state of war, not only with the rest of the world, but with itself. What condition that people-pushers are quick to identify as a "social problem," does not carry with it proposed legislation to forcibly restrict how others are to live their lives?

For reasons largely explainable as a reaction to the increased decentralization that threatens the institutional order, our formal systems—as well as those who take direction from them—are becoming increasingly sociopathic. The day may soon be upon us when cannibalism will emerge as the "politically correct" solution to all our problems; with Hillary writing a cookbook; and *The New York Times* editorially praising her for her "bold" program to "serve her fellow man." In that day, cable news channels may continue to challenge our minds with inquiries into the fate of the teenage girl in Aruba.

CHAPTER 28

Obama Revives a Tradition

I don't know why so many people are getting agitated over the Obama administration's acknowledged use of a "secret panel" to order the killing of Americans without any judicial due process. The practice is an old American tradition, one particularly resorted to in time of such economic downturns as the Great Depression of the 1930s. Like the Obama reinstitution, the earlier model operated in secret and without any legislative authority or judicial supervision. The members of such agencies were not made public, nor were the criteria by which victims were chosen for assassination identified. Presumably, the current panel will attract the same kind of "socially responsible" members as did its predecessor: prior to his appointment to the United States Supreme Court by FDR, Hugo Black had been a member of this secret organization.

Like their earlier counterparts, members of the secret Obama death panel will take all necessary steps to hide their identities. Operating under the National Security Council will provide them with many means of concealment. For added precaution—and to reinforce the sense of tradition upon which this new agency rests—they might want to consider using the tool of secrecy employed so effectively in past generations: *bedsheets* to cover their bodies, and with eye-holes in their percaled hoods to allow them to see!

President Obama will now be able to boast that, in addition to being the nation's first black president, he has restored an old American tradition for dealing with "undesirables." At long last, "equality" has come full circle!

CHAPTER 29

The Irrelevance of the State

I continue to receive responses from readers who cannot understand why I do not have a "what can we do?" answer to the problems that beset not only America, but the entire world. There is a sad, childlike quality to many of these e-mails, as though there were some authority figure—be it a politician or a writer—who could offer a magic solution to any difficulty. When I suggest to them that there *is* nothing that anyone "in authority" can do to change any of this, and that the only change that can begin to correct our present course is to be found within their *own thinking*, their shattered confidence in me to offer yet *another* "bold new program" turns to frustration and anger. We have for so long abdicated individual responsibility for the direction of our lives, that any suggestion that it is now timely to reclaim it meets with cries of contempt.

For those who have not yet gotten the message that our present condition is beyond institutional repair, and that civilization itself has run out of "solutions" to the problems it has created and is now in a state of collapse, you might wish to consider the warnings of a top CIA official. In an address at Duke University on April 11, 2002, CIA Deputy Director for Operations, James Pavitt, declared: "Now for the hard truth. Despite the best efforts of so much of the world, the next terrorist attack—it's not a question of if, it's a question of when."[1] Even though, today, his agency has "more spies stealing

---

1   *Rense.com/general24/cc.htm; Central Intelligence Agency: Speeches and Testimony.* cia.gov/news

more secrets than at any time in the history of the CIA," Pavitt noted that "with so many possible targets and an enemy more than willing to die, the perfect defense isn't possible." To his credit, he added that increased counter-terrorism measures would require the sacrifice of so many liberties as to turn America into a system "not worth defending."

Pavitt's words confirm one of the central theses of "chaos" theory: complex systems are too unpredictable to be controlled in furtherance of a given objective. This is why the Soviet Union and other systems of pervasive state planning have either collapsed or are in a state of disrepair. When this man declared "we in the government of the United States could (sic) neither prevent or precisely predict the devastating tragedy of the September 11th attacks"[2] he was, knowingly or not, confirming the irrelevance of the state in a complex world.

There you have it, from someone at the top of the political food-chain: short of turning America into the kind of vicious police-state so familiar to KGB and SS operatives of the past, *there is nothing that the most powerful nation-state in the history of the world can do to prevent more attacks such as occurred on September 11th*. Out of respect for this man's candor, please do not deluge *him* with e-mails berating his stance. Take his words as yet another wakeup call to your own sense of responsibility. *You* and *I* are the only persons who can bring about any fundamental changes in the butcherous madness that now besets our world. And our only means of doing so requires *you* and *me* to go deep within our own thinking, in order to identify—and discard—the divisive, conflict-ridden, and destructive assumptions whose ancestral voices we continue to channel.

Each of us must learn to *energize* our minds, to give up our habits of passively recycling the lies that are told us—as well as the truths that are withheld—by institutional voices. We must cease the practice of allowing *others* to formulate what should be *our* questions, heeding the warning of Andre Malraux: "[A] civilization can be defined at once by the basic questions it asks and by those it does not ask."[3] We must also give up our eagerness for quick and easy answers—which any sharpie is well-equipped to provide—recalling the words of Milton Mayer: "the questions that can be

---

2   Ibid.

3   Dev.iwise.com/ykeiM

answered are not worth asking."[4] In short, each one of us must pursue what we most dread in this world: our own sense of responsibility.

The apparatus of the state has neither the capability nor the inclination to protect any of your interests. To the contrary, *you* are expected to provide the means—including your very lives—in order to protect the *state*. This is why wars have *always* increased the *powers* of political systems as they diminish individual *liberties*. The state is as dependent upon wars as orthodontists are on overbites, or lawyers are on disputes, or physicians and nurses are on illness.

While the ostensible enemy is always portrayed as faceless "others," in reality every war is conducted by the state against its own citizenry. If you doubt this, ask yourself these questions: whose liberties have been more greatly curtailed since September 11th, members of al-Qaeda or yours? Whose belongings are being searched at airports and other public buildings; whose telephone, computer, credit card, medical, bank, and employment records are being monitored: terrorist operatives or yours? Whose taxes will be increased and whose children will be called upon to die in this eternal war: leaders of the Islamic Jihad or yours? And who does the state have in mind as the object of a current federal bill to require driver's licenses to contain computer chip records of the details of your life: Saddam Hussein or you?

If you have not already figured out the essential nature of the state, it is time for you to do so. *Every political system is a racket*, run by and for the benefit of the most disreputable people in any society, and employing those methods that, to any decent folk, represent the lowest qualities in human behavior. Lying, threatening, coercing, killing, corrupting, deceiving, are such common characteristics in political life that we scarcely comment upon it anymore. And yet, if your child grew up exhibiting such traits, you would rightfully regard yourself as a parental failure!

Government schools have conditioned us in the belief, long ago stated by Thomas Hobbes, that without the direction and supervision of the state, our lives would be "nasty, brutish and short."[5] Might this man have been doing anything more than projecting onto all of mankind his own "dark side" fears? How is it even conceivable that a society organized *not* around

---

4   Milton Mayer, *Man v. The State* (Santa Barbara, Calif.: The Center for the Study of Democratic Institutions, 1969), dedication page.

5   Thomas Hobbes, *Leviathan* (1651), in William Ebenstein, *Great Political Thinkers*, 2nd ed. (New York: Rinehart & Company, 1956), p. 346.

the political principles of monopolistic violence, but of voluntary cooperation and exchange, could begin to match the dehumanizing horrors that
define the history of states? Might the surviving victims of the massive
bombings of Hiroshima, Nagasaki, Dresden, Tokyo, London, Hamburg,
Wurzburg, Vietnam, Iraq, to mention the more familiar examples, have
anything to tell us about Hobbes's delusions? Might any of them raise the
question unasked by this dystopian speculator, namely, what individuals—
not enjoying the collective power to forcibly direct the lives or exploit the
wealth of others—would have either the capacity or incentive to produce
the weapons, prisons, torture facilities, or other dehumanizing and life-
destroying tools? The trillions upon trillions of dollars necessary for such
a system would depend upon practices that could only reduce mankind to
the dreary image foreseen by Hobbes.

We have been told that, while we are incapable of managing our own
lives, we *are* capable of electing wise leaders to do this for us! We have
learned how to recite all of our socio-political catechisms with nary a glitch
in meter. We laugh at notions of "political correctness," not realizing that
the joke is on *us*: our minds have become little more than a mélange of
contradictory beliefs and bromides about the necessity for the political
domination of our lives. How many among us, while chortling over some
bureaucratic nonsense, are prepared to admit to the absurdity of *all* of politics? *"The Emperor's New Clothes"* is a story that every parent should not
only *read* to his or her children, but should *discuss* with them its significance.

The "War on Terror" is the clearest expression of the failure of the state
to foster a harmonious and orderly society. Having a diminished appeal to
the minds and souls of increasing numbers of people, the American state
has had to resort to ubiquitous fear and violence in an effort to sustain
its authority. In so doing, it has revealed its *own* terrorist inclinations, the
"dark side" of its character that it prefers to project onto *others*.

There are many otherwise intelligent people declaring that the attacks
of September 11th were occasioned *not* by policies and practices of the
United States government, but by some combination of "evil," petulance,
and cultural envy! According to this view, some dozen and a half "terrorists" carefully plotted and carried out the destruction of the World Trade
Center—knowing full well that they were going to be killed in the process—for no other reason than resentment of the fact that we have MTV
and Calvin Klein jeans and women who can go out into public without

being covered by a tent. In the end, their sandbox syllogism comes down to nothing more than this: "*we*" are "*good*," but "*they*" are "*evil*."

These same babblers are quick to condemn any who would doubt the validity of the party line. To suggest that these attacks were brought on by American government policies, they intone, is to *justify* them; a proposition reflecting not only an intellectual bankruptcy, but their ignorance of Newton's "third law of motion" (i.e., that for every action there is always an equal and opposite reaction). The men and women who died in the WTC collapse no more "deserved" to die than did those killed by an earthquake or tornado. If one is to speak intelligently about such matters, he or she ought to have proper respect for distinctions between *causation* and *justification*.

But intellectual clarity is not what these apologists for statism have in mind. I suspect that they are aware of the deeper implications these attacks have for the future of the state. The order and liberty that most people have been conditioned to expect from hierarchically structured political systems has been called into grave doubt by a handful of men armed only with box-cutters. Many of those who had been trained to believe that an all-powerful state could protect them from any threat, are now beginning to ask the sorts of questions left behind on government school playgrounds.

Having just completed a century that witnessed the state-caused deaths of some 200 million human beings in wars and genocidal practices; and having become aware of how politicians have manipulated wars and other crises in order to advance state powers, many of us have been looking elsewhere for the peace, liberty, and order that is not to be found in political systems. But to the statists, such inquiries are to be discouraged. And so, we are witnessing a spate of attacks upon "libertarian" thinking of late—some of it even coming from those with pretensions of libertarian sentiments. Those of us who understand that war has always been the greatest threat to liberty, have been accused of being "people who hate America," "delusional," "anti-American," "naïve," and "anti-business," by men and women with a more restricted sense of what it means to live freely.

One can only ponder the vision of humanity shared by those who can, simultaneously, support the marketplace as a regulator of our economic needs while embracing the war system that negates the value of human beings. Do they believe that the collective exercise of deadly force is the essence of human values? Are missiles, invading armies, and F-16 fighter-bombers what they conceive of as *market forces*? Shall this become the mantra of the incestuous marriage of political and economic systems—to be emblazoned on allegedly "libertarian" think-tank T-shirts—"General Electric: Love It or Leave It"?

Perhaps the silliest attack on libertarianism came from the conservative Francis Fukuyama, a man whose earlier misprognosis of "the end of history" has not dissuaded him from offering *this* self-contradictory twaddle: after noting "the hostility of libertarians to big government," he declared that

> Sept. 11 ended this line of argument. It was a reminder to Americans of why government exists, and why it has to tax citizens and spend money to promote collective interests. It was only the government, and not the market or individuals, that could be depended on to send firemen into buildings, or to fight terrorists, or to screen passengers at airports. *The terrorists were not attacking Americans as individuals, but symbols of American power like the World Trade Center and Pentagon.*[6]

One must accumulate the benefits of many doubts in Mr. Fukuyama's favor in endeavoring to explain this absurd paragraph. Perhaps he was lacking in the study of both history and evolutionary biology when he declared, earlier, that human history had come to an end; or perhaps he has an insufficient understanding of basic physics, chemistry, or engineering, giving him a diminished understanding of *causality*. Then, again, perhaps his parents never read *"The Emperor's New Clothes"* to him when he was a child. That he could fail to recognize that *his own words confirm* the libertarian critique of the state is remarkable. "The terrorists were attacking . . . symbols of American power" on September 11th, and *this* is why the libertarian criticism of state power is flawed? Perhaps Mr. Fukuyama should read Mr. Pavitt's assessment not only of September 11th, but of the capacity of the state to prevent *future* attacks!

There is desperation in the voices of those statists who hope that, by declaring libertarian thinking dead, they will have a clear field for what is the core premise of their social thinking: *the subjection of human beings to domination by the state.* They may have differing ideas as to how much leg chain to give to each of us—so that we may enjoy the *illusions* of liberty—

---

6   Francis Fukuyama, "The Fall of the Libertarians," *Wall Street Journal*, May 2, 2002, (emphasis added).

but share that attribute so well observed by Hayek: "a fear of trusting un-controlled social forces."[7]

In this outpouring of writings about the demise of libertarian thinking, one is reminded not only of Shakespeare's admonition about people who "protest too much," but of Mark Twain's retort that reports of his death had been "greatly exaggerated." There is more wishful thinking than credibility in such assessments, not unlike that of the Elvis worshippers who would have us believe that he is really *alive*.

By any standard with which you judge the efficacy of any system, *the state is irrelevant*. Neither your health, economic well-being, the education of your children, the protection of your life and property, are in any way fa-cilitated by the state: to the contrary, such interests are *threatened* by politi-cal institutions. Every political system is constructed on a rationalization for theft, and depends upon a recognized sovereign authority to compel obedience. In one of those last remaining functions that defenders of the state have clung to—i.e., national defense—events of 9/11 have shown the utter uselessness of the state, a fact that finds confirmation in the remarks of the CIA's James Pavitt.

The state may not be able to survive in a world of instant global com-munication, decentralized decision-making, and computerized "virtual realities." If so, its demise will come about not through "terrorists" or vio-lent revolutionaries, but out of a sense of *boredom*; it will simply cease to entertain. The statists understand this. They know that, in a world of com-peting amusements, they must stage a Cecil B. DeMille extravaganza—a never-ending war against the entire world—if the boobs are to be induced to keep buying tickets.

While working on my uncle's farm as a child, I recall seeing him behead chickens. The birds flapped and fluttered about, spattering blood wherever their dying bodies took them. They made a mess of everything and a lot of noise, giving every appearance, to a young child, of purposeful behavior. But the chickens' fates were sealed. So too, I believe, is that of the state, which insists in going out with the same bloody fanfare as the chickens.

In this age of decentralizing systems, there remains only one state function of which free men and women would readily approve: *to go out of business*. Its functions are no longer relevant to a complex and interrelated

---

7   F.A. Hayek, *The Constitution of Liberty* (Chicago: University of Chicago Press, 1960), p. 400.

world. Politicians, bureaucrats, police officers, judges, prison officials, tax collectors, one and all, would then be freed up from the burdens of "public service." In the words of Lysander Spooner, they could then return to their homes, and "content themselves with the exercise of only such rights and powers as nature has given to them in common with the rest of mankind."[8]

---

8   Lysander Spooner, "A Letter to Thomas F. Bayard," in *No Treason: The Constitution of No Authority* (Larkspur, Colo., 1966), p. 69 (letter originally published 1882).

CHAPTER 30

The Hitler Test

In previous years, and on the first day of class, I have given my new students a ballot, indicating that "it is time to elect the leader of a great nation," and offering them two candidates, A and B.

Candidate A is identified as "a well-known critic of government, this man has been involved in tax protest movements, and has openly advocated secession, armed rebellion against the existing national government, and even the overthrow of that government. He is a known member of a militia group that was involved in a shoot-out with law enforcement authorities. He opposes gun control efforts of the present national government, as well as restrictions on open immigration into this country. He is a businessman who has earned his fortune from such businesses as alcohol, tobacco, retailing, and smuggling."

Candidate B is described thusly: "A decorated army war veteran, this man is an avowed nonsmoker and dedicated public health advocate. His public health interests include the fostering of medical research and his dedication to eliminating cancer. He opposes the use of animals in conducting such research. He has supported restrictions on the use of asbestos, pesticides, and radiation, and favors government-determined occupational health and safety standards, as well as the promotion of such foods as whole-grain bread and soybeans. He is an advocate of government gun-control measures. An ardent opponent of tobacco, he has supported increased restrictions on both the use of and advertising for tobacco products.

Such advertising restrictions include: (1) not allowing tobacco use to be portrayed as harmless or a sign of masculinity; (2) not allowing such advertising to be directed to women; (3) not drawing attention to the low nicotine content of tobacco products; and, (4) limitations as to where such advertisements may be made. This man is a champion of environmental and conservationist programs, and believes in the importance of sending troops into foreign countries in order to maintain order therein."

The students are asked to vote, anonymously, for either of these two candidates. I employ this exercise only every other year, at most, so that students will not have been told to expect it. Over the years, the voting results have given candidate B about 75 percent of the vote, while candidate A gets the remaining 25 percent. After completing the exercise and tabulating the results, I inform the students that candidate A is a composite of the American "founding fathers" (e.g., Sam Adams, John Hancock, Thomas Jefferson, George Washington, etc.). Candidate B, on the other hand, is Adolf Hitler, whose advocacy for the programs named can be found in such works as Robert Proctor's *The Nazi War on Cancer*.[1]

In one of my classes a few years ago, we were discussing the *Schechter*[2] case, in which the United States Supreme Court struck down the cornerstone legislation of the "New Deal," the National Industrial Recovery Act. I was explaining to the students how this legislation had transformed American commerce and industry into a system of business created but government-enforced cartels. I also pointed out to them how popular fascist/socialist programs were throughout much of the world at that time. There was Stalin in the Soviet Union, Mussolini in Italy, Hitler in Germany, and Roosevelt in the United States. Franco came to power in Spain in 1939.

I then informed my class how Winston Churchill had, in 1938, praised Hitler, as had such luminaries as Gandhi, Gertrude Stein (who nominated him for the Nobel Peace Prize), and Henry Ford (who was pleased to work with the German leader).[3] One of my students could take it no more. "How

---

1   Robert Proctor, *The Nazi War Against Cancer* (Princeton, N.J.: Princeton University Press, 1999).

2   *Schechter Corporation v. United States*, 295 U.S. 495, 55 S. Ct. 837 (1935).

3   Re: Gandhi, see Cerf and Navasky, *The Experts Speak: The Definitive Compendium of Authoritative Misinformation* (New York: Pantheon Books, 1984), p. 283; re: Churchill, see *The London Times*, November 7, 1938; and www.rense.com/general51/strange.htm; re Stein, see rense.com, ibid, and *New York Times Magazine*, May 6, 1934; re: Ford, see en.wikipedia.org/wiki/Henry_Ford.

can you say that so many people could support such an evil man as Adolf Hitler?," she pleaded. "You tell me," I responded, "just two weeks ago 78% of you in this class voted for him!" Some twenty seconds of pure silence settled into the classroom before we moved on to the next case.

I later introduced a new group of students to this exercise. After they voted—again, anonymously—I tabulated their votes and discovered that, once again, Hitler had prevailed, but by a much narrower margin than in earlier years. In my two classes, Hitler won by a 45-41 combined total of votes (nor did he require the Supreme Court to validate his victory). His support, in other words, had fallen from previous averages of 75 percent to about 52.3 percent.

One of my students wrote on his/her ballot "leaving ballot blank, or writing in a socialist candidate if one exist." At the following class meeting, I read this notation aloud and told the class that a "socialist candidate" *did* exist: candidate B, in the person of Adolf Hitler. The word "Nazi" was derived from the formal name of Hitler's party: the National Socialist German Workers' Party. That so many of Hitler's policies have become the essence of modern "political correctness," as well as "mainstream" Republocratic platforms, is a sad reflection on just how far the American culture has deteriorated in recent decades.

Still, there may be some basis for optimism in this latest response from these students, who had never had a class with me before. When close to half of these young people were more comfortable siding with the kind of men whose thinking was reflected in the Declaration of Independence, there may be healthy signs that support for the Bush/Cheney/Ashcroft/Ridge form of fascist state is starting to wane.

Additional evidence of a diminishing enthusiasm for Leviathan can be seen in the resolutions passed by over one hundred city/town councils—plus one state legislature—stating their opposition to, or even refusal to abide by, the Patriot Act! The lobotomized voices that insist upon passive submission to authority, may find themselves screeching to a rapidly depleting audience. They, and their statist overlords, may be able to count on the continuing complicity of a round-heeled Congress, but many thoughtful men and women may be peeling the "love it or leave it" bumper-stickers off their minds and cars.

Having had a brief taste of the brown-shirted culture of the present administration, perhaps enough Americans are rediscovering the significance of their own history. As the media lapdogs continue to recite their scripts and slobber on cue, it may prove to be the case that the "spirit of

'76," with its love of liberty and distrust of governments, is still sufficiently engrained in the fabric of our society.

CHAPTER 31

Impeach
the American People!

Perhaps the sentiments contained in the following pages, are not yet sufficiently fashionable to procure them general favor; a long habit of not thinking a thing wrong, gives it a superficial appearance of being right, and raises at first a formidable outcry in defence of custom. But the tumult soon subsides. Time makes more converts than reason.

—Tom Paine
Common Sense

Now that George Bush's marbled columns of support have turned to sand, there is talk of impeachment and, perhaps, even criminal prosecution, along with that of his coterie of unprincipled administration thugs and advisors who helped turn America into the twenty-first century equivalent of 1939 Germany. If Bill Clinton was to be impeached for lying about his oval office peccadilloes, the bill of particulars against Mr. Bush and his fellow barbarians rises to exponential levels of insistence.

I refuse to take part in this whooping and hollering. It is driven by the same refusal of men and women to examine what they have made of themselves that allowed Mr. Bush to mobilize their "dark side" energies into murderous attacks upon hundreds of thousands of innocent people; to torture and detain—without hopes of trial—anyone the administration saw fit to deprive of their liberties; and to turn America into the kind of dystopian police-state that was beyond the fertile imaginations of Messrs. Orwell and Huxley. It is, in a word, just another collective exercise in scapegoating.

This is not to suggest that Mr. Bush and his fellow butchers are not deserving of punishment. While "justice" amounts to little more than the redistribution of violence, those who consider themselves called upon by God to slaughter, torture, and otherwise destroy the lives of their fellow humans, need to be held accountable for their actions. But I resent any notion that they ought to be answerable to the same people who, over the past five years, could not find enough flags to wave, bumper-stickers to attach to their cars, or angry vitriol to direct at what few of their neighbors retained a sufficient sense of maturity and integrity to resist the collective madness that now defines America.

If this gang of criminals is to be held answerable to the rest of humanity, the case against them ought not be advanced by those who, by their lynch-mob enthusiasm, helped facilitate these wrongs. The stench of hypocrisy would be far too suffocating, making a mockery of the moral principles to which the emerging ersatz outrage appeals for support. It would be like Mafia hit-men wanting to bring the leading figures of organized crime to justice for their violent ways.

No, if anyone is to be impeached for the atrocities of this past semi-decade, it ought to be most members of the American public who should stand in the dock. The politicians and military leaders did no more than what politicians and military leaders always do: use as much violence to accomplish their ends as their victims will allow them to exercise. Like putting a bowlful of candy in front of children, mature adults ought to know what to expect when self-interested pursuits are not checked by an insistence upon the inviolability of the boundaries of others.

I want to make clear that I am not offering any collective indictment of all Americans. From 9/11 onward, there have been numerous voices of opposition to the Bush-leaguers from men and women whose moral principles never lost focus. People like Cindy Sheehan, Lew Rockwell and others at lewrockwell.com, Gore Vidal, Chris Hedges, Justin Raimondo and his associates at antiwar.com, Lewis Lapham of *Harper's*, Bob Higgs and his colleagues at the Independent Institute, Glenn Greenwald, and Amy Goodman, are just a few of the more prominent voices to "just say 'no'" to tyranny and butchery. Republican Congressman Ron Paul remains a consistent 434-1 voice against these practices, while Democratic Senator Russ

Feingold stood up early and often to oppose statist measures that his complaisant fellow legislators were always eager to support.

But most Americans went into a moral slumber, and dreamt the illusions put into their heads by Bush, Cheney, Rumsfeld, et al, along with members of the mainstream media who, in parroting every word and nuance provided by their establishment masters, confirmed that brothels are not restricted to seamy red-light districts. "Founding Fathers" such as Thomas Jefferson, Sam Adams, and James Madison, were well aware of the danger of ordinary people coming to trust power. The likes of Alexander Hamilton, however, counted on such weakness, being aware that, in the market for human integrity, it was always wise to sell short. As the Bushites continued to unfold the details of their dictatorship, the words of Ben Franklin echoed. When asked what kind of government the framers had created, Franklin replied: "a republic, if you can keep it."[1]

I have long discounted the myths upon which governments are based. The reality that the state is no more than a product of conquest has long dissipated the fairy-tale of some alleged "social contract." Still, if the practitioners of modern government insist upon the fabled version, I shall be pleased to confront them on their own terms. Perhaps it is the lawyer in me that sees the advantage in using the opposition's case to discredit their own arguments.

No more succinct characterization of the "social contract" theory of the state has been offered than by Edmund Burke, who regarded the state as "a partnership not only between those who are living, but between those who are living, those who are dead, and those who are to be born."[2] The U.S. Constitution—in its preamble alleging to be the product of "We the People"—resorts to this contractual rationalization for state power. The Declaration of Independence, however, is far more explicit about such matters, stating that governments derive "their just powers from the consent of the governed; that whenever any form of government becomes destructive of these ends, it is the right of the people to alter or abolish it."

If one is to try to justify any relationship on the basis of a contract, it is important to understand what is implicit in a contractual undertaking. Contracts involve what is termed a "meeting of the minds" of two or

---

1   John Bartlett, ed., *Familiar Quotations*, 16ᵗʰ ed. (Boston: Little, Brown, 1992), p. 310.

2   Edmund Burke, *Reflections on the Revolution in France* (1790), in Ebenstein, *Great Political Thinkers*, p. 469.

more people, each of whom has certain rights and duties as spelled out in the agreement. If the Constitution, for example, is thought of as a *bilateral* contract between state authorities and "the people," the state acquires its legitimacy only by adhering to the terms of the instrument that conferred power upon it. As with any other contract—such as for employment, or the buying and selling of merchandise or real estate—there is a burden upon those who are to be subject to state rule to insist upon adherence to the contractual terms. It is the obligation of members of the public to maintain vigilance over state officials and to make firm and timely objections when they exceed their authority. If I were to purchase a car, I would be obliged to make payment, just as the dealer would have a duty to deliver the car to me. In order to protect my self-interests in the transaction, the onus would be upon me to insist that the dealer deliver to me that which the sales contract prescribed as well as to perform other specified duties.

In recent decades—and particularly during these past five years—most Americans have utterly failed in their contractual undertakings. They have treated this alleged "social contract" not in *bilateral* terms—where each have duties to perform—but as a *unilateral* transaction, in which performance is all one-sided. To most people, government may have been established by contract but, once created, the state became a free agent, able to extend its decision-making authority in any direction it chose, without any check upon its power from those it ruled. The obligation of "the people" to insist upon its rulers abiding by the terms of the "agreement," dissolved into the duty to be obedient to whatever state authorities mandated.

I do not discount for a moment the vicious and wicked deeds of the White House sociopaths who have, with only token objection from others, behaved like drunken SS-officers on a holiday for butchers. But it is time not only for Americans, but for the subjects of other nation-states as well, to look themselves in the face and ask why they have been willing not only to sanction such destructiveness, but to insist upon it as the highest expression of the "greatness" of the society in which they live.

Those who drafted the Declaration of Independence had an inherent distrust of power. Rather than see this as a reason to not create state systems, they believed that members of an enlightened, skeptical, and constantly observant public could and would insist upon state authorities restraining their appetites, lest they be driven from office. If men like Jefferson, Sam Adams, and Franklin were around today, they would understand, perfectly, what those in power are doing and why they are doing it. They would be sadly disappointed, however, in the docility of most of the American sheeple eagerly lining up to be fleeced, proudly sending their children off to be slaughtered on behalf of interests of which they are unaware, and equating obedience to their rulers with social responsibility.

Most Americans have failed to live up to their responsibilities under this alleged "social contract." This includes most Democrats who, during the George W. Bush administration, have done little more than opportunistically await the day that they might recover the White House in order to continue the same statist agenda "under new management." Nor have you seen the Democrats proposing repeal of the Patriot Act—or any of the other recently enacted additions to police-state powers—or the dismantling of the Homeland Security system. Neither have they done what any morally decent person would do in the conduct of a war against wholly innocent people: stop the killing. Democratic and Republican leaders are in agreement that more money will always be needed for the military, and the troops will be brought home but only after they have achieved victory.

It is counterproductive not only to look to the Democrats to bring about any fundamental change in governmental behavior, but to fantasize about bringing George W. Bush to "justice." There is something cowardly about failing to confront a bully when he enjoys strength, but then joining with others to pounce on him when he has fallen into a weakened condition.

Furthermore, to demand retribution from members of this crowd is but to reinforce the process by which political systems energize themselves, namely, to project our self-directed fears and other shortcomings onto others. We shall never end our self-destructive subservience to power by indulging in the pretense that, by punishing such wrongdoers, we can not only absolve ourselves of the painful feelings of our moral cowardice, but sanitize the political system—to which we remain attached—from any future transgressions.

So, forget about impeaching George Bush and his moral reprobates. They—along with his predecessors—have breached whatever "social contract" Americans like to delude themselves into thinking they have with the state. It is most Americans who ought to be impeached. As the purported real parties in interest in this arrangement, their breach has been the most egregious. They have utterly failed, not only in their obligations to their children and grandchildren to restrain state power but, what is worse, to give a whit that such a state of affairs has arisen in a country that was once looked upon by the rest of the world as a symbol for peace, liberty, and decency.

CHAPTER **32**

What Did bin Laden "Deserve"?

> GABRIELA: *And you believe everything the authorities tell you?*
> FRANZ KAFKA: *Well, I have no reason to doubt.*
> GABRIELA: *They're authorities! That's reason enough.*
> —From the movie *Kafka*

My recent article on the U.S. government's assassination of Osama bin Laden elicited many favorable responses, along with a negative one that advised me that this man "got what he deserved." The reader went on to ask "how dare you imply that we owed him the 'right' to be captured and brought to justice." How effortlessly we make our judgments when our minds are in the default mode, and we need only parrot the words of those in authority!

The media has long been an echo chamber for the avoidance of independent thought and judgment. It is easy to repeat the party line that the state's enemy du jour "got what he deserved" when one refuses to ask the question "what does *any* of us 'deserve'?" What do I "deserve?" Do you know what *you* "deserve," and for what actions? From what set of facts do we draw when we make such judgments about the conduct of others? I am neither a fan nor a defender of bin Laden, but those who are so anxious to invoke "closure" as an excuse for evading inquiries into the nature of governmental policies, might ask themselves why they are so willing to embrace his murder.

An answer to the question "what did bin Laden deserve?" depends upon one's perspective. Leaving aside the obvious responses that his Al Qaeda sympathizers would make, even patriotic Americans might have differing opinions, depending upon the time period of one's assessment. When the Reagan administration found bin Laden and Al Qaeda useful agents to help rid Afghanistan of Soviet military forces, American politicians took turns posing with these "freedom fighters" for self-serving photo-ops. Their combined efforts drove the Soviets from that country, and helped bring about the collapse of the Soviet Union and the end of the Cold War. For his part in all of this, did bin Laden "deserve" having a statue built to him in Washington, D.C., or a boulevard named for him?

But when his usefulness to American interests terminated—or even became hostile—he was quickly relegated to the character of "villain." This is a tactic long predating Machiavelli, having been useful, in recent years, to transform Saddam Hussein from Donald Rumsfeld's smiling photo-op "friend" to a lynch-pin in the axis of evil; to Muammar Gaddafi's mercurial foe/friend/foe role of convenience in American foreign policy. That most Americans insist on remaining so dupable—if not outright stupid—as the state plays out its games of "endless enemies" at their expense, is remarkable.

What *did* bin Laden "deserve" in all of this? What do any of us "deserve" in our dealings with one another? Is there any principle to which we can turn to help us answer such questions? Do we "deserve" to be coerced, robbed, or killed whenever someone with superior strength is able to do these things to us? Is this the highest social standard to which we can repair? Have the playground bully and the brutalizing parent become the "founding fathers" of our "New World Order?"

If the defenders of state assassinations believe they have found a defensible tactic for resolving disputes—or just promoting their own preferences—should it become more widely available for all of us to employ? If two neighbors have a long-standing dispute as to the ownership of rose bushes along their property boundaries, should they resort to murder to settle the matter? Do we not understand that the problem of urban street-gangs is but politics in the neighborhood; that Obama's drive-by shooting in a house in Abbottabad differs from such a killing in south-central Los Angeles more in terms of geography than substance? If the political establishment is willing to embrace such methods as a way of eliminating political enemies in foreign countries, should the same practices be acknowledged as appropriate within America? Might we want to rethink the "lone-nut-with-a-gun" explanations most of us eagerly swallowed to explain the deaths of the Kennedy brothers, Martin Luther King, Malcolm X, et al, as well as the failed attempts on the lives of Ronald Reagan and George Wallace?

For decades, I have tried to discover whether there is some principle upon which all people can agree to define the propriety of our actions; a proposition that rises above arbitrary subjective preferences. Politically-defined laws will not suffice, since the state—being defined by its use of violence—exists to promote and enforce *conflicts* among people. Neither have I found so-called "natural law" principles much help, as their content seems to vary from one advocate to another.

As we have seen, the state has often been able to overcome the seemingly universal aversion we have to our victimization by appealing to the anti-libertarian doctrines of "egalitarianism" and "procedural due process of law." Most of us are inclined to succumb to our own predation provided others will share in the same mistreatment, and that some regularized system will be employed against us. But would the moral stature of Hitler's or Stalin's regimes be elevated by a showing that everyone was subject to the same levels of oppression? Furthermore, what is the "process" that will be "due" an individual, and who will determine that standard?

The idea that the military and/or the police—the enforcement arms of the state—could undertake arbitrary and deadly force against any person, finds support among most conservatives. This is why the market for flags and "support the troops" decals blossoms whenever the emperor finds a new "enemy" to attack. It is also why so many conservatives—and even a number of so-called "liberals"—can get their diapers so knotted over the suggestion that Osama bin Laden should have been brought to trial rather than murdered. It is the same mindset that allows police officers to gun down "suspects" without, themselves, being held to account in a court of law.

Suppose a man is "suspected" of having committed a heinous crime (e.g., sexually assaulting and then murdering a small child)? Suppose this man is found and arrested by the police, who then take him into a back alley and kill him? Did he "get what he deserved?" Would you raise any objection to this—unless, of course, you were the suspect—or would you regard demands for a public trial to be only a "loophole" that might allow him to "escape" his punishment? Is a jury determination of *"innocence"* to be regarded as a "legal technicality?" Is "suspicion" or "accusation" the equivalent of "guilt?" Should "criminal procedure" classes in law school be required to address such matters as "how to organize a lynch mob?" Should a Ku Klux Klan Grand Dragon square off with an ACLU activist to debate the question "is justice delayed, justice denied?"

Don't you understand that if the bin Laden's of the world can be "brought to justice" by government hit-men who, like their Mafia counterparts, then dump the bodies into the ocean, so can you? Insistence upon state-defined "due process of law" is no guarantee that the innocent shall not be punished, but it's an improvement over assassinations, torture, trips to hidden prisons around the world, and the denial of habeas corpus. Jury trials often result in wrongful convictions, but I'd rather take my chances with twelve men and women with no sinister agendas of their own, than with decisions made behind closed doors by the politically unscrupulous. Bin Laden "deserved" a public trial for the same reasons you and I would.

With each passing month, it becomes increasingly evident that the United States of America—as a formal system—is about finished. The Constitution has become virtually meaningless as a means of conducting the business of the state. The "separation of powers" of the various branches of government—which we used to pretend would limit the ambitions of each—has given way to notions of "empire," with the president playing the role of "emperor," able to start wars on his own motion (and without congressional approval); to torture or imprison without trial, or order the assassination of any persona non grata of his designation; to give away hundreds of billions of dollars to his corporate friends; ad nauseam. Over many decades, the *powers* granted to government in the Constitution—which, far from being *limited*, speak of "general welfare," "necessary and proper," and "reasonable"—have been given very expansive definitions by the courts. By contrast, the *rights* reserved to individuals have been accorded very restrictive meanings. In the treatment of bin Laden—as well as the continuing incarcerations at Guantanamo—we see further confirmation that what we once thought of as an inalienable right to a public trial is another illusion sacrificed to the empty rhetoric of "national security."

As the "United States of America" continues its collapse, we may have the opportunity of discovering that a *nation* and a *government* are not synonymous terms. The success the political establishment had in merging "society" and the "state" may unravel in the decentralization now occurring. If we can revisit the basic assumptions that underlay the "founding fathers" pre-Constitution efforts, we may discover why conditions in which peace, liberty, and respect for life must take precedence over edicts offered by rulers who smirk and strut as they demand obedience to their very whim.

In the course of such inquiries, we may discover why bin Laden—along with every one of us—*deserved* to not be dealt with in such an arbitrary, coercive manner. *Institutionalized violence* is the essence of every political system, and is in the process of destroying Western Civilization. But as *secession* and *nullification* enjoy an increasing interest among thoughtful people, members of the establishment power structure may find themselves regarded as the new "Red Coats." Like their predecessors, they may then be urged to follow Lysander Spooner's advice to join a society of free men and women *not* as part of a domineering force, but as cooperative neighbors.

CHAPTER 33

Wind Power

Political language . . . is designed to make lies sound truthful and murder respectable, and to give an appearance of solidity to pure wind.

—George Orwell

Whenever I drive east of Los Angeles toward Palm Springs, I encounter the hundreds of gigantic propellers whose stated purpose is to transform wind into electrical power. I wonder about the efficiency of these devices: does the enormous cost of constructing and maintaining them generate a sufficient amount of electricity to make them a profitable investment? Or, as I often suspect, do these towers serve a more secular religious purpose; a modern ziggurat expressing a commitment to a new sacred orthodoxy? Having grown up in farm country, I am aware of the beneficial use farmers have made of windmills to pump water. On the other hand, if the output from these modern wind machines exceeds their costs, why do they not appear across the country, wherever strong winds prevail? Whenever I hear people preach of the importance of some costly technological program they want the state to undertake, my economic understanding always asks the question: if this is such a worthwhile and productive project, why have profit-seeking entrepreneurs not already entered the field?

171

These and other related thoughts are with me whenever I watch C-SPAN coverage of congressional hearings on the Federal Reserve policies and practices or, of late, inquiries into the government expenditure of hundreds of billions of dollars to benefit the major corporate interests who are the de facto *owners* of American society. I have watched Treasury Secretary Timothy Geithner perform his Professor Harold Hill act[1] before an increasingly unimpressed body of Republican and Democratic representatives. ("Oh yeah, we got troubles; that's trouble with a capital 't' and that rhymes with 'b' and that stands for the 'billions' we gave to AIG!")

In his own way, Geithner—along with his predecessor Henry Paulson, as well as Ben Bernanke, et al.—has been generating his own form of wind power in an effort to disguise the corporate-state-serving ends that have, for decades, underlain government economic policies. There is an increased public consciousness of the realpolitik at work in the halls of state that makes it difficult for intelligent minds to any longer indulge the establishment-serving media's explanations of governmental behavior. Hollywood film studios would, today, be unable to produce a *Mr. Smith Goes to Washington* with a straight face.

The giggling must have commenced even in the congressional hearing room when Mr. Geithner began his public catechisms about how the conferral of hundreds of billions of dollars on AIG was undertaken for the benefit of American taxpayers. Nor was his self-contradiction more evident than when he first declared that trust in the financial system required disclosure and transparency, but later warned that it would be a grave mistake to make public the machinations of the Federal Reserve Board. Such actions (i.e., exposure to the American people about how the Fed actually operates) would destroy this agency's "independence." There was even some suggestion that the cause of "national security" had been invoked early on when the AIG bailout was being considered! Such are the consequences whenever hot air is disguised as cool reasoning.

Geithner—along with his boss, Mr. Obama—added to the gross domestic product of pure wind in declaring that they "took responsibility" for their respective actions. I am forever annoyed by people who make such empty statements; what do they mean? What cost does each intend to incur in taking such "responsibility"? If I accidentally run you over with my car, and then claim "responsibility" for having done so, it

---

1   From Meredith Wilson's *The Music Man* (Warner Brothers, 1962).

would be expected that I would compensate you in some manner for my actions. Will either man resign his office in atonement? This is what the president of Japan Air Lines did, a number of years ago, when one of their planes crashed, killing many passengers.[2] Such statements by Geithner and Obama unencumbered by personal costs, are gestures as meaningless as Abraham Lincoln's "emancipation proclamation" which, by its very terms, declared slavery to be abolished in those states that were "in rebellion" (i.e., those regions not under federal control). A modern edict of comparable impact could be expressed by President Obama declaring Tibet to be independent of Chinese authority!

When I used to teach students on their first day in law school, I would begin with the following exercise: "you are passengers on a cruise ship that has just sunk, and are afloat in the water with a lifeboat that will only hold half of our numbers [there might be forty students in this class]. If twenty of you get into the boat, you will survive; if more than twenty of you try to do so, the boat will capsize and all of you will drown. You have thirty minutes to make a decision. Good luck!" I left the classroom, later returning to hear their decision. I was always less interested in what they decided, than in the question of how they decided to decide. Invariably, I would get one or two students—almost always males—who announced that they volunteered to stay in the water and let the others survive. Their answers as to why they made such choices gave me the opportunity to discuss how we often say things of an abstract nature, in order to look good in the eyes of others, but whose costs we do not expect to bear. "But would you make this self-sacrificing decision if there were real-world consequences associated with it? Oh, by the way, did I tell you that the twenty people who managed to stay in the boat would each have ten points added to their final exam grades?"

We have learned to expect meaningless gesturing from Washington. Many of us have even learned to regard government officials as personal grantors of benefits ("the president gave us" some stated amount of money), as though they were distributing their own resources to us. But those who scramble for coins tossed from the speeding carriages by the ruling elite will never be in the same league as those favored few—members of the establishment—who have mastered the art of investing in the industry of wind that *is* Washington, D.C. If you are content to obtain a meager government

---

2   See en.wikipedia.org/wiki/Japan_Airlines_Flight_123. Going further, the maintenance manager for JAL committed suicide over this tragedy.

contract, or a sinecure in this setting, you can compete with your fellow humans for the paltry dregs remaining after the trough has been emptied by the well-connected hogs.

But if it is your purpose to be a big-time player in this environment, you must be prepared to help empower the wind industry with your very sense of being; to commit yourself to a life of bromides, contradictory thinking, and the ability to tell lies with a straight face. Political capitals have always been the factory-towns where hyperbole, fraud, deceit, lies, and empty promises provide the necessary foundation for statism. As I write this article, I have been informed that the Pentagon is proposing the establishment of what it calls an "Office of Strategic Deception."[3] (Who do you suppose is to be the target of such falseness?)

But beyond consigning your soul to a life of corruption, you must be willing to invest vast sums of money in the effort, being mindful that the secret of understanding realpolitik in this country is to be found in the phrase "follow the money." Don't bother asking your stock-broker for investment details or strategies: the chances are he is either too honest or too far out of the loop to be able to inform you. Nor will you find "balloon-juice futures" listed on any of the commodities markets. Ownership shares in this industry are bought and sold *not* in the open market, but behind closed doors in the hallowed halls of state; with the currency of exchange consisting of government-issued decorated paper rather than more substantive values.

If you want more evidence of how success is obtained in this multi-trillion dollar racket, continue to watch the politicians and government officials as they twist and squirm in their efforts to convince you that their nakedness is really the latest fashion; watch and read the mainstream media, and then reverse whatever they tell you; and pay attention to the Internet and the alternative voices who may provide you with the kinds of questions you have been trained not to ask.

---

3   From *Wired*, January 26, 2010. wired.com/dangerroom/2010/01/pentagon-report-calls-for-office-of-strategic-deception/

CHAPTER 34

Life is Destroying the Planet!

N ews stories advise us of yet another contributor to the menace of global warming, this one arising from the flatulence produced by cows. The metabolic processes engaged in by our bovine neighbors produce methane, one of the greenhouse gasses against which the environmentalist faithful are ever vigilant. Methane is also produced through the breakdown of organic matter (e.g., manure, dumpsites) and, other life forms.[1] In his book *Gaia* the renowned chemist, James Lovelock, analyzed how methane, produced in the guts of termites, is an essential factor in the self-regulating nature of the earth's atmosphere.[2]

The notion that "self-regulation" could account for the orderliness found in social, economic, or biological systems is a heresy to people-pushers of all doctrinal faiths, including the secular theology of high-church

---

1 *LA Times*, October 15, 2007. latimes.com/2007/oct/15/opinion/ed-methane15

2 James Lovelock, *Gaia: A New Look at Life on Earth* (Oxford: Oxford University Press, 1982). Lovelock later expanded his thesis into a more holistic work in his *The Revenge of Gaia: Earth's Climate in Crisis and the Fate of Humanity* (New York: Basic Books, 2006). Lovelock—long a supporter of "climate change" threats, has recently admitted that he, Al Gore, and others, were "alarmist" about such fears. In words reflecting the uncertainties inherent in the study of chaos and complexity, Lovelock added: "The problem is we don't know what the climate is doing. We thought we knew 20 years ago." (http://nextbigfuture.com/2012/04/jameslovelock-admits-he-and-others.html)

environmentalism. A people-pusher can be thought of as a person with a leash, in search of a dog. Like chameleons, they can undergo superficial changes to accommodate the circumstances in which they find themselves: the persecution of witches or infidels, the fostering of state socialism, or, modernly, the salvation of the planet. It matters not to the zealots of any particular denomination whether their belief system is grounded in substantive truth; only that it provide a plausible rationale for the imposition of authority over the lives of others. The disciples of environmentalism have shifted from being prophets of a coming "ice age," to "global warming," to the compromise position of "climate change" as the empirical basis for their claims continue to be called into question by scientists.

If flatulence from cows is to be regarded as a threat to be regulated—or even prohibited—by institutionalized people-pushers, what next? Shall Mexican restaurants or Texas barbecues become future targets? In their efforts to subject every facet of the diets and lifestyles of others to their detailed scrutiny, shall these sociopaths finally reveal their ambition to rule as a collective god over all of creation?

Ever since childhood, I have had a strong interest in geology. I long ago learned of the turbulent origins of the earth; of how plate tectonics and continental drift have shaped and reshaped the planet; of the effects occasioned by the invasion of comets, asteroids, solar flares, and meteors; of periodic polar reversals and ice ages; and, more interestingly, how the earth has been resilient enough to respond to such tumult. Many who share this understanding of what our planet has been through over billions of years can appreciate the late George Carlin's treatment of those innocent souls who want to "save the planet" from such relative inconveniences as plastic bags and aluminum cans!

The volcanic activity that has introduced great quantities of gasses into the earth's atmosphere must be attributed to the planet itself, and not to the presence of organic life. This conclusion is even more compelling when one considers that the cause of most of the disruptive conditions occurred during the Precambrian period (i.e., before life emerged on Earth). Thus, living systems cannot be held to blame for all "wrongs" to the planet in the environmentalists' growing bill of particulars.

Of course, we must bear in mind that it is humanity against which the environmentalists rail in their secular version of original sin. How often do we hear it said that mankind must limit its involvement with the rest of creation lest we "upset the balance of nature?" That our species is to be severed from the rest of nature reflects the conflict-ridden character of this ideology. Likewise, continuing criticism of our "carbon footprint" reflects the attitude that we are collective trespassers upon the planet, with the environmentalists in the role of police inspectors in an ongoing crime scene search for evidence of our criminal intrusions against the property interests of some ill-defined owners.

But as mankind cannot carry out its wrongdoing against the planet without the complicity of other species, it is evident that—like the search for "terrorists"—a much larger net must be cast more broadly. When cows passing gas becomes yet another threat to arouse the global-warmingists, you begin to sense that this new orthodoxy has, at its core, a hostility to life itself. The life process—whether exhibited by humans, other animals, or plants—involves the transformation of all kinds of resources to serve the entropy-reducing needs of living beings. Life feeds on other life and, because none of us are one hundred percent efficient in this process, we invariably end up producing entropic byproducts that may be quite beneficial to other life forms. In such ways do plants emit oxygen which, in turn, is inhaled by animals who complete the exchange with the plant world by exhaling the carbon dioxide upon which they depend.

One would think, from such an example, that the symbiotic relationships that exist among so many species on the planet, might inspire even the environmentalist faithful to reconsider their hostility to life processes. A reading of Michael Pollan's wonderful book, *The Botany of Desire*,[3] might awaken them to how humans have entered into relationships with such plant life as tulips, apples, marijuana, and potatoes, to the mutual benefit of one another. Pollan's description and analyses of how these species have served their self-interests through one another, is in sharp contrast to what might be a Marxist's interpretation of human "exploitation" of plant life. Has mankind "exploited" tulips and apples, or have these plants engaged in "exploitation" by making their qualities attractive so that humans would want to cultivate them? Are the mutually beneficial processes of exchange that define the human marketplace also at work *inter*-specially in ways that are more apparent than we realize? Contrary to our divisive thinking, mankind is related to all forms of life through our common ancestor, DNA.

Politically-driven environmentalists are uncomfortable with questions premised upon symbiosis, self-regulation, cooperation, spontaneous organization, and other informal systems of order. Such inquiries would be

---

3   Michael Pollan, *The Botany of Desire* (New York: Random House, 2001).

fatal to the people-pushers, whose ambitions depend upon nurturing the mindset that our relationships with one another are irreconcilable other than through their interventions. To such minds, political structuring is the universal solvent for every condition to be exploited for their power interests.

And so, we are to forget that the carbon dioxide we humans—and other animals—expel in our continuing effort to survive becomes the nourishment for the plants that produce all of the oxygen and much of the food upon which we rely. We may soon hear from the apocalyptic wing of the environmentalist church that the relationship between "plant" and "animal" species is what poses a threat to the planet. It is not just we humans who are to blame, but the plants and animals of the earth who conspire with us to continue this destructive oxygen/carbon dioxide cycle. It is the life process itself, the environmentalists will soon be informing us, that threatens the stability of the planet.

Taken to their logical and empirical lengths, the environmental dogmas lead to endless wars against the efforts of the life force to manifest and sustain itself on Earth. But life is a disruptive force, forever transforming the environment into other forms. And all of this change, we are told, is a threat to the planet, which must now make adjustments—as George Carlin reminded us—to incorporate plastic bags into its being.

The assumption that underlies much of environmentalism is that maintaining equilibrium conditions is beneficial to a system. This is the same attitude that leads most established business interests to want to stabilize the conditions under which competition is to take place. But with any living system—be it an individual, an enterprise, or a civilization—stabilization is the equivalent of death. In the words of the noted botanist, Edmund Sinnott, "[c]onstancy and conservatism are qualities of the lifeless, not the living."[4] The only time your body will be in an equilibrium state is when you are *dead*; your biological system will have ceased to make life-sustaining responses to the changes in your environment. Not even the marketplace manifests equilibrium conditions. The laws of supply and demand tend *toward* equilibrium pricing—an increase in demand or a shortage in supply will raise prices which, in turn, encourages the greater production that will lower prices—but without ever achieving stability as a fixed state.

---

4   Edmund Sinnott, *The Biology of the Spirit* (New York: The Viking Press, 1955), p. 61.

In contrast to those who insist on sterilizing the planet—vaccinating it from the virus of mankind—may I suggest an alternative metaphor, drawn from the biologist Lewis Thomas. In his wonderful book, *The Lives of a Cell,*[5] Thomas proposes a more holographic metaphor that sees the Earth *not* in the mechanistic, fragmented image to which our politicized thinking has accustomed us, but as an integrated system. Like a cell that functions through horizontal interconnectedness rather than vertically-structured direction, the planet may be seen as a self-regulating, mutually-supportive life system energized by the spontaneity and autonomy of its varied participants. So considered, those who insist upon severing this interconnectedness and fragmenting life into categories of controllers and the controlled, pose the greatest threat to the viability of the planet.

---

5   Lewis Thomas, *The Lives of a Cell: Notes of a Biology Watcher* (New York: Bantam Books, 1974).

CHAPTER 35

The Real World Order
is Chaotic

*Chaos is found in greatest abundance wherever order is being
sought. Chaos always defeats order because it is better organized.*
—Terry Pratchett

M y last words on the gallows will be to praise the study of chaos.
For the sake of our very survival as a species, the destructive
and dysfunctional nature of our highly-structured world may
soon force humanity into an outburst of intelligence. Should
that occur, an understanding of the creative and orderly processes of chaos
may save us from the consequences of our collective hubris.

What can be more insane than mankind's continuing belief that the
intricacies and variability of our complex world can be fully comprehend-
ed and rendered manageable by wise leaders. In a world caught up in the
madness of wars, genocidal campaigns, economic depressions, and the resort—by some—to the despair implicit in suicide bombings, there is no
better occasion for us to consider a major paradigm shift in our thinking.

"Desperation" may well be the best word to describe our current responses to the ubiquitous malfunctioning of social systems premised on
the necessity for vertically-structured, top-down, command-and-control
organizational forms. Western Civilization collapses all around us, yet

most of us continue to insist upon a renewed commitment to variations of the Platonic vision of a world made orderly by philosopher-kings.

Perhaps the clearest expression of just how desperate mankind has become in its efforts to restore social order without, in the process, deviating from the premise of centralized authority, was seen in President George W. Bush's usurpation of personalized decision-making power. Having tested the water to see if there was any significant objection to his stated preference for political dictatorship—of which there was little—Mr. Bush proceeded to turn the direction of American society to whatever whim or vision fascinated him at the moment. If war was an attractive course, he would declare it on his own initiative—constitutional grants of such authority to Congress notwithstanding. Nor did it seem to matter to *Boobus Americanus*, or the media, or the corporate owners of American society, what the pretext or identification of enemies for such wars happened to be.

And as decades of government economic planning, direction, and other interventions began playing themselves out in the dislocations that now threaten to pull the marketplace into the destructive vortex of a black hole, resort is once again had to the premise of centrally-directed political power. Far from even pretending to the status of philosopher-kings trying to rationally manage the present crisis, the president, members of Congress, the Federal Reserve Board, and other government officials operate upon no greater insight than the unstated assumption "let's try *this* and see what happens!" Having long been accustomed to believing that no problem was too considerable that could not be overcome by the infusion of money, Congress and the executive branch began sending *trillions* of dollars to their corporate sponsors. Contrary to the presumed premises of "economic planning," there were no announced directions as to how such money was to be spent, or what specific consequences were anticipated. It was enough that members of the corporate-state hierarchy were in menacing straits, and that the federal government owned a printing press that could alleviate such difficulties! The ancient saying, "desperate times call for desperate measures," were invoked to rationalize this grand-scale looting. But in so doing, the political system inadvertently confessed to its incapacity to efficaciously plan in a world of complexity.

Boobus—unaccustomed to thinking outside the circle of his institution-serving conditioning in the necessity for centralized authority—has been unable to envision any alternative other than replacing a failed wizard with a new and improved model. Barack Obama became the establishment's well-hyped candidate, being packaged and sold not as yet another failed philosopher-king, but in the nature of a god-king. Gods, after all, are looked upon as both omniscient and all-powerful, capable of transcending the limited capacities of mere humans to deal with the uncertainties of complexity. Obama promised "change" to a beleaguered public without, in the process, altering any of the fundamental practices or structures that produced the disorder. Indeed, as announcements of his forthcoming cabinet revealed the names of many of the political retreads whose past efforts helped to produce our current problems—including Obama's retention of President Bush's present Secretary of Defense!—expectations of "change" eroded to little more than the placing of corn flakes in a more attractive box. When Obama proves as incapable as his predecessors of imposing greatness upon the country; and his presumed godliness evaporates to reveal just another ambitious politician; I wonder if his idolatrous followers will be as inclined to deal with him as fiercely as Daniel Dravot was treated by the denizens of Kafiristan in Kipling's *The Man Who Would Be King*?[1]

At no time do I recall such a frequent recitation of the definition of "insanity" as "continuing to repeat the same behavior, expecting a different result." Perhaps this reflects a growing awareness of the need for a major transformation in how we think about the nature of social systems. The Ron Paul phenomenon seems to have tapped into an undercurrent of energy—particularly among people in their twenties, thirties, and forties—that goes far beyond opposition to war, the burdens of taxation, and government regulatory and fiscal policies. I was in Minneapolis for the Ron Paul alternate convention, and was stunned to hear an audience of some twelve thousand people cheer Tom Woods' reference to the "Austrian theory of the business cycle." The kids know that "the system" just doesn't work anymore; that it cannot deliver its promised order; that they will simply continue to be ground up in the machinery that serves only a privileged elite, and not themselves.

The foundations of Western Civilization are fast crumbling. Like hillside homes caught in a landslide, there is little that rational people can do other than distancing themselves from the descent while, at the same time, helping to establish more peaceful, free, and cooperative ways of working with others. In the words of the science historian, Thomas Kuhn, mankind

---

1   Rudyard Kipling, *The Man Who Would be King*, in *The Phantom Rickshaw and Other Eerie Tales* (Allahabad: A.H. Wheeler & Co., 1888).

is in need of a fundamental "paradigm shift" in our social thinking.[2] An increased familiarity with the nature of "chaos" may provide the catalyst for such a change.

We humans have long allowed ourselves to be dominated by *linear* thinking. We have become too attached to structured forms of thinking (e.g., regarding emotional expression as inferior to logic and rational thought; treating the literal as superior to the metaphoric), which has led us to prefer *structured* organizational forms to the more *informal*. Linear thinking has also led us to the worship of *technology* as the principal means by which to improve our quality of life. None of this is to condemn such thinking outright—if I were going in for major surgery, I would want the surgeon to approach the operation in a linear fashion rather than as a "stream of consciousness." It is, however, to suggest a more integrated relationship between linear and non-linear thinking.

The study of chaos makes us more familiar with the non-linear nature of complex systems. From our own bodies to social systems to the rest of the physical universe, our world is far more characterized by spontaneous, informal, and unplanned behavior than our linear thinking chooses to acknowledge. Even giving institutional officials the benefit of the doubt as to their motives, we are fated to play out the "unintended consequences" of our best of intentions. This was the essence of Ron Paul's debate quarrel with Rudy Giuliani concerning the "blowback" of American foreign policies that led to the events of 9/11. Paul was but applying Newton's "third law of motion" (i.e., for every action there is an equal and opposite reaction), a proposition that a thoroughly institutionalized Giuliani was unable to grasp.

The forces of chaos will continue to play themselves out, regardless of the self-righteous arrogance with which they are opposed by politicians, public opinion polls, and the babblings of journalism-school trained news "reporters." The trillions of dollars of "bailout" funds will have unforeseen "trickle-down" consequences long after the checks have cleared the Treasury. Learning how to function within a world whose forces are indifferent to our demands is the opportunity provided by the study of the order that lies hidden within chaotic systems. It is a field of inquiry whose insights will prove discomforting to members of the political class, the philosopher-kings and god-kings who will continue to ignore its teachings to the peril of us all.

---

2   Thomas S. Kuhn, *The Structure of Scientific Revolutions*, 2nd ed. (Chicago: University of Chicago Press, 1970; originally published 1962).

CHAPTER 36

Blogs or Blotto?

Heavier-than-air flying machines are impossible.
—Lord Kelvin (1895)

Video won't be able to hold onto any market it captures after the first six months. People will soon get tired of staring at a plywood box every night.
—Darryl F. Zanuck, head of
Twentieth Century Fox (1946)

I can assure you on the highest authority that data processing is a fad and won't last out the year.
—Business books editor at
Prentice-Hall (1957)

The foregoing quotations are to be found in a delightful book, *The Experts Speak*, by Christopher Cerf and Victor Navasky.[1] Described as a "compendium of authoritative misinformation," it illustrates how even highly respected authorities in their fields of endeavor can get tripped up and embarrassed by the unexpected outcomes of creative behavior.

If another edition of that book is forthcoming, the authors would be well-advised to pay attention to the whining coming from members of the

---

1   Cerf and Navasky, *The Experts Speak*, pp. 208, 209, 236.

established media, who are doing their best to convince us that Internet "blogging" is just another fad that will soon go the way of the hula-hoop and the hokey-pokey. Members of the mainstream media periodically attack "blog power" as an unreliable source of information, focusing their criticisms on the fact that there are so many sources, so much conflicting data and analysis, and so much error inherent in the blogging process that readers are burdened in their efforts to discover the truth of things. The mainstreamers rarely make mention of the lying, distortions, and propagandizing that has long infected traditional news outlets; nor is credit sufficiently given to blog-sites for catching and correcting a number of these institutional deviations from truthfulness. The search for truth and understanding depends upon a constantly energized mind that searches, weighs, and analyzes, all with an enduring skepticism as to what one finds.

In the face of so much competing and conflicting information, Harvard University's Alex Jones contrasted the behavior of organizations such as Wikileaks with "the mainstream media, the responsible media" whose role has been "to make sure that real [government] secrets are not being released."[2] Was he implicitly suggesting that people would be better advised to rely on the "mainstream media" for their news? He might just as well have added: "you have been content to let us do your thinking for you; why do you want to undertake such tedious and unceasing work? Let us continue to tell you what we think you should know!" That PBS and Harvard University are two "mainstream" institutions, the self-interested nature of his comment expresses the empty desperation of the practitioners of an information system model that is rapidly dying. Is not the nature of institutionalized news reporting better reflected in the comment a radio newscaster friend, Jeff Riggenbach, told me he was tempted to use on the air: "good morning! And here are the lies your government would like you to believe today!"

The image that comes to mind when I think of the present institutional order, is that of the stegosaurus, the bell-curve-shaped dinosaur with plated armor along its spine. The stegosaurus was so large that it had two brains, one in its head the other in its tail. It is said that a stegosaurus might have been fatally attacked at its backside, while the frontal brain—due to

---

2   Alex Jones, director of Joan Shorenstein Center for Press, Politics and Public Policy at Harvard University. From *PBS Newshour* broadcast of July 27, 2010, pbs.org/newshour/bb/media/july-dec10/wikijournalist_07-27.html

the sluggish nature of the animal's nervous system—might have continued munching tree leaves, not knowing that its fate was already sealed.

So it seems with denizens of the institutional order, particularly those in the news media. The minds at the major television networks, newspapers, and other "mainstream" purveyors of information, either (a) don't understand that the vertically-structured information model—which operates from the premise "we will tell you what we think you ought to know"—is in as terminal a state as our stegosaurus; or (b) they *do* understand this, but hope that, by denying the inevitable, they can forestall the fatal consequences.

There is nothing "faddish" about the collapse of *vertically*-structured institutional systems, and the emergence of *horizontal* networks of interconnected individuals. *Centralized* systems are rapidly becoming *decentralized*, producing a fundamental change in how people will organize themselves in society. Because of the Internet, the information-genie has escaped its institutional confines—where it has been controlled, manipulated, and hidden from view, in furtherance of institutional interests to monopolize the content of the minds of subjugated men and women.

The role of the "mainstream media" has long been the same as that of the government school system: to condition minds to not only *accept*, but to *desire* having society organized just as it is. As the United States' wars against Afghanistan and Iraq progressed, major news outlets were preoccupied with propagandizing the Bush administration's party line. One retired general after another—most employed by defense contractors!—was brought on camera to assure the American people that the war policy was justified and the military strategy was in competent hands. Critics of the war were not to be seen or heard, save for the one channel that has preserved its journalistic integrity: C-SPAN.

American television, in particular, has so diluted the substance of "newscasts" as to render them virtually meaningless to thoughtful men and women. While bloggers, Internet websites, and individual e-mailers were often making factual and analytical challenges to political policies and programs, network television was anesthetizing minds with prolonged coverage of the Scott Peterson trial, entertainment world gossip, or trivial events writ large as the "lead story" of the day. Driving down the Pacific coast the other day, my wife and I listened to a BBC News show on satellite radio—a phenomenon that is carrying decentralization into the realm of broadcast radio. It was refreshing to hear newscasters discussing something other than who had won what particular "Grammy" award the night before!

The establishment media is so intellectually bankrupt that the most informative television news program is "The Daily Show, With Jon Stewart" on the "Comedy Central" channel. When *satire* becomes the most effective means of understanding human events, it is a sign that established society may be in an irreparable state of collapse. Air-headed television voyeurs who partake of the sociology of men and women transported to a remote island, or locked up in a suburban house—shows peddled to the American public as "reality"—overlook the reality that such mindless programming represents: the continuing failure of an establishment media to appeal to intelligent minds.

News reports abound of the sharp declines in television viewing and newspaper subscriptions. Men and women intent on understanding the world in which they live are increasingly turning to the Internet, a system that expresses the phrase "marketplace of ideas" as no other has up to this point in time. Websites and bloggers are learning the same lessons that now beleaguer the established media: in a rapidly decentralizing world, men and women will develop their *own* demands for information that serves *their* interests. With the Internet, people need no longer be passive recipients of what institutional authorities regard as the "politically correct" content of their minds!

Perhaps the self-interest motivations of members of the broadcast media sense this popular demand for "news" that is something more than statist propaganda. Recently, we have seen the emergence of such successful television programs as the Fox News Channel's *The John Stossel Show*, and Judge Andrew Napolitano's *Freedom Watch*. This channel, at least, seems to recognize that a healthy future does not lie in remaining a buggy-whip manufacturer in the face of the oncoming automobile!

Established interests have always been discomforted by innovation and change. In the face of the Internet challenge, I suspect that many media chieftains would find comfort in the sentiments of a Michigan banker who, in 1903, opined that "the horse is here to stay, but the automobile is only a novelty—a fad."[3] Because, as the study of chaos informs us, complex systems generate unpredictable outcomes, "blogging" may, indeed, be a short-term phenomenon. But as long as the channels for the flow of information remain unrestricted, today's blogs will likely evolve into more sophisticated, horizontal processes that allow *individuals* to freely

---

3 Cerf and Navasky, *The Experts Speak*, p. 228.

communicate their understanding to one another, without the need for institutionalized oversight and control. Individuals who are both the producers and consumers of information will have incentives to create more effective systems and mechanisms for the pursuit of understanding.

Such establishment shepherds as Hillary Clinton will continue their pleas for Internet "gatekeepers" to keep the marketplace of ideas as subject to rigid regulations as attend other economic activity. Nor will there be a shortage of institutional voices imploring the ovine herds to give up their wanderings into uncertain territories and return to the fold wherein minds are soothed and left untroubled by events they are told are beyond their ken.

But such efforts will not avail the institutional order. Gutenberg put the establishment on the defensive centuries ago, demonstrating the creative consequences that flow from a loosening of monopolies on information. The Internet—with its proliferation of websites and bloggers, and the continuing collapse of the vertical into the horizontal—has taken the Gutenberg revolution to exponential dimensions. How far this will extend and what forms may arise are completely unknown, which makes the process all the more exciting. Perhaps, sooner than we think, we shall be witness to a new "reality" show, wherein Hillary and Alex Jones find themselves on an island with a group of bloggers. Who would be the likely "survivor" in such a real-world setting? I know upon whom I would *not* be betting!

CHAPTER 37

Bring Back Discrimination!

ardly a week goes by without a news report of such senseless acts as a kindergarten boy being charged with sexual harassment for kissing a classmate on the cheek; or a grade schooler disciplined for violating an anti-drug policy by offering a friend an over-the-counter cough drop; or young boys threatened by the state with "assault with a weapon" prosecution for using their fingers as make-believe guns to play cops-and-robbers. The latest contribution came from the criminal conviction of a teenager for shooting a "spitball" at a classmate, hitting him in the eye.

Practices of this sort are usually defended, by school officials, as part of a "zero tolerance" policy for violence, or drug use, or sexual harassment. Unfortunately, what "zero tolerance" often comes down to in practice is an admission that "I am unable to think clearly and to make distinctions between an uninvited kiss and a violent assault, between a cough drop and a tablet of LSD, between boys pointing their gun-like fingers at one another and a full-blown knife fight." "Zero tolerance," in other words, becomes synonymous with "zero critical analysis."

When I was a youngster, the attempted criminalization of such conduct would likely have been met with questions about the competency of school officials to supervise the learning of children. It would have been understood that the process of growing up involves experimentation and testing of the boundaries of appropriate social conduct. It was also accepted that learning how to establish suitable relationships with others came about through trial and error, and the feeling out of the expectations of *one's peers*, more so than having one's conduct constantly micromanaged by supervising adults. Only if conduct morphed over into the realm of viciousness was it thought appropriate to consider the transgression in criminal terms.

The "spitballer" was given a six-day jail sentence—even though prosecutors reportedly sought an eight-year prison term; while the "cough-drop kid," the finger-pointing "gunman," and the "kindergarten kisser" may have to spend the rest of their lives acknowledging, to colleges or employers, their respective "offenses" of "drug-dealing," "attempted assault," and "sexual harassment." Again, how does one satirize absurdity?

The underlying cause of such nonsense is not to be found in either wickedness or a penchant for being overly-protective. I suspect that the school administrators who engage in such Draconian measures truly mean to do well by the children entrusted to their care. The problem, instead, can be traced to one of the underlying shortcomings of our culture—one for which, coincidentally, government schools have been the primary culprits—the ongoing *war against discrimination*. We must remember that most of the school officials who cannot distinguish between a pointed finger and a .38 caliber revolver are, themselves, products of government school training.

There was a time when it was considered the highest compliment to tell another that he or she had a "discriminating" mind. Today, such is an *accusation*. One who learned to distinguish *truth* from *fashion*; to critically analyze a given set of events on the basis of intellectually sound criteria; to have both an empirical and rational basis for his or her opinions; to be able to separate fact from fallacy; to have one's mind well grounded in such fields of study as the sciences, history, economics, the classics, psychology, and the humanities; and, above all else, to have both a sense of humility about what we know and a recognition of the human need for transcendent experiences; that person was worthy of being called a "discriminating" individual.

Not only are such qualities not *developed* in schools and colleges today, they are actively *opposed*. One who dares to suggest that the works of Shakespeare are superior to the folktales of some primitive tribe is likely to be charged with cultural chauvinism. To dissent from American foreign policy practices in the Middle East is to invite an accusation of "anti-Semitism" (even though truly *discriminating* minds would note that Arabs are also Semites). To challenge the legitimacy of welfare programs, "affirmative action," or any of a variety of other government policies, is to run the risk of being labeled a "racist" or peddler of "hate." Such absurdities helped to make up the world of "political correctness," a phrase that boils down to the failure of its practitioners to engage in discriminating thought.

At this point, some may respond that I am only setting up a straw man to knock over; that racial, ethnic, and religious bigotry exist in our world, making discrimination a problem to be overcome. I disagree. The person who uses *race* as a determining factor in deciding who to hire or otherwise associate with is *not*, in most instances, *discriminating*, but *failing to discriminate*!

"Discrimination" is closely tied to another misunderstood practice: "prejudice." Whenever we act, we do so on the basis of our prior experiences. We "prejudge," based upon the past events in our lives, what we believe will occur in the future. Let us suppose that, while walking down a dark street one evening, I am mugged by a man wearing a purple hat. In the future, I might very well be fearful of men in purple hats, believing that there was some connection between hat color and my victimization. This is a common response of small children who, having once been frightened by a barking dog, might thereafter fear all dogs.

But as I encounter more and more people wearing purple hats who do *not* assault me, I begin to modify the basis for my prejudgment (i.e., "prejudice") about purple-hatted people. In a word, I learn to *discriminate*, based upon factors more directly relevant to my being victimized, and may eventually come to the conclusion that purple-hattedness has nothing to do with the commission of violent acts. Focusing upon purple hats becomes a distraction to clear thinking.

Our prejudices can serve us well or ill depending upon how proficient we become at making distinctions that help to further what we seek to accomplish. If, for instance, I would like to find a restaurant that sells pizzas, my past experiences lead me to *prejudge* that I am more likely to find pizza in an *Italian* than in a *Szechuan* restaurant. It may be the case that, in this city, the best pizza is made at a Szechuan restaurant, but information costs being greater than the benefits I might derive from trying to locate such a place, I content myself with an Italian eatery.

When factors such as race, religion, or ethnicity enter into our decision-making, however, there seems to be an enhanced likelihood that such considerations will prove detrimental to our objectives. More often than not, prejudging others on such grounds will fail to predict for outcomes that we favor. The employer who refuses to hire a woman, or a black, to operate a punch press *because* of such criteria—rather than the applicant's demonstrated skill at handling the machine—will have to forego the added profitability from having the most *competent* people working for him.

On the other hand, there are times when being prejudiced on the basis of race or other such factors is quite rational: I suspect that, when Spike Lee was casting for the *Malcolm X* film, neither Robert Redford nor Whoopi Goldberg were given the slightest consideration for the lead. Lee "discriminated" by casting Denzel Washington. Was Lee "prejudiced" in his decision? Of course: he "prejudged" that Denzel Washington would be a more believable Malcolm X—thus adding to the quality of the film—than would Robert Redford. He made a perfectly intelligent decision; he exhibited the qualities of a "discriminating" mind: he knew when race and gender were relevant factors in his decision-making.

Racial and ethnic bigots, on the other hand, fail to make such relevant distinctions. In their minds, such factors become central to all forms of decision-making. Percaled Ku Klux Klansmen and the most ardent champions of "affirmative action" programs have this in common: for each, another person's race or ethnicity is a deciding characteristic. The quantity of melanin in one's skin determines whether a targeted individual will be brutalized or given a preference, depending upon the nature of the group making the decision. It is *not* that such people *discriminate*, but that they *do not know how to discriminate*!

Nor is this problem confined to these more vulgar forms of expression. A friend of mine was a high-level executive for a major American corporation. One of their divisions was having major cost problems, and he was sent to find out what was wrong. His first act was to pull the personnel files on the top twenty or so executives in that division and discovered that each was a retired Naval officer. Upon further inquiry, he learned that the official in charge of hiring within that division was, himself, a retired Naval officer, and when he saw an applicant with such a background, *that* fact became the basis for his hiring decision. That there was no causal connection between being a Naval officer and a competent business executive led to employment policies that hindered corporate purposes.

The catastrophic events of 9/11 provided what has thus far proven to be a missed opportunity for clear, discriminating thinking. Rather than treating the attack as a criminal act, President Bush and other government officials reacted with unfocused anger against a vaguely defined "enemy" who, upon closer inspection, became "anyone who's not with us" in a unilaterally declared "War on Terror." Without any evidence of Afghan involvement in the WTC attacks, the Bush Administration started bombing Afghanistan, and putting together lists of "enemies" and possible nuclear targets—whose identities were both interchangeable and subject to continuing amendment. A number of countries were identified as an "Axis of Evil," an appellation reflecting an unfamiliarity with basic geometry. Draconian police state measures were also announced that would greatly restrict individual liberties, but only for the duration of the "war" which was, of course, to go on forever!

Those who suggested that the WTC attacks might have been in response to American foreign policies and military actions were lambasted by the booboisie who, unable to distinguish between an *explanation* and a *justification* of events, accused such critics of *defending* the attacks! Bill Maher—host of the TV program, *Politically Incorrect*—offered one of his few genuinely "politically incorrect" observations when he rejected President Bush's comment that the 9/11 attackers were "cowards." Referring to American actions, Maher declared that "lobbing cruise missiles from two thousand miles away, that's cowardly."[1] For his honest comments, he was pilloried by those whose inability to discriminate gets expressed in terms of *distinctions without meaning.*

The failure to make intelligent distinctions among competing choices or explanations is not confined to more newsworthy events. I have observed the practice, in a number of restaurants, of requiring customers ordering alcoholic drinks to present proof of their adult status, even in situations in which the patron is well into his or her sixties or seventies! The implicit notion that a waiter or waitress might inadvertently mistake a twenty-year old for a person who had reached majority and, therefore, require that employee to challenge the age of grandparents, is but one more reflection of a dying culture.

These are just a few examples of the consequences of abandoning the pursuit of critical thinking. Analysis and reasoning have given way to flag-waving, bumper-sticker slogans, and public opinion polls. If you are unable to assess the propriety of a given course of action, then ask *other* equally confused people what *they* think. Let us pool the ignorance!

---

1   en.wikipedia.org/wiki/Bill_Maher

As the study of mob behavior informs us, when self-righteous rage suppresses intelligence, an unfocused mindlessness emerges. Collective insanity has a way of escalating quite rapidly. When top government officials in Washington can casually discuss "first strike" nuclear attacks against other nations, and warn dissenters to watch what they say, you can be assured that discriminating minds are not in charge.

Perhaps intelligent thinking will begin to assert itself over the official madness that now prevails. There may be sufficient remnants of discriminating thought within the life force itself to impress upon even the most rabid of Washington warmongers that, no matter how horrific and inhumane the attacks of 9/11, they do not justify either a massive police state or a nuclear firestorm capable of obliterating all of humanity.

Arthur Koestler suggested that mankind might have been an evolutionary mistake.[2] A killer ape with a highly developed brain might not be a recipe for species longevity. That same brain, however, provides us the means to evaluate the nature of our behavior, and to make choices that either advance or diminish our lives. But how does one make choices without discriminating among alternatives? And if we are to make life-fulfilling choices, upon what grounds shall we discriminate? Do purple hats really matter?

---

2   Arthur Koestler, *The Ghost in the Machine* (New York: Random House, 1982) pp. 272–80.

CHAPTER 3 8

Saving a Dying Corpse

An Associated Press news report told of 1,900 sheep following one another over a cliff in Turkey, resulting in the deaths of 450.[1] The sheep had been grazing when, without explanation, some members of the herd began leaping from the cliff. The others followed the lead, providing an example of "sheepish" behavior.

What a fitting metaphor for the herd-oriented behavior of humans. Political systems—along with various corporate interests that produced the homogeneous corporate-state—have succeeded in getting people to organize themselves into opposing herds. These multitudes are placed under the leadership of persons who function like "Judas goats," a term derived from the meat-packing industry. Judas goats are trained to lead sheep to the slaughterhouse, slipping safely away as the others are led to the butcher. Political leaders take their flocks to the deadly precipice, depart to the safety of their bunkers, and allow herd instincts to play out their deadly course. With the help of the media, Bush, Blair, Cheney, Wolfowitz, Rumsfeld, Rice, et al., perform the Judas goat function quite well, rousing the herds into a "let's you and him fight" mindset without occasioning the loss of their own blood. You will not see any of these smug, arrogant creatures

---

1   *USA Today*, July 9, 2005. usatoday.com/news/offbeat/2005-07-08-sheep-suicide_x.htm

in the front lines of battle: that is the purpose served by the "masses" (i.e., the "herds").

But what happens when this herd-hustling game begins to break down—when the consequences become so destructive as to threaten the herd itself? What happens when the sheep begin to suspect that there are alternatives to their present condition and that their lives might have a greater purpose than to be part of a pile of corpses? What if they should learn of greener pastures elsewhere, entry to which is not restricted to a privileged few, the enjoyment of which requires only a breaking away from the restraints of the herd? What if word of such life-fulfilling options begins to spread among herd members?

This allegorical reference seems apropos to modern society, whose vertical structures continue their collapse into more horizontal networks. One cannot grasp the meaning of the established order's admittedly endless war on "terrorism" without understanding the much deeper question: how is a free and creative society to be organized? Under what sorts of systems will men and women live, work, play, cooperate, and raise children? The institutionally-centered forms with their command-and-control mechanisms that have long represented Western societies are eroding; and the established interests that have benefited from such systems are in a life-and-death struggle to resist their demise.

Having become ends in themselves, institutions must resist behavior that threatens their interests. Once men and women have been conditioned to accept the supremacy of institutional interests over their own, it is an easy matter to get them to sanction the use of state power to protect and promote established interests. *Corporate* interests become synonymous with *societal* interests; concerns for "security"—whether "national," "homeland," "job," "social," or "airport"—justify governmental restrictions on individual liberty and other processes of change that threaten the status quo.

Business firms have been the principal forces behind the promotion of governmental regulation of the economic life of this country. Through competitive and trade practice standards; licensing and other limitations on entry into the marketplace; tariffs and taxation policies; government research subsidies and defense contracting; and various other uses of the coercive powers of the state to advance private interests, the business community has fostered rigidities that help to insulate firms from the need to remain creatively resilient and adaptive to change.

As I have previously observed, a number of historians have shown how such institutionalizing practices contribute to the decline of civilizations. If a society is to remain creative and viable, it must *encourage*—not simply *tolerate*—the processes of change. At this point, the creative interests of *society* (as people) comes into conflict with the structuring interests of *institutions* (as organizational systems). Whether the autonomous and spontaneous processes of change will prevail over the preservation of established institutional interests, may well determine the fate of the American civilization!

The forces of institutional dominance—with their centralized, vertically-structured, coercive systems of control—have encountered the decentralized, horizontally-connected, voluntary methods of cooperation. Mankind is in a life-and-death struggle not simply for its physical survival, but for its very soul. The contest centers on the question of whether human beings shall continue to be servo-mechanistic resources for the use and consumption of institutional interests, or whether they shall be their own reasons for being. Will *institutional* or *individual* interests be regarded as the organizing principle of society?

It is this confrontation that underlies the so-called "war on terror." "Terrorism"—like "international communism" that preceded it—is but another specter held up to a gullible public to enlist their continuing support for institutional hegemony. "Terrorism" is a tactic, not a competing political institution, a tactic that reflects the inability of the state to predict and control events. Even the British Home Secretary, Charles Clarke, admitted that there was no governmental measure that could have prevented the 2005 London subway bombings.[2] One former CIA analyst has asserted that unpublicized U.S. government figures show an increase in terrorist acts in the world from 175 in 2003 to 625 in 2004,[3] hardly a ringing endorsement of the efficacy of the "war on terror."

In numerous ways, humanity is slipping out of the grasping hands of the state, a prospect that does, indeed, "terrorize" institutional interests. Parents are increasingly turning to home-schooling and other forms of private education as alternatives to government schools; alternative medicine and health-care systems continue to prosper; the Internet—with its myriad and interconnected web and blog sites—is increasingly relied upon by men

---

2   Opendemocracy.net/understanding_suicide_attacks. June 21, 2007

3   Newsinsider.org/92/us-losing-grip-in-the-middle-east/. April 25, 2005

and women for all kinds of information, with a corresponding decline in newspaper readership and network television news viewing. These are just a few of the more prominent examples of a world that is becoming increasingly decentralized, spontaneous, and individualized.

The difficulties we face often arise from our failure to ask relevant questions. This may help explain the institutional establishment's lack of awareness of its apparent fate. A CNN news show reported on the increased popularity of Internet blogsites, explaining their growth as a public demand for getting news out more "quickly,"—then urging viewers to continue watching CNN for the fastest reports. However, it is not information *speed* that attracts people to the Internet, but increased *options* in *what* is reported. When the Iraqi war was on center stage, television networks trotted out retired generals, admirals, or colonels to explain—and favorably comment upon—the government's war strategies. If one wanted to find thoughtful criticism of the war—such as provided by Bob Higgs, Lewis Lapham, Justin Raimondo, Lew Rockwell, Chalmers Johnson, Alexander Cockburn, John Pilger, Karen Kwiatkowski, Alan Bock, Seymour Hersh, Glenn Greenwald, Chris Hedges, or numerous other thinkers—one had to go to the Internet.

The latent forces of complexity and chaos, coupled with the adverse consequences of increased organizational size, will doubtless continue these decentralizing trends. Secession movements, along with an increased willingness of state and local governments to openly challenge federal government policies, reflect a growing interest in decentralizing political power. Even the Iraqi insurgency forces and various "terrorist" attacks attest to war itself becoming decentralized.

The institutional order could, of course, try to adapt to such changes. Many business organizations have, in fact, discovered the enhanced productivity to be found in the adoption of more decentralized managerial policies in which day-to-day decision-making is more widely distributed throughout the work force. But few have been willing to extend the logic of centrifugence to broader social environments such as the marketplace. They—and most of the rest of us—fail to understand that the spontaneous and autonomous processes that enhance the creativity and profitability of a *firm*, also foster the viability of *society* itself.

Creativity has always posed a threat to those who refuse to adapt themselves to more productive alternatives. Because we have learned to regard institutions as *ends* to be preserved, rather than *tools* to be utilized, fundamental changes that threaten the institutional order must be resisted. Such is the case with the worldwide shift from vertically-designed and hierarchically-structured systems of centralized control, toward more decentralized, horizontally-networked social systems. Feudalism—grounded in politically-defined privileges, rights, and status—was unable to sustain itself in the face of an Industrial Revolution that rewarded people on the basis of exhibited merit in a free marketplace. So, too, the neo-feudal, politically-structured institutionalized order, will be unable to resist the oncoming liberalizing trends.

Like the Luddites who fought the Industrial Revolution, the established order will not give up its privileges without a fight. Efforts to revive the dying corpse of centralized power structures have taken on paramount importance. With the demise of the Soviet Union as its symbiotic partner for the rationalization of state power—itself the victim of decentralist forces—the United States has had to find a new threat with which to keep Americans as a fear-ridden herd. The statists believe they have found this eternal danger in the specter of "terrorism," which they hope can be manipulated to justify endless wars and unrestrained police powers.

But if you can cut through the veneer of propaganda as "news," and begin to ask such questions as how U.S.-supported persons and organizations (e.g., Saddam Hussein, Osama bin Laden, the Taliban) could suddenly became threats to America, you will begin to understand the nature of the herding game being played at your expense.

What government officials and the media have labeled the "war on terror" has, I believe, a more encompassing target: the decentralizing processes that are eroding institutionally-controlled social behavior. "Terrorism" is the state's new scarecrow, erected to ward off the changes that threaten the interests of the rigidly-structured political establishment. What is now drifting away into diffused networks of freely developed, alternative forms and practices, must be resisted by a state system that insists upon its centralized, coercive control of the lives of us all. As has always been the case, the life-sustaining processes of spontaneity and autonomy are being opposed by the life-destroying forces of coercive restraint.

With its newly-concocted perpetual war upon an unseen enemy—combined with greatly expanded police powers—the established order seeks to force free men and women back into the herd upon which its violent control over life depends. That we may take our places in the serried ranks set out for us by the state so that we remain subservient to the state, is the purpose underlying the present "war on terror." As with the sheep in Turkey, the consequence will be that we will follow one another over cliffs leading to our mutual destruction. In the tapestry of human history, it is but the latest expression of the state's continuing war against life.

CHAPTER 39

The Slave Mentality

A slave is one who waits for someone to come and free him.
—Ezra Pound

Many Americans are under the illusion that the 13th Amendment to the U.S. Constitution abolished slavery. Its words certainly *sound* as if it did: "Neither slavery nor involuntary servitude, except as a punishment for crime whereof the party shall have been duly convicted, shall exist within the United States, or any place subject to their jurisdiction." The language sounds quite clear. Neither "slavery" (defined by one dictionary as "submission to a dominating influence") nor "involuntary" ("compulsory") "servitude" ("a condition in which one lacks liberty esp. to determine one's course of action or way of life") shall exist within the United States.[1]

But words are abstractions, and must always be interpreted. As Orwell made clear to us, unless we pay attention to what is being said, scheming men and women with ambitions over the lives and property of others, will interpret words in such ways as to convey the opposite meaning most of us attach to those words. This is true with the American state—particularly

---

1   *Webster's New Collegeiate Dictionary*, pp. 1091, 609, 1060.

through its definers and obfuscators in the judicial system—in telling us the "true meaning" of the 13th Amendment. This provision was only intended to prohibit *private* forms of slavery; the state was not intended to be bound by its otherwise clear language. Thus, the 13th Amendment did not *end* slavery, but only *nationalized* it. The state is to have a monopoly on trafficking in slaves! Evidence for this is found in the current corporate-state prisons-for-profit system. Some *six million* Americans are now under the control of the state's prison/correctional apparatus, most having been convicted of victimless crimes. This number exceeds those imprisoned in Stalinist-era gulags! Those who cling to the myth that the Civil War ended slavery should consider this fact: there are more black men trapped in this prisons-for-profit racket today than were enslaved on plantations in 1850.[2]

Compulsory systems of military conscription, jury-duty, school attendance, and road-building duty, have long been upheld by the courts as not being barred by the 13th Amendment. So, too, has that most far-reaching form of involuntary servitude, taxation. When the *state* desires your non-consented services, the courts—consistent with their record of expanding state power while giving very restrictive interpretations to individual liberty—are quick with the "newspeak."

As the war in Iraq continues apace, and with Massa Bush suggesting a seemingly endless presence in that country, proposals for expanding the present state-slavery racket are being voiced. Bills have been introduced in the House (H.R. 163) and the Senate (S. 89) by so-called "liberal" Democrats urging a renewal of military conscription. What is worthy of note is that a number of the sponsors of this proposed legislation are African-Americans—Charles Rangel, Sheila Jackson-Lee, John Conyers, Eleanor Holmes Norton, Elijah Cummings, and Alcee Hastings, among others. Jesse Jackson has also urged a reconsideration of the draft.

On first impression, one might wonder why blacks, whose identities are so wrapped up in ancestral slavery, would be advocating a return to a system of conscripted labor. But Rep. Rangel and other blacks have expressed another purpose. They have defended this proposal as a way of focusing attention on whether blacks, Hispanics, and low-income people would—as in the Vietnam War—bear a disproportionate share of the burden of military service. If conscription were applicable to all, with no special exemptions or

---

2   See, e.g., Adam Gopnik, "The Caging of America," in *The New Yorker*, January 30, 2012. www.newyorker.com/arts/critics/atlarge/2012/01/30/120130crat_atlarge_gopnik

deferments allowed, it is argued, the system could be operated in a "fair" manner.

"Fair" is one of those four-letter "f" words that I discourage in my classroom. Within a few days of being introduced to my strange ways, students learn to omit that word from class discussions. The word "fair" is an expression of teenager justice, carrying no more meaning than to say "I don't like it." "If you consider something to be 'unfair,'" I ask my students, "tell me, specifically, why you think such a state of affairs is wrong." It is more important to ask whether the state should be impressing *anyone* into forced servitude than it is to debate the "fairness" of who is selected for sacrifice!

And yet, it is to the doctrine of "equality" that many advocates of the "fairness" argument repair. Those who regard *liberty* and *equality* as synonyms—instead of understanding their contradictory, irreconcilable nature—tend to believe that, as long as an oppressive measure is forced upon all, without regard to distinctions, there is no problem. Such attitudes are generally shared by statists, whose responses to a tax, a restriction, or a mandate that is borne by only one group, is to urge governmental impositions upon *all*. The chuckleheaded branch of "feminism"—whose members cringe in terror at any expression of "liberation"—insist that, as a matter of principle, women should share with men the abuse by the state, including military conscription. To egalitarians, the "equal protection of the laws" is to be furthered by *universalizing* oppression, rather than ending it as to everyone! Had Hitler not singled out minority groups for his tyrannical practices—had he, in other words, oppressed everyone equally—the egalitarians would have been hard put to find grounds for objection.

I don't want to leave you with the impression that black politicians are the principal promoters of this renewed system of state slavery. They are not. Nebraska Senator Charles Hagel is also championing a return to conscription.[3] While Rep. Rangel and others may be somewhat forgiven for their misplaced strategies in using conscription as a way of focusing on other issues, Sen. Hagel has no such ulterior purposes. In expanding his openness to conscription to include other forms of "mandatory national service"—which might include involuntary servitude on behalf of some other governmental function—Hagel made clear his commitment to state collectivism.

---

3   Thefreelibrary.com/A+step+back+from+a+draft.a0124258300. See, also, watchmanscry.com/forum/archive/index.php?t-440.html

Hagel picked up the egalitarian chant about conscription imposing an equal burden upon "the privileged, the rich," not being clear whether he intended these as synonymous or separate words. If he means to attack "the rich," generally, such an appeal to class-warfare rhetoric is rather peculiar from one who, as a Midwest Republican, I assume would not openly count himself a foe of private capitalism. If, on the other, it is his purpose to criticize "privilege," he might want to begin with a definition of that term. One dictionary defines it as "a right or immunity granted as a peculiar benefit."[4]

"Granted" by whom? As a long-standing member of the U.S. Senate, it should be evident to this man that it is the *state*, of which he is a key member, that involves itself in conferring benefits and immunities upon its well-connected supporters, just as Congress grants to itself and its members special privileges not enjoyed by the rest of society. If it is his desire to end such special dispensations, he might begin by cleaning up his own house. Rather than universalizing state power over people's lives, Sen. Hagel might consider joining Rep. Ron Paul—and the seven cosponsors of his H.R. 487—in a bill that would *permanently* end the system of military conscription, for the rich as well as the poor.

To statists, of course, anyone who owns property is regarded as a "rich" target for their plundering pursuits. Collectivists—a word applicable to all defenders of state power—consider *all* property subject to their preemptive authority to direct, destroy, or consume as suits their preferences. Sentiments for the oft-expressed phrase—"eat the rich"—are not confined to modern Marxist ideologues, but provide bipartisan support to all who harbor ambitions of power over others, be they "rich" or "poor."

A conservative Bill Buckley,[5] and such more "liberal" persons as Robert McNamara, President Obama, former President Bill Clinton, and others,[6] have previously clucked the virtues of service to the state, a fact that should help you understand why, in the words of a friend of mine, the late James J. Martin, the political "Left" and "Right" are simply "two wings of the same bird of prey." All political systems and ideologies have, at their base, an implicit belief that human beings are expendable resources to be exploited on behalf of whatever ambitions those in power might have. If the state needs more money, tax those who produce wealth. If the state wants to conduct a

---

4   *Webster's Third New International Dictionary*, p. 1805.

5   www.fff.org/freedom/0491a.asp

6   www.cato.org/pubs/pas/pa190.pdf. www.whitehouse.gov/agenda/service

war, appropriate the lives of hundreds of thousands of young people to be slaughtered in its service. If the state wants privately owned land, take it, without regard to whether the owner chooses to part with it.

If we wish to put an end to the systematic exploitation and enslavement of people, we must confront the underlying premise upon which all of this is grounded: that our lives belong to the state, to be consumed in whatever manner and for whatever purposes state officials choose. We must confront and move beyond the delusional thinking that a responsible and meaningful life is to be found in participating in coercive governmental undertakings. Sen. Hagel is but one of many overseers on the state's plantation, whose entreaties on behalf of enforced service must be resisted with the same determined spirit that led many antebellum slaves to walk away from their servitude.

The first case I have students read in my Property Law class is *Dred Scott v. Sandford,*[7] in which a slave raised the question of whether he ought to be considered a "person" under the U.S. Constitution. The U.S. Supreme Court ruled that he could not, that he was the property of his slave master. I then demonstrate to my students how "ownership" is a function of "control" over an item of property; that whoever is able to effectively control property is its owner, regardless of what some document might suggest.

As we saw in Schumpeter's distinction between owner-controlled and manager-controlled businesses, troublesome consequences arise when *ownership* is separated from *control.* This problem is also at the center of the inevitable social conflict generated by political systems. Government regulation of the lives and property of people, taxation, eminent domain, and other acts of state, bifurcate one's ownership *claim* (i.e., to be an exclusive decision-maker over an item of property) from the effective *control* that gives meaning to ownership. When the inviolability of claims is respected—the condition essential to peace—control over the property of another can arise only through such voluntary means as contracts and conveyances of ownership claims. What continues to be hidden in news stories about political, religious, ethnic, tribal, and other expressions of organized violence throughout the world, is that societal conflict will always result when control over property is acquired by force.

I go on to ask my students if they claim "self-ownership." "Do you own yourself?," I inquire. I then warn them about their answer to this question,

---

7   *Dred Scott v. Sandford,* 61 U.S. (19 How.) 393 (1857).

and how we shall have occasion to visit the implications of their answers throughout the school year. "If you *do* claim self-ownership," I ask, "how do you tolerate the state controlling your life through various laws? And if you do *not* claim self-ownership, what possible objection can you raise to anything another might choose to do to you? If you do not want to own yourself—and to insist upon the control that goes with such a claim—should you be surprised that *others* might choose to assert a claim of ownership over that which you have rejected?"

If Sen. Hagel and his fellow slavers have their way, what will be your response when the roundup of vassals begins? Will you—like the people who watch or babble on FoxNews—rejoice at your good fortune to live in a country where you enjoy the "freedom" to be a slave, or will you exhibit the good sense to reject the system? The state will have its modern version of the Fugitive Slave Laws to hunt down, punish, and return you to the plantation; legislation that Sen. Hagel and most other members of Congress will eagerly endorse.

It is frightening enough to hear proposals for our universal enslavement coming from people who pretend to be representatives of our interests. It is equally disturbing that such dehumanized thinking can be defended by so many out of what can only be regarded as a twisted sense of community. Those who embrace such offerings without giving much thought to their meaning should understand that the most important quality we hold in common with our neighbors is a need to defend one another's individuality. Being converted into humanoid servo-mechanisms of the state perverts, not fosters, our sense of community. There is something very sad about a society whose members think otherwise, and who acquiesce in the collectivist premise that their lives, and the lives of their children, are the property of the state; that they are to be the cannon fodder, tax-cows to be milked, and inflatable Bozo clowns to absorb the brutal anger of police officers; that they amount to no more, in the political scheme of things, than fungible resources to be collected, counted, catalogued, warehoused, and shipped off to whatever location, and exploited for whatever purposes that serve the interests of their institutional owners.

CHAPTER **40**

Running on Empty

Conservative, n.: A statesman who is enamored of existing evils, as distinguished from the Liberal, who wishes to replace them with others.

—Ambrose Bierce

It is not surprising that, when a culture is in collapse, so too is the level of thinking upon which it is based. This is doubtless the social equivalent of the proposition that water can never rise higher than its source. For a civilization to be creative and to thrive, it must have a substructure capable of producing the values that can sustain it. Our present civilization is dying because it no longer has such a base of support.

Western society has become so thoroughly politicized that it is difficult to imagine any area of human activity that can be said to be beyond the reach of the state. People's diets, weight levels, child-raising practices, treatment of pets, how one can express anger, whether one can make alterations to his/her home, including replacing a lawn with rocks or plants, these are but a handful of private decisions intruded upon by the state. Other than complaints voiced by those directly affected by the state's intervention, there are few who consistently defend the liberty of individuals to live as they choose.

A culture that has to resort to threats, coercion, and other forms of violence to accomplish collective ends, is having to oppose and repress a great deal of human energy and self-interested action seeking other ends. Political systems—as well as the institutions that pursue their purposes through the coercive machinery of the state—are inherently at war with life itself. A free, orderly, and productive society is held together *not* by the armed might of the police and military, nor by the dictates of rulers or the edicts of judges, but by a shared sense of the conditions that *foster* rather than *inhibit* life. At the core of such thinking is a belief in the innate worthiness and inviolability of each person, an attitude that manifests itself in terms of respect for one another's property boundaries, within which each of us is free to pursue our respective self-interests. Peace and liberty are the inevitable consequences of living in a society so constituted.

Sadly, as our world has become increasingly infected by the virus of institutionalism—and its coercive agent, the state—men and women have intensified their attachments to these organizational forms. As we see in the repeated failures of government schools and the criminal justice system to meet the expectations so many have of them, people continue to invest heavily in the promotion of such governmental interests. The more such agencies fail, in other words, the more most people are willing to support them, an absurdity that provides such programs with an incentive to fail.

As the business world has experienced the consequences of moving from the self-disciplining nature of a free market system to the mercantilist coziness of the modern corporate-state arrangement, we find the same institutionally-serving impulses to use governmental force to benefit failing firms. Under the mantra "too big to fail," the corporate-state establishment has been able to bamboozle most Americans into believing that it is in their individual interest to be forced to support business enterprises that lack the resiliency, creativity, and other capacities to respond to competition; that they should be compelled to do what more and more of them would not choose to do in the marketplace.

I went to an Internet site and found a listing of now-defunct American auto manufacturers. Their numbers ran to some *fifty-one* pages. I am certain that, at their demise, the owners of such firms might have wished for the kinds of government-funded bailouts that their successors now enjoy. I can understand—although do not accept—the kind of thinking that would like to be on the receiving end of such state largess. It is not unlike Linus—in an early *Peanuts* cartoon—contemplating his death. After declaring "I'm too young to die," he finally admits "I'm too *me* to die!"

What I do not understand, however, is the innocence—the gullibility, if you prefer—of so many men and women who have brought themselves to share in the institutional mindset that the organizational system is to be more highly-valued and defended than the marketplace processes that created such enterprises in the first place. Such thinking is a symptom of just how deeply the virus of institutionalism has infected American society.

For various reasons that go beyond a principled criticism of our centrally-directed, vertically-structured social systems, the institutional order is in a state of turbulence. Political, corporate, and educational systems are increasingly unable to meet even the most meager of popular expectations. Our world is becoming more and more decentralized, with *vertical* systems being challenged—and even replaced—by *horizontal* networks governed by autonomous and spontaneous human activity. In the face of such changes, the establishment has become desperate to reinforce its crumbling walls. Because its essence is so wrapped up in violent behavior, it is not surprising to see it escalating the use of brute force in an effort to maintain its position.

Because the state depends upon the war system to maintain its support from *Homo Boobus*, governments find it to their interest to maintain environments of perpetual hostility. Whether wars be undertaken for so-called *defensive* or *preventive* purposes is no longer a relevant consideration. The core offense at the Nuremberg Trials was the *starting* of a war; such aggression now serves, among many Americans, as an occasion for slapping bumper-stickers on their cars with the vulgar message: "support the troops." The war frenzy brings forth such displays of flag-waving as will cause the statists to give serious consideration to using nuclear weapons against Iran, as well as for John McCain to warble idiotically: "bomb, bomb, bomb Iran" during the 2008 presidential campaign!

The general absence of criticism over "preventive warfare" has led the defenders of statism to extend the practice to "preventive detention," by which men and women can be thrown into prisons and held without trial—or even charges filed against them—and without benefit of the writ of habeas corpus. That such persons *might* be inclined to engage in criminal acts is regarded as a sufficient basis for their incarceration. While being so held, the captives may be subjected to all kinds of torture, a practice the statists wish to disguise by giving it different names!

In an effort to plumb the shallowness of the minds of most Americans, the statists have reiterated the proposition, first enunciated by George W. Bush and continued under the Obama administration, that American citizens could be targeted for assassination as part of the "global war on terror." Just who the targeted persons might be, or who would have the authority to authorize their murder, was left unsaid. Again, Pogo Possum reminds us of our "identity" in the political scheme of things.

What's next in the offing? Shall we soon be hearing of concentration camps, complete with gas chambers, to which Americans—or anybody else—might be sent for the "final solution" to the terrorism problem? Of course, the terminology will have to be cleaned up a bit, just as it was for the Japanese-Americans who, during World War II, were sent to "relocation centers" for the offense of having politically-incorrect ancestors! As a recent bumper-sticker reads: "there will never be concentration camps in America; they'll be called something else."

Nor would modern death-camps have to be specialized to the elimination of so-called "terrorists." What about *other* enemies of governmental programs? After all, if former Secretary of State Madeleine Albright can rationalize the deaths of 500,000 Iraqi children in furtherance of her more mundane policies, how many millions might be sacrificed to such nobler ends as, well, *saving the planet*?

At last! A project to which Al Gore could be put in charge; one that would allow him to realize his life's dream: to be in control of all life on the planet. How better to reduce carbon emissions on the planet than to systematically exterminate their contributors (i.e., human beings)? Of course, enough people would have to be left living in order to provide the energies with which to serve the state. But this is simply a matter of careful calculation to be engaged in by neo-philosopher-kings!

Will there be no end to the efforts of statists to keep upping the ante in their quest for absolute control over their fellow humans? Is there any indecency or atrocity that most Americans would be unwilling to embrace? Is there a moral threshold that most would refuse to cross?

As America continues to unravel, expect even more intensive efforts by the statists to regain and solidify their power. Look, further, to increasing numbers of your neighbors who sense that something is terribly wrong—quite evil—in America that must be resisted. To whom can we look for an assessment of the problem? Do the *conservatives* have anything to offer? Sadly, they are still too strongly attached to the kinds of thinking that got us where we are (e.g., the war system and police-state authority). As I read or listen to them, I find little more than name-calling, jingoism, and fear-mongering coming forth from those who lost their passion for liberty once the Soviet Union collapsed.

For the time being, at least, most of the *liberal* community is still in too much of a stupor over the election of a black president to be of much use in confronting the wrongdoing of the current state. The so-called *moderates* (i.e., the worst of all "extremists," who congenitally insist upon compromises between equally untenable positions) are, as in most matters, of little benefit. Nor will much assistance be found within most of academia, so many of whose members are in a terminal state produced by the institutional virus. The mainstream media will likewise prove to be a dry hole for enlightenment. They are the voices of the establishment; their job is to reinforce your institutional commitments. The Internet, by contrast, continues to be the best source of alternative thinking, what with entry into this medium being so easy. It is, perhaps, the best spur to individualized thinking since Gutenberg upset the established order of his day.

How much causation is concealed in the details of events in our lives? Intelligent minds must attend to this inquiry in contemplating the future. I don't know of anyone—including myself—who has a monopoly on "all the *answers*" to what plagues us, both personally and socially. What we need to focus on, instead, are those who might have a better set of *questions* to ask as we try to distill a free, peaceful, and orderly society out of the carefully-organized insanity into which we find ourselves twisted and knotted. Perhaps it would do us well to recall the lesson from an etymological dictionary: that the words "peace," "freedom," "love," and "friend," have interconnected histories. Might our ancient ancestors have known what we have long-since forgotten as we traipse about in search of one divisive ideology after another?

CHAPTER 41

A Black Hole on $10 Billion a Day

I am striving . . . to discover whether man still has a place in this tangle; whether he still has any authority among these colossal masses in movement; whether he still can exert any force whatever on the statistics which are slipping from his hands into the abstract and the unreal. Can he have a place, authority, and possibility of action on a better basis than ill-founded declarations of hope or blind acts of unreasonable faith?

— Jacques Ellul

A friend of ours has observed that one of the consequences of having children and grandchildren is that "they give you more people to worry about." As both a father and grandfather, I must confirm that her observation is correct. I have long been of the view that a parent has a moral obligation not to allow his or her children to live under tyranny. My adult life has been preoccupied with this duty but, while I believe my efforts have produced some marginal benefits, Leviathan still reaches out to devour all within its grasp. My continuing focus on this danger has, at least, helped my daughters—and hopefully, in time, my grandchildren—to develop an awareness of the threat to their well-being posed by political systems and the uncertainties that lie before them.

It is interesting—albeit not pleasant—to witness the collapse of Western Civilization. A vibrant system that once was productive of the material and intangible values supportive of human well-being, has reached a terminal state. Civilizing principles and practices that found sufficient—albeit inconstant—expression in Western societies, have deteriorated into an acceptance of corruption—provided it is carried out in high places—and the celebration of violence—provided it is directed against plausible categories of wrongdoers. In such ways has the multi-trillion dollar looting of taxpayers on behalf of an entrenched corporate-state plutocracy combined with the ongoing conduct of endless wars against endless enemies to send a morally, intellectually, and economically bankrupt culture to an awaiting black hole.

As I watched politicians, members of the mainstream media, and selected academicians discuss the self-styled "stimulus" plan designed to transfer trillions of dollars to the establishment's favored institutions, I found myself recalling those early days following the Bush administration's bombing of Baghdad, with thieves engaged in the wholesale looting of artifacts from the National Museum of Iraq. How fitting that Americans, with their insistence upon procedural due process, should content themselves with watching Congress carry out such pillaging on C-SPAN, with the regularities of "Roberts Rules of Order" being faithfully observed.

The desperation with which presidents Bush and Obama urged this grand-scale despoliation was breath taking, with Mr. Bush going so far as to threaten a declaration of martial law should Congress not accede to his plan. Even the terminology underwent a rapid transformation: what began as a "bailout" quickly took on a bad name, and was changed to "stimulus." But who or what was to be "stimulated" remained open to question. The more uncertainty that underlay this program, the more Boobus suspected something untoward. In an effort to allay such fears, Mr. Obama spoke—in the haziest of words—about some "plan" being put together to save America from the effects of Newton's "third law of motion." After all, if Ozymandias is to have credibility among the dupable, its wizards must appear to be capable of designing and carrying out effective "plans." That the "plans" under consideration are but photocopies of the previous programs that created our present difficulties, is to be overlooked. The study of economics or history might inform Boobus of the vicious circle within which he is ensnared. But Mr. Obama has cautioned against listening to "ideologies," or focusing upon the past!

To characterize this so-called "stimulus" as a plan that can rectify decades of programs and policies against which free-market advocates had long warned, is to corrupt the rational and informed nature of intelligent planning. At best, the supporters of this program have offered little more than a hodge-podge of guess-work that boils down to "let's try this and see if it works." Neither is the undertaking an "investment" on behalf of taxpayers, as politicians insist on characterizing it. I recently saw a figure that the total cost of the many "bailout" packages given to corporate interests, totals some $9,700,000,000,000. If my math is correct, this so-called "investment" comes out to almost $33,000 per American. Do you expect to receive any dividend checks from these corporations, or be allowed to attend annual stockholder meetings to vote on new management?

There is no doubt that the corporate recipients of this booty are "stimulated" to get as much money as they can. But the stumbling and bumbling uncertainty as to how the program will work, what criteria will be employed to determine recipients, or how the money will be used, illustrates that this program is not so much a rationally-based *plan*, as it is a *scheme*. Any pretense of this being a carefully calculated solution to a ubiquitous problem clouds its sordid reality: a last-ditch effort on the part of institutional interests to ransack the governmental treasury before the entire system collapses. The prognosis for a restoration of the economic health of the country resulting from it is no better than your submitting to brain surgery at the hands of a college freshman who has just received a B+ in a first-year biology course!

This "plan"—like the wars whose costs have so greatly contributed to our economic woes—is but another expression of the moral, intellectual, and economic bankruptcy that is destroying Western Civilization. The notion that a society can be rendered free, peaceful, productive, and orderly through the use of institutionalized violence belongs to a distant past. Nor can a civilization continue to countenance governmental policies of plundering the fruits of the labors of an entire population, and redistributing it to the institutional friends of those in power.

I apologize to my children and grandchildren for failing in my moral duty to protect you from the ravages of tyranny. I shall continue in my efforts, of course, recognizing that only peaceful methods can produce a peaceful world. In the meantime, I offer you this advice: (1) never believe anything the government tells you; (2) never believe anything the mainstream media tells you; (3) pay attention to—but be skeptical of—those whose ideas do not conform to consensus-based definitions of reality; (4)

master the art of contrary thinking, and learn to stay away from herds as well as from those who insist upon herding others into destructive, lemming-like stampedes; (5) do not put your trust in those who offer you "hope," but seek out those who will help you develop *understanding*; (6) be prepared—as were your ancestors—to move to new frontiers that are better suited to both your liberty and material well-being; (7) find, support, protect, and defend like-minded friends, being mindful of the shared origins of the words "peace," "freedom," "love," and "friend;" (8) avoid being drawn into the black hole to which our civilization is destined; whose vacuuming force is made possible by the collective energies of your neighbors; and, (9) mindful of all the above, avoid all sense of despair by combining your intelligence and emotions to help in the creation of a new civilization grounded in peace, liberty, and respect for the inviolability of the individual.

CHAPTER 42

The New Geometry and the New Math

They [feminist groups in Iraq] *are very strong. Their approach is unique because they have no leaders. They do not have a head or branch offices. . . . This movement is made even stronger by not having leaders. If one or two people lead it, the organization would weaken if these leaders were arrested. Because there is no leader, it is very strong and not stoppable.*

—Shirin Ebadi
2003 Nobel Peace Prize Recipient

For a number of years, I have been writing and speaking about the de-centralizing forces that are bringing about the collapse of our highly-structured, institutionalized society. Such warnings must always be listened to with skepticism, as we confront the often incomprehensible nature of an ambiguous world.

Nonetheless, events of recent years provide confirmation of my prognostications. Alternative schooling, dispute resolution, and health-care practices; political secession and nullification movements; the decentralization of management in business organizations; news-reporting moving from the centrally-controlled, top-down model of traditional media, to the more dispersed, horizontally-networked Internet; individualized technologies such as personal computers, cell-phones, iPods, video cameras, and other innovations that enhance person-to-person communication, are just the more evident examples of how our social systems are undergoing constant centrifugation.

To express this phenomenon in terms of solid geometry, the *pyramid* is being replaced by the *sphere*. Plato's hierarchically-structured world directed by *philosopher-kings*—long the favored model of the intellectual classes who fashioned themselves fit to sit at the institutional apex—has proven unfit for ordering the affairs of human beings. It is not better *ideas* that are transforming how we organize with one another, but real-world *pragmatism:* the life system simply cannot operate on the principle of being directed by centralized authorities!

The pyramid expresses the essence of a world premised on vertical power, in which interpersonal relationships are yoked together in systems of domination and subservience. No more poignant image of a top-down world—one in which institutional violence operates as a kind of ersatz gravitational force—exists than this. Members of the institutional hierarchy—who long ago learned that they could more readily benefit by *coercing* their fellow humans than by *trading* with them—have seen to it that others be inculcated in a belief in the necessity of pyramidalism. Our entire institutionalized world—from the more violent political organizations to more temperate ideologies—is premised on the shared assumption that only in vertically-structured institutionalized authority can mankind find conditions of peace, liberty, and order. If you doubt the pervasiveness of such thinking, recall your own learning—from childhood through adulthood—and identify *any* voices who *tolerated,* much less *encouraged,* your questioning of this article of faith.

How foolishly we cling to the belief that the state, for instance, exists to protect our lives, liberty, and property interests, even as it continues to slaughter millions of people, restrain their liberties, and despoils their wealth. The life system, itself, constantly pushes the fallacy of pyramidal thinking into our unconscious and often conscious mind. As we look around our communities and the rest of the world and discover how much better decentralized systems perform in providing what political agencies only promise, faith in the pyramid collapses. Not willing to allow its violence-based interests to decompose due to a change in human consciousness, the state—along with the corporate interests that have long benefited as politically-created parasites—desperately reacts to shore up its crumbling foundations. To do so requires a restoration of the falsehoods and contradictions upon which its power depends. Truth—and the free flow of information against which the state is in constant war—becomes a "security risk" or an appeal to "treason." In one personage or another, the state calls upon its modern Joseph Goebbels who, as Hitler's Propaganda Minister, advised:

> The lie can be maintained only for such time as the State can shield the people from the political, economic and/or military consequences of the lie. It thus becomes vitally important for the State to use all of its powers to repress dissent, for the truth is the mortal enemy of the lie, and thus by extension, the truth becomes the greatest enemy of the State.[1]

The demonstrations taking place in such Middle Eastern countries as Egypt, Tunisia, Bahrain, Yemen, and Libya, carry a much deeper meaning than what the institutionally-serving news media have expressed. When millions of men and women can peacefully come together in the center of major cities to protest the legitimacy of their being ruled by others, one ought to ask whether we might be witnessing what the pyramidalists would most fear: *an open expression of the decentralization of our common interests, not as "citizens," but as human beings.* We witnessed an earlier example of this when, on the eve of the American government's decision to wage an unprovoked war on Iraq, millions of people gathered in cities throughout the world to protest.

I long ago discovered the writings of the Swiss psychiatrist, Carl Jung, and the British physiologist, Rupert Sheldrake. Jung did much of the pioneering work in the study of the "collective unconscious,"[2] wherein he posited that, in addition to the individualized content of both our conscious and unconscious minds, human beings also share an inherited—and identical—content of our unconscious minds. In an inquiry that parallels Jung's, Sheldrake has developed the study of what he calls "morphogenetic fields," in which members of given species connect up—both spatially and temporally—to determine subsequent biological forms and behavior.[3] If there is validity to their respective conclusions, might their inquiries be expanded to explore the question: is it possible for humans to have unconscious channels of communication that might motivate us to express our common need to resist the forces that war against life itself?

---

1   www.whale.to/b/goebbels_h.html

2   Carl Jung, *The Undiscovered Self* (New York: American Library, 1959).

3   Rupert Sheldrake, *A New Science of Life* (Los Angeles: J.P. Tarcher, Inc., 1981).

I must admit to having no conclusions in this regard, although I believe, given the destructive and dehumanizing history we humans have thus far generated, it is imperative that we expand the range of our questioning. Perhaps it is reflective of mankind's capacities for tool-making that, rather than plumbing the depths of our thinking, we have created *technologies* that allow us to share the contents of our respective conscious and unconscious minds. Our computerized technologies are not only the *products* of our thinking, but the *means* for expanding its content to exponential levels of awareness. They have done more than anything else to dismantle the pyramid and give life to the sphere. In contrast with the linear and vertically-structured design of the pyramid, the *sphere* is a model for social systems that have no top-down locus of centralized authority. Interpersonal connections arise *horizontally*, there being no preferred position from which people can exercise power over one another. As such horizontal technologies are helping us discover, there is nothing quite so liberating, creative, and life-enhancing as the free flow of information!

Not only is the *geometry* of our world being transformed, so is the *mathematics*. Decentralizing information makes it much easier for more *individuals* to communicate with millions of other individuals. The number of Internet websites in the world has been estimated at 100,000 in 1996 to 1,300,000,000 by 2010.[4] The capacity of the *millions* to generate information and ideas heretofore confined to the *thousands*, has proven discomforting to members of the institutional order. Each one of us now enjoys the technological means to communicate directly with *every person on the planet*, provided (a) they have a computer linked to the Internet, and (b) desire to communicate with *us*. In other words, mankind enjoys what the political establishment regards as that most destabilizing influence: a genuine marketplace in ideas.

From speech codes, to censorship, to the enforcement of political-correctness, to the punishment of pornography,[5] to government efforts to control or shut down the Internet, the institutional order has long been at war with free expression. *Words* are the carriers of *ideas*, and ideas that are not supportive of institutional interests can prove destabilizing to the status quo. The decentralization of *what, how, and by whom* alternative in-

---

4   www.starpoint.net/index.php?option=com_content...id...-; and http://www.eq-solutions.com/google-ranks-your-website-using-site-speed/

5   David Paletz and William Harris, "Four-Letter Threats to Authority," in *The Journal of Politics* 37(1975): 965 ff.

formation and ideas are expressed, keeps the political establishment in a state of constant fear.

What this has done is to unravel the mindset upon which the state has depended to maintain its control over people: the belief that political change could only come about through the so-called "democratic process." "Democracy"—the illusion that my wife and I, combined, have twice the political influence of David Rockefeller!—is premised on the proposition that any meaningful political reform must secure the electoral support of tens of millions of individuals, a situation most unlikely to occur. How often have any of us given up on the prospects of "working within the [rigged] system" to bring about change, when we are reminded that we must get 51% of our neighbors to vote with us? The difficulties associated with organizing precincts, trying to get ballot-access, and as Ron Paul has discovered, trying to be heard within political parties and the media bent on maintaining the status quo, discourage most people. We quickly discover the truth of Emma Goldman's observation that "If voting changed anything, they'd make it illegal."[6]

To those who cling to the idea that social change can only arise through "majority rule" processes, I ask if they have heard of Plato, Aristotle, Moses, Jesus, Leonardo da Vinci, Shakespeare, Dante, Newton, Darwin, Einstein, et al. And did such more recent individuals as Maria Montessori, Bill Gates, Steve Jobs, Ayn Rand, Mark Zuckerburg, Julian Assange, and numerous others, have to rely on the outcome of public opinion polls to certify the worthiness of their ideas?

The advantages of massive size and numbers that keep the powerful immune from the protestations of the subservient, lose their forcefulness in the face of the unrestrained flow of information. This is why—as Goebbels reminds us—the state has had to resort to such practices as censorship, the crushing of dissent, and the "secret" classification of documents exposing its corrupt behavior. It also explains the efforts of so many establishment politicians to control, if not destroy, the Internet; as well as their resistance to Ron Paul's proposals to audit the Federal Reserve!

The Internet has changed the mathematics from "51%" to the lone individual as the catalyst for change. Because of the herd-oriented nature of the political mind, the state has always enjoyed a symbiotic relationship

---

6   thinkexist.com/quotation/if_voting_changed_anything-they-d_make_it_illegal/204480.html

with an organized mass of people. In the words of Doctor Murnau, in the movie *Kafka,* "A crowd is easier to control than an individual. A crowd has a common purpose. The purpose of the individual is always in question."[7] The truth of Murnau's observation was seen when Julian Assange—the founder of "Wikileaks"—used the Internet to make known to the world some of the "secrets" the state did not want revealed to its citizens. Assange was allegedly assisted in this effort by an army private, Bradley Manning, who had access to some of this information. Two individuals—not a "silent majority" or even a *vocal* one—not only "spoke truth to power," but to the *powerless,* whom it has always been the state's purpose to keep uninformed and subservient.

As members of the establishment do their best to destroy the liberating influences of the Internet, others remind us that technology, itself, may have its own immune system to protect this life-serving network from the statist virus. Columbia University law professor, Eben Moglen, advocates a more *decentralized* Internet technology, in which the mechanics for what has become known as the "social media" are dispersed into the hands of each of us. The current technological forms he tells us, "are too centralized; they are too vulnerable to state retaliation and control." In words that Shirin Ebadi would welcome, Moglen adds:"It is not hard, when everybody is just in one big database controlled by Mr. Zuckerberg [of Facebook], to decapitate a revolution by sending an order to Mr. Zuckerberg that he cannot afford to refuse."[8]

As the math changes, so does the geometry by which we organize ourselves. What is almost humorous to consider is that the defenders of the dying order—be they the neo-Luddites trying to destroy the Internet, or those who would confine the Bradley Mannings and Julian Assanges to a modern Tower of London—don't grasp the reality of what confronts them. The statists operate on the notion that these two men are to blame for the revelations that are inherent in the new technology. For all of their supposed wisdom that they believe entitles them to sit atop Plato's pyramid, they are in truth as lost as "flat-earthers" sharing their collective ignorance in trying to calculate the sun's revolutions around the Earth!

---

7   *Kafka* (Miramax Films, 1991).

8   Jim Dwyer, "Decentralizing the Internet So Big Brother Can't Find You," *New York Times,* February 15, 2011; online at nytimes.com/2011/02/16/nyregion/16about.html

What Is Anarchy?

I have mixed feelings about the use of labels to describe philosophical views, whether of myself or others. It is difficult to avoid doing so because our efforts to understand and communicate about the world necessarily involve the use of words, and words are, as Alfred Korzybski warned us[1], abstractions that never equate with what they are meant to describe. His insights offer a caveat whose implications for confusion are further compounded when addressing such unsettled topics as political philosophy.

One philosophical abstraction that seems to befuddle most people is "anarchy." To those challenged by complexity—such as radio talk show hosts and cable-TV "newscasters" who seem convinced that all political opinions can be confined to the categories "liberal" and "conservative"—the word anarchy evokes an unfocused fear of uncertain forces. Images of bomb-throwing thugs who smash and burn the property of others are routinely conjured up by politicians and the media to frighten people into an extension of police authority over their lives. "Disorder" and "lawless confusion" are common dictionary definitions of this word.

---

1   In Ken Wilber, *The Spectrum of Consciousness* (Wheaton, Ill.: The Theosophical House, 1977), p. 41.

That there have been some, calling themselves "anarchists," who have engaged in violence on behalf of their political ambitions, is not to be denied. Nor can we overlook the *provocateuring* often engaged in by undercover policemen—operating under the guise of "anarchists"—to justify harsh reprisals against political protests. But to condemn a philosophic viewpoint because a few people seek to exploit it for their narrow advantage, is no more justifiable than condemning Christianity because a man murders his family and defends his acts on the grounds "God told me to do it!"

As long as a president continues to rationalize war against the Iraqi people as "operation freedom;" as long as the Strategic Air Command insists that "peace is our profession;" and as long as police departments advertise that they are there "to serve and protect," intelligent minds must be prepared to look behind the superficiality and imagery of words to discover their deeper meaning. Such is the case with the word "anarchy."

The late Robert LeFevre made one such effort to transcend the popular meaning of this word when he declared that "an anarchist is anyone who believes in less government than you do."[2] But an even better understanding of the concept can be derived from the Greek origins of the word (*anarkhos*) which meant "without a ruler." It is this definition of the word that members of the political power structure (i.e., your "rulers") do not want you to consider. Far better that you fear the hidden monsters and hobgoblins who are just waiting to bring terror and havoc to your lives should efforts to increase police powers or budgets fail.

Are there murderers, kidnappers, rapists, thieves, and arsonists in our world? Of course there are, and there will always be, and they do not all work for the state. Nor has the state—with its hundreds of billions of dollars purloined from taxpayers—exhibited any magic for preventing such crimes. Ask the ghosts of John F. Kennedy or Lee Harvey Oswald—both murdered in the presence of hundreds of police and Secret Service agents—whether this is so. It is amazing that, with all the powers and money conferred upon the state to "protect" us from such threats, they continue to occur with a regularity that seems to have increased with the size of government! With fear as a primary factor in getting people to sanction political power over them, thoughtful minds are beginning to question whether it would even be in the state's interests to eliminate victimizing

---

2   en.wikipedia.org/wiki/Robert_LeFevre

crime from society. Considering the fact that governments have long been micro-managing people's lives in order to prevent harms (e.g., food and automobile production, investment and banking practices, child safety, the licensing of drugs, etc.) is it not remarkable that injuries still arise despite such regulations, and that the state is able to use its *failures* as a rationale for extending its powers?

Nor can we ignore the history of the state in visiting upon humanity the very death and destruction that its defenders insist upon as a rationale for political power. Those who condemn anarchy should engage in some quantitative analysis. In the twentieth century alone, governments managed to intentionally kill—through wars, genocides, and other deadly practices—more than 200,000,000 men, women, and children.[3] This figure does not include those who died as unintended consequences of government regulatory systems. How many people were killed by anarchists during this period? Governments, not anarchists, have been the deadly "bomb-throwers" of human history!

Because of the disingenuous manner in which this word has been employed, I endeavor to be as precise in my use of the term as possible. I employ the word "anarchy" *not* as a *noun*, but as an *adverb*. I envision no utopian community, no "Galt's Gulch" to which free men and women can repair. I prefer to think of anarchy as a way in which people deal with one another in a peaceful, cooperative manner; respectful of the inviolability of each other's lives and property interests; resorting to contract and other voluntary transactions rather than coercion and expropriation as a way of functioning in society.

I am often asked if anarchy has ever existed in our world, to which I answer: almost all of your daily behavior is an anarchistic expression. How you deal with your neighbors, coworkers, fellow customers in shopping malls or grocery stores, is often determined by subtle processes of negotiation and cooperation. Social pressures, unrelated to statutory enactments, influence our behavior on crowded freeways or grocery checkout lines. If we dealt with our colleagues at work in the same coercive and threatening manner by which the state insists on dealing with us, our employment would be immediately terminated. We would quickly be without friends were we to demand that they adhere to specific behavioral standards that we had mandated for their lives.

---

3   See, e.g., R.J. Rummel, *Death By Government* (New Brunswick, N.J.: Transaction Publishers, 1994, reprinted 2010).

Should you come over to our home for a visit, you will not be taxed, searched, required to show a passport or driver's license, fined, jailed, threatened, handcuffed, x-rayed or groped, regulated, or prohibited from leaving. I suspect that your relationships with your friends are conducted on the same basis of mutual respect. In short, virtually all of our dealings with friends and strangers alike are grounded in practices that are peaceful, voluntary, and devoid of coercion.

A very interesting study of the orderly nature of anarchy is found in John Phillip Reid's book, *Law for the Elephant.*[4] Reid studied numerous diaries and letters written by persons crossing the overland trail in nineteenth century wagon trains going from St. Joseph, Missouri, to Oregon and California. The institutions we have been conditioned to equate with "law and order" (e.g., police, prisons, judges, etc.) were absent along the frontier, and Reid was interested in discovering how people behaved toward one another in such circumstances. He discovered that almost everyone respected property and contract rights, and settled whatever differences they had in a peaceful manner, all of this in spite of the fact that there were no "authorities" to call upon to enforce a decision. Such traits went so far as to include respect for the property claims of Indians. The values and integrities that individuals brought with them were sufficient to keep the wagon trains as peaceful communities. Modern-day examples of anarchistic practices are found in such settled communities as the Amish.[5]

Having spent many years driving on California freeways, I have observed informal orders amongst motorists who are complete strangers to one another. There is a general—albeit not universal—courtesy exhibited when one driver wishes to make a lane change and, in spite of occasional noncooperative drivers, a spontaneous order arises from this interplay. A major reason for the cooperative order lies in the fact that a driving mistake can result in serious injury or death—or just damage to one's car—and that such consequences will be felt *at once*, and by the actor, unlike political decision-making that shifts the costs to others.

One may answer that freeway driving is regulated by the state, and that driving habits are not indicative of anarchistic behavior. The same response

4   John Phillip Reid, *Law for the Elephant: Property and Social Behavior on the Overland Trail* (San Marino, Calif.: Huntington Library Press, 1980).

5   See, e.g., John A. Hostetler, *Amish Society,* 3rd ed. (Baltimore: The Johns Hopkins University Press, 1980); Steven M. Holt, *A History of the Amish* (Intercourse, Pa.: Good Books, 1992).

can be made concerning behavior generally (i.e., that government laws dictate our conduct in all settings). But this misconceives the causal connections at work. The supervision of our moment-to-moment activities by the state is too remote to affect our actions. We are polite to fellow shoppers or our neighbors for reasons that have nothing to do with legal prescripts. What makes our dealings with others peaceful and respectful comes *from within ourselves*—as expressions of our social needs with one another—not from beyond. For precisely the same reason, a society can be utterly destroyed by the corruption of such subjective influences, and no blizzard of legislative enactments or quadrupling of police forces will be able to avert the entropic outcome. Do you now understand the social meaning of the "Humpty-Dumpty" nursery rhyme?

The study of complexity, or chaos, informs us of patterns of regularity that lie hidden in our world, but which spontaneously manifest themselves to generate the order that we like to pretend authorities have created for us. There is much to discover about the interplay of unseen forces that work, without conscious direction, to make our lives more productive and peaceful than even the best-intentioned autocrat can accomplish. As the disruptive histories of state planning and regulation reveal, efforts to impose order by fiat often produce disorder, a phenomenon whose explanation is to be found in the dynamical nature of complexity. Terry Pratchett's words are recalled.[6]

"Anarchy" is an expression of social behavior that reflects the individualized, self-directed nature of life which, at the same time, is enhanced by our social needs for cooperation with others. Only as living beings are free to pursue their particular interests in the unique circumstances in which they find themselves, can conditions for the well-being of all be attained. Anarchy presumes decentralized and cooperative systems that serve the mutual interests of the individuals comprising them, without the systems ever becoming their own reasons for being. It is this thinking, and the practices that result therefrom, that are alone responsible for whatever peace and order exists in society.

Political thinking, by contrast, presumes the supremacy of the systems (i.e., the state, as well as the corporate interests that control it) and reduces individuals to the status of resources for the accomplishment of their ends. Such systems are grounded in the mass-minded conditioning and behavior

---

6   Terry Pratchett, *Interesting Times* (HarperCollins e-books, 2003).

that has produced the deadly wars, economic dislocations, genocides, and police-state oppressions that comprise the essence of political history.

Men and women need nothing so much right now as to rediscover and reenergize their own souls. They will never be able to accomplish such a purpose in the dehumanizing and dispirited state systems that insist upon controlling their lives and property. In the sentiments underlying anarchistic thinking, people may be able to find the individualized sense of being and self-direction that they long ago abandoned in marbled halls and citadels.

CHAPTER 44

Anarchy in the Streets

Chaos often breeds life, when order breeds habit.
—Henry Adams

How often do discussions on the prospects of a stateless society produce the response that, without government, there would be "anarchy in the streets"? To many people, the streets are symbolic of society, and with good reason: they are the most visible networks through which we interact with one another. They are much like the major arteries (we even use that word to describe streets), veins, and capillaries that transport blood throughout our bodies. Each can be thought of as the carrier of both food and waste to and from individual cells.

The thought that city streets—upon which we depend for daily functioning—could ever become disorderly, leads most people to accept, without much questioning, a governmental policing function of such avenues. We imagine that without speed limits, traffic lights at busy intersections, and all of the varied warnings plastered on tens of thousands of signs that encumber streets in our cities, driving would become a turbulent and destructive undertaking.

For a number of years now, various cities in Europe have been experimenting with the removal of *all* traffic signs—including traffic lights, stop signs, speed limit directives—and with surprising results. Towns in the

Netherlands, Germany, Belgium, Sweden, New Zealand—even the UK!—have joined in the experiment. Contrary to the expectations of those who might expect multi-car pileups throughout the cities, traffic accidents have been dramatically *reduced* (in one town, dropping from about eight per year to fewer than two). Part of the reason for the increased safety relates to the fact that, without the worry of offending traffic sign mandates, or watching for police speed-traps, or checking the rear-view mirror for police motorcycles, drivers have more time to pay attention to other cars and pedestrians.[1]

The architect of this experiment, the late Hans Monderman, attributed its success to the fact that "it is dangerous, which is exactly what we want." "Unsafe is safe" was the title of a conference held on this practice. Monderman added that this effort "shifts the emphasis away from the Government taking the risk, to the driver being responsible for his or her own risk." Equally significant, drivers now focus more of their attention on other motorists—taking visual cues from one another, informally negotiating for space, turning into an intersection, etc.—instead of mechanistically responding to signs and electronic machines. Monderman stated: "When you don't know exactly who has right of way, you tend to seek eye contact with other road users. You automatically reduce your speed, you have contact with other people and you take greater care." He added: "The many rules strip us of the most important thing: the ability to be considerate. We're losing our capacity for socially responsible behavior." In words so applicable to the rest of our politically-structured lives, he declared: "The greater the number of prescriptions, the more people's sense of personal responsibility dwindles." Monderman expressed the matter more succinctly in saying: "When you treat people like idiots, they'll behave like idiots."[2]

We have too many rules governing us. Formal rules divide us from one another; the more rules that are imposed upon our conduct, the greater the distances among us. Of course, this is the logic upon which the state always acts: to insinuate itself into our relationships with others, substituting its

---

1   www.gadling.com/2009/10/21/can-reducing-the-number-of-traffic-signs-reduce-the-number-of-ac/

2   En.wikipedia.org/wiki/Shared_space; www.telegraph.co.uk/news/uknews/1533248?Is-this-the-end-of-the-road-for-traffic-lights.html;forums.finalgear.com/general-automotive/trial-of-traffic-sign-ban-in-europe-cities-14914; nytimes.com/2009/02/London- seeks-to-reduce-congestion-by-eliminating-traffic-ligl; csmonitor.com/World/Global-News/2010/0331/What-happens-when-you-remove-all-traffic-sig; spiegel.de/international/Spiegel/0,1518,448747,00.html

coercively-enforced edicts for our interpersonal bargaining. We become conditioned to look upon strangers as threats, and to regard political intervention as our only means of looking after our own interests. Imposed rules not only generate disorder, but deprive us of the autonomy and spontaneity that help to define life; they dehumanize us.

One sees this mindset of social impotence expressed throughout our lives. I am fond of asking my students why they do not negotiate with retailers for groceries, clothing, and other consumer items. They look at me as though I had suggested they attend movies in the nude. "You can't do that," they instinctively respond. I then offer examples of persons I have known who make a habit of such bargaining, managing to save themselves hundreds or more dollars each year. Incredulity still prevails. On one occasion, a student raised his hand to inform the class that he had been an assistant manager of a major retail store in Los Angeles, adding "we did this all the time."

How easily we give up on our own social skills, and at what costs. These experiments with traffic-sign abandonment remind us how much we rely upon informal methods of negotiating with other drivers, and the socially-harmonious benefits of our doing so. My own freeway driving experiences provide an example: if another driver signals to move into my lane, or I signal to move into his, more than a simple lane-change takes place. From that point on, there is nothing this other motorist can do—short of intentionally crashing into my car—that will cause me to feel anger toward him. He's "my guy," and I will feel a sense of neighborliness to him that will generate feelings of protectiveness toward him. "Neighborliness" is a good word to use here: how many of us could honk our horn or make angry hand-gestures at another driver we recognized to be someone that we know?

This is one of the unintended consequences of taking the state out of the business of directing our traffic: we regain our sense of society with others; strangers lose their abstractness, and become more like neighbors to us. If you doubt the pragmatic and social benefits of these experiments, try recalling those occasions in which a traffic light goes out at a major intersection. Motorists immediately—and without any external direction—begin a "round-robin" system of taking turns proceeding through the intersection. One of my seminar students related her experience in this connection. She was parked at the curb, waiting to pick up her mother. She noted that traffic was flowing quite smoothly, and without any significant delays. Then a police officer showed up to direct the traffic, with gridlock quickly ensuing.

A number of years ago, an op-ed piece in a Los Angeles newspaper reported on a major Beverly Hills intersection where some six lanes of traffic converge. There were no traffic lights governing the situation, with motorists relying on the informal methods of negotiating with one another. The writer—who lives in the area—commented upon the resulting orderliness, going so far as to check police records to confirm just how free of accidents this intersection was.[3]

How counter-intuitive so much of this is to those who have become conditioned to think that the *state* is the creator of order in our lives. In much the same way that people are discovering how widespread gun ownership *reduces* violent crime in society, putting power back into the hands of individuals is the most effective way of fostering both the responsible and harmonious relationships we have so childishly expected to arise from our dependence upon, and obedience to, external authorities.

What if the idea of living without coercively imposed rules were to spread from the streets into *all* phases of our lives? What if we abandoned our habits of looking to others to civilize us and bring us to order, and understood that obedience to others makes us irresponsible? As government people-pushers continue their efforts to micro-manage the details of our lives—what foods and drugs we may ingest; how we are to raise and educate our children; the kinds of cars we may drive and light bulbs we may use; the health-care we are to receive; our optimal weight levels; how we are to provide for our retirement; ad nauseam—might we summon the courage to end our neurotic fixations on "security?"

Might the quality of our lives be greatly enhanced by the transformation in thinking implicit in these traffic experiments? Might they offer flashes of insight into how the individual liberty to assess our own risks and freely act upon the choices we make provide the necessary basis for a life that is both materially and spiritually meaningful? As our institutionalized subservience and dependency continues to destroy us, can we learn that what we and our neighbors have in common is our need to negotiate with and to support one another as autonomous and changing people in a changing and uncertain world?

---

3   Bernard Weissman, "On This Corner, Anarchy Rules (and So Politely)," *Los Angeles Times*, September 5, 1991, p. B7.

CHAPTER 45

An Outbreak of Order in NYC

A few years ago, I was on an airliner about to make a landing in Denver. As any experienced flyer knows, a landing at this airport is always subject to the turbulence of air coming in over the mountains. But on this day, the turbulence was extraordinary; some of the worst I have experienced as a passenger. So troublesome was it that the pilot aborted his first landing try and went around for a second effort.

A woman sitting next to me was rather perturbed by the experience, and asked me "do you think we'll ever get on the ground?" "I guarantee it," I responded. "I know enough about physics to be able to assure you that we will not be floating around up here forever. The forces of gravity will see to it that we will end up on the ground. What shape we will be in is another matter!" She laughed and, bumpiness and all, the pilot made a safe landing.

This event reminded me of an oft-ignored truth: *pilots* do not land airplanes; *gravity* lands airplanes. A skilled pilot has learned how to maneuver and manipulate many thousand pounds of metal in order to trick gravity into reducing the harshness of its mandate that objects fall at an accelerating rate of 9.8 meters per second squared. The pilot is not simply a machine responding in some programmed manner, but is engaged in a kind of performance art. As with any artist, a competent pilot is able to combine his or her learned, mechanical skills with judgments gained from years of experience in playing with gravity's seemingly inexorable rules.

One hundred fifty-five passengers and five crew members of a U.S. Airways flight were fortunate to have been in a plane under the control of a highly skilled pilot, Chesley Sullenberger III. His now-famous landing of a powerless jet on the Hudson River provides more than simply evidence of his mechanistic skills—as great as those were—but of his *judgment* in deciding for a watery landing. A less experienced—though equally skilled—pilot might have opted for the suggestion made to him of trying to nurse what had now become a glider to a nearby airport. Had that decision been made, we might now be reading of more than 160 fatalities following the plane crashing into a row of apartment buildings. Capt. Sullenberger was a performance artist—a man who is also a glider instructor—who, carrying out a judgment that in this instance only he was capable of making in response to the peculiar circumstances which he faced, completed his dance with gravity's indifference to outcome, albeit in an unexpected venue.

Upon landing in the river, and with the fate of 160 people in the balance, rescue efforts immediately began. Officials of the FAA, Homeland Security Secretary Michael Chertoff, New York Mayor Bloomberg, and Senator Hillary Clinton, all descended on the scene to begin helping passengers to safety. No? It didn't work out that way? But it *must* have been so. Is it not an integral part of our thinking that social order can be fostered and sustained only by a political system that can plan for responses to troublesome events? Wasn't this the logic upon which federal, state and city governments acted in New Orleans, following hurricane Katrina? Do we not elect politicians who, in turn, create bureaucracies to make our lives secure?

Initially, the only seen presence of government at the site of the U.S. Airways emergency landing involved police helicopters interfering with rescue efforts by keeping the water around the plane churned up. These helicopters were of value to the state, of course, as a visual symbol of its superintending presence above a scene in which its practical role was nonexistent. Like a president or state governor flying over an area hit by a tornado or flooding, such an aerial presence reinforces the vertically-structured mindset upon which political authority depends. After rescue efforts were substantially completed—with no loss of life—New York and New Jersey police officials arrived (those whom the New Jersey governor incorrectly described as the "first responders").

The real work of rescuing passengers and crew members was left to the sources from which the only genuine social order arises: the spontaneous responses of individuals who began their day with no expectation of participating in the events that will henceforth be high-water marks in their lives. After the airliner came to a stop, one private ferry-boat operator, sensing the danger of the plane's tail submerging, began pushing up on the tail in an effort to keep it elevated. Other private ferry-boat operators—whose ordinary work involved transporting people between New York and New Jersey—came to the scene in what became a spontaneously organized rescue under the direction of no one in particular. Photos of the area show the plane surrounded by ferryboats on all sides.

On board the plane, passengers were making their own responses. CNN's Wolf Blitzer—a man who has probably seen one-too-many Irwin Allen films—later interviewed a passenger, asking whether those aboard the plane were yelling and screaming at their plight. "No," the man replied, going on to describe how calm and rational was the behavior of his fellow passengers; removing exit doors; putting on life vests; and helping one another get out onto the wing of the plane.

This man's words reminded me of so many other descriptions I have heard from those who find themselves involved in catastrophes. A few weeks after 9/11, I spoke with a man and a woman who had been in one of the World Trade Center buildings on that day. I asked them how those leaving the damaged building behaved. Each replied that people were calm but determined as they left the building; they saw no screaming or yelling persons running frantically. In *Calculated Chaos*, I have provided a description of the informal, spontaneous responses of many Omahans to the damage inflicted by a tornado upon that city in 1975.

One of the more telling distinctions between informal and formal responses to problems was seen in Capt. Sullenberger's being the last person to leave the plane but, before exiting, making two trips through the aircraft to be certain that everyone on board, for whom he felt responsible, had gotten off. Few government officials would likely have deigned to exhibit such a personal sense of responsibility: they would have been too busy conducting press conferences!

Whether we are considering the patterns of regularity found in the marketplace, or from our relationships with strangers on streets and highways, or, in this case, the aftermath of a disaster or near-disaster, so much of the order that prevails within society arises, without anyone's intention, as a result of our pursuing other ends. Our politicized training—reinforced by media and government officials—leads most of us to believe that social order is the product of the conscious design of wise leaders, whom the political process allows us to identify and elect. In the face of the wars and economic collapse that are now destroying our world, it is difficult for intelligent men and women to any longer embrace such childlike thinking that is probably a carryover from a dependence on parental authority.

As the events of that day slowly fade, those most immediately affected will recite, for others, their recollections. Capt. Sullenberger will doubtless enjoy his well-deserved hero status with appearances on television and radio programs. The ferryboat operators will likewise enjoy their earned fifteen minutes of fame. Other than memories, nothing permanent will come of this event. Those directly involved will return to their normal work: Capt. Sullenberger piloting other flights; ferryboat operators transporting people across the Hudson.

But the statists will figure out ways to exploit all of this for their narrow ends, insinuating their non-existent roles in the rescue. In an effort to reinforce the illusion that their authority carried the day, the politicians—along with Homeland Security officials—will likely concoct statutes or other rules in an effort to repeat, in the future, the kinds of spontaneous responses that arose, without design. Hearings will probably be conducted on behalf of some proposed "Water-ditching of Aircraft" regulations—to be administered by a newly-created federal agency to be housed in the Department of Homeland Security. Thereafter—and reflecting the governmental responses in New Orleans—woe be unto any future Capt. Sullenberger who dares to exercise his independent judgment should it conflict with government-mandated conduct. Nor shall this agency be inclined to tolerate the unapproved efforts of ferryboat operators—or others—who might dare to act, without prior authorization to save lives.

I will be surprised if the bureaucratic control freaks fail to see this event as an opportunity to expand their forced ministrations upon human affairs. The National Transportation Safety Board will make its routine "investigation"—to reinforce the supervisory mindset that, in finding out "what went wrong," the government will be able to "keep this from happening again." What will be overlooked in all of this is the fact that volumes upon volumes of FAA regulations already micro-manage air travel, and that such directives played no part in this emergency landing.

Those who believe themselves capable of directing complex systems for the achievement of desired ends, are unaware of the fact that the separate—but interconnected—events in our lives are underlain by numerous influences peculiar to given situations. The forces that combined to create the situation to which Capt. Sullenberger made his spontaneous response, will likely never recur. On the other hand, there will be another pilot who, on some future day, will have to deal with unforeseen and even bizarre circumstances to which he—like the good captain in this case—will have to be flexible enough to respond.

But as the politically-minded seek to exploit this near-tragedy into some "what if" hypotheticals to rationalize their ongoing quest for power over others, 155 passengers, 5 crew members, and their families, can celebrate the fact that they owe their lives not to government planning, but to the playing out of a spontaneous order for which no planning was possible.

CHAPTER 46

The Virtues of Smallness

Whenever something is wrong, something is too big.
                                              —Leopold Kohr

Recent events in Japan once again bring to mind Leopold Kohr's book, *The Breakdown of Nations*, wherein he develops the "size theory of social misery." In words that help to explain the processes of decentralization that are transforming *vertically*-structured organizations into *horizontal* networks, Kohr tells us that "only relatively small bodies—though not the smallest, as we shall see—have stability. . . . Beyond a certain size, everything collapses or explodes." He adds that "the instability of the too large . . . is a *destructive* one. Instead of being *stabilized* by growth, its instability is *emphasized* by it."[1] An economist of Austrian birth, and with a strong anarchist bent, Kohr was a great influence on E.F. Schumacher, best known for his book, *Small Is Beautiful.*[2]

Kohr's views confront, head-on, the alleged virtue of "bigness" in which our institutionally-directed culture has been thoroughly indoctrinated. The benefits that derive from "economies of scale;" the "bottom-line" authority

---

1   Kohr, *The Breakdown of Nations*, pp. 83, 84 (emphasis in original).

2   E.F. Schumacher, *Small Is Beautiful: Economics As If People Mattered* (London: Blond & Briggs, 1973).

of "power" to resolve difficulties; the ego-gratification that some people find in being part of a world-dominating "empire"; are just some of the attractions that seduce us into embracing the cult of size. What sound is more prevalent at sporting events than the chant "we're number one"?

But a principle that was not sufficient to sustain the dinosaurs into the present, is being challenged in the nature of the systems by which we humans organize with one another. While giant nation-states, and sprawling multi-national corporations, express—in the minds of many—an article of faith, there is a growing sense that our vertically-structured world no longer meets our expectations for both liberty and order. Decentralized technologies are causing us to rethink and redefine what we mean by "society."

The Internet—which occupies center-stage in our decentralizing world—was midwifed by a continuing scaling down of computer technologies. In the 1940s and 1950s, there was a sense that computers were destined to be so monolithic that only a handful of major institutions could afford to develop and use them. This was the feared model that directed Orwell's *1984* dystopian tyranny. Computers of ever-increasing capacities would require the ever-increasing size of buildings to house them. IBM's Thomas J. Watson expressed this sentiment when, in 1943, he said: "I think there is a world market for about five computers."[3] As late as 1977, the president of a major computer manufacturing firm declared: "There is no reason for any individual to have a computer in their home."[4] What could not be foreseen by such men was the process of miniaturization that produced transistors, microchips, microprocessors, integrated circuits, and other innovations that decentralized and individualized computer technologies. These transformations, in turn, helped generate video cameras, cell-phones, and continuing additions to digital technologies, all of which are adding to the centrifugal processes that are providing greater access to, and control over, information to hundreds of millions of individuals.

The unanticipated implications associated with size appear in other areas as well. Some of the unforeseen consequences of the 2011 9.0 earthquake in Japan are providing empirical support for Kohr's warnings. There are lessons waiting to be learned from the literal "fallout" of radiation from the damaged nuclear facility. The unexpected problems produced at this site by the quake should cause thoughtful minds to question *not* nuclear

---

3   Cerf and Navasky, *The Experts Speak*, p. 208.

4   Ibid., at p. 209.

power per se, but the practice of centralizing the production and distribution of electrical energy. There are more considerations involved than just calculating the scale economies associated with huge power generators connected into national grids. Not only are such structures subject to the uncertainties that attend all intricate systems—periodic blackouts will be recalled—but the same implications that attend *political* centralization are present. I read a wonderful quotation from Jacques Ellul—neither the origins nor the exact wording I recall—which said, in essence, "show me how *electrical* power is distributed in a society, and I will show you how *political* power is distributed." It is no idle coincidence that political authority and electrical energy are each spoken of in terms of "power."

I don't know whether the aftermath of the nuclear-power-plant meltdown in Japan will prove harmful or neutral to those outside the immediate area. I do suspect that those in the higher echelons of the corporate-state establishment are busy formulating an "official" prognosis that will best serve its interests. If establishment interests in protecting nuclear power predominate, we will be told that there will be no adverse radiation consequences for Americans. On the other hand, if it will further promote government interests in regulating the production, transportation, and sale of foods, I can imagine our being told that such radiation poses too much danger to Americans—particularly "the children"—to allow independent farmers to avoid detailed regulation of their produce. Keeping in mind George Carlin's comment that "I never believe anything the government tells me," each of us will bear the burden that we have heretofore ignored, namely, to bore deeply into the question "how do we know what we know?"

There is a cryptic message in this disaster which, predictably, will not be addressed by institutional voices, but whose decipherment may be aided by a synthesis of Kohr's and Ellul's insights. At a time when the decentralization of social systems has taken on great importance, it is timely to consider the advantages that could arise from a more localized—perhaps even individualized—source of electrical power. A principal benefit arising from both a free market system and the private ownership of property—concepts that are corollary expressions of each other—is that both individual liberty and social order are maximized when decision-making authority diverges into independent persons, rather than converging into centralized elites. A major problem with institutionalized systems—particularly the state—is that the adverse consequences of their actions are multiplied, exponentially, and the range of their activities are increased.

If, for example, electrical power is produced and generated centrally, problems that arise will have a much wider range of consequences (e.g., might affect an entire region of the country) than if it is produced locally. The same dynamics are at work in other areas of economic activity: if an individual businessman makes an error in judgment, he and those with whom he associates will suffer the loss. If a governmental agency (e.g., the Federal Reserve) makes such an error, the entire economy will likely suffer the effects.

So, too, if an individual, a neighborhood, or a small community, operating its own electric power system, makes a mistake, the consequences will be experienced more locally than when the power source is centralized. What better illustration of this than the Japanese incident: the meltdown of a nuclear-power plant could send radiation over many thousands of miles, adversely affecting people on other continents. This contrast is made even greater by the realization that only in large, centralized systems is electricity going to be produced by nuclear energy. An individual or neighborhood system is not likely to employ a power source requiring so much investment and involving such potential for external harm.

I have no particular case to make either for or against nuclear power, other than of my concern for the institutionalization of the system, and the likelihood that, as with other large corporate undertakings and their propensity for employing the coercive powers of the state, there will be a more widespread socialization of costs. It may be that the very nature of nuclear power necessitates largeness and concentration in its generation. In the same way that only powerful nation-states—and not your next-door neighbor—would desire to own nuclear weapons, there is a life-threatening quality that inheres in the marriage of power and massive size. Leopold Kohr's admonitions must be given serious attention, as humanity continues to get crushed by the weight of institutional monoliths. Jacques Ellul gets to the essence of my objections when he sees the connection between electrical and political power.

As I watched television reports that warned of the possibilities of nuclear radiation flowing from Japan to the United States, I could not avoid the allegorical symmetry in which Japan—the victim of intentional nuclear attacks by America in 1945—might, unintentionally, be providing a literal form of "blowback" (i.e., Newton's "third law of motion") to the country whose government unleashed the atomic secrets that would have been best kept from the destructive hands of state power.

As I witness our world giving in to the "dark side" forces of our humanity, I am reminded of the film *Koyaanisqatsi.*[5] Produced in 1983, the film is an unspoken collection of photographic images—many in exaggerated slow motion—and Philip Glass music. The film takes its title from a Hopi Indian word meaning "life out of balance," and provides a strong visual and emotional sense of the insanity of how we live. While watching news reports from Japan, my unconscious mind, dwelling on the atomic bomb, kept reminding me of the Hopi phrase that appears in this film: "a container of ashes might one day be thrown from the sky, which could burn the land and boil the oceans."

I was reminded, as well, that two of the people who had helped inspire this film were Leopold Kohr and Jacques Ellul!

---

5   *Koyaanisqatsi: Life Out of Balance* (Metro Goldwyn Mayer, 1983).

CHAPTER 47

Increase Your Carbon Footprint

There are today on the plains of India and China men and women, plague-ridden and hungry, living lives little better, to outward appearance, than those of the cattle that toil with them by day and share their places of sleep at night. Such Asiatic standards, and such unmechanized horrors, are the lot of those who increase their numbers without passing through an industrial revolution.

—T.S. Ashton
The Industrial Revolution (1961)

O ur two-year old granddaughter was at our house recently. She was joyously stomping her feet, in rhythm to some piece that had been performed in her music class. The delight with which she carried out her highly-energized dance reflected a spirit that is particularly evident among small children, an approach that the adults in their lives are often quick to squelch. Our birth certificate announces to the institutional order the arrival of another conscript to be molded into servo-mechanisms programmed to serve "obligations" that are neither of our origins nor to our benefit: dancing and other joyous expressions that serve no institutional ends are to be discouraged.

As I watch my grandchildren pursue their spontaneous senses of learning, pleasure, and action that inhere in life itself and require no abstract affirmation, I am reminded of the many misanthropic humanoids who will beset them with demands to restrain their sense of well-being and to temper their happiness. Unable to find meaning within themselves, such pathetic beings endeavor to compensate for this shortcoming by seeking power over others. They do so by identifying with and becoming agents of *institutions*, those well-organized entities that are destructive of both individual lives and civilizations. It is on behalf of the interests of such instrumentalities that most of our social pathologies get played out.

This campaign to draw children into the vortex of personal and societal destructiveness will initially be undertaken by parents whose best-of-intentions are matched by their own lifelong conditioning in the cult of duty. Soon thereafter, the child will be brought into schools and churches for further inculcation, while the media and, ultimately, the state await with their more persistent and forceful reinforcement.

If there were but one message I would hope readers would draw from my writings it would be an awareness of how we condition our minds to make our lives subservient to institutional interests. With the emergence of the current forces of perpetual war, ubiquitous policing, and state-managed economic dislocation that are combining to bring about the collapse of American civilization, there is no more opportune time in which to examine the mess we have made of ourselves.

Even as the virus of institutionalism continues to spread its deadly influences—dangers to life that far exceed the hyped threats of "swine flu"—a sense of desperation emanates from within the establishment. Even *more* regulations, *more* surveillance, *more* weapons of torture and suppression, and *more* laws to be enforced by *more* police, *more* prisons, and longer sentences are demanded by those who rule from the heights of a failed system. Even with a polychromatic display of "terror alerts," the specter of bogeyman "terrorists" no longer entertains most Americans. In a nation saturated with fear-objects used for political control, threats of a more far-reaching nature than child abductors, street-gangs, or drug-dealers must be dredged up. The power-seeking reasoning behind such efforts was well developed in *Report From Iron Mountain*.

Until the collapse of the Soviet Union, the "communist menace" was sufficient to get Americans to part with their liberties, wealth, and intelligent judgment to support the corporate-state in its fear- and war-mongering ventures. But with the disappearance of this bogus threat, a new peril had to be introduced in order for the political establishment to maintain and extend its power over people. The winning candidate became "climate change." Originally concocted as the "coming ice age," and later morphed into "global warming," the threat of "climate change" serves as a compromise that accommodates *any* deviation from a fixed point of reference! Recent revelations of the dishonest and institutional-serving "science" underlying this campaign, may force the political establishment to go in search of a new "threat." Perhaps we shall soon be told that, as the space-films warned us, there *are* extra-terrestrials out there waiting to attack us with their weapons of mass destruction.

It must be noted that there is nothing fundamentally new in the practice of controlling people through fear. Tribal leaders learned how easily their fellow tribesmen could be rendered subservient by reminding them of the threat of the "Nine Bows" from across the river—dangerous men who would certainly come in and destroy their village but for the protection provided by their chief. Some of the brighter tribal members soon figured out that they could profitably employ their minds to avoid the difficult and dangerous work of a hunt by convincing their fellows that they had a special pipeline to the cosmic forces that governed the earth; and that their powers could be used to foster the good of the tribe. Does anyone not see the modern parallel to this practice in Federal Reserve chairmen who presume the capacity to promote the economic well-being of a nation by controlling the supply of money?

I suspect that Johann Gutenberg's invention of movable type made possible the second stage of the information revolution that quickly spread its liberating influences to the rest of humanity. The Renaissance, the Reformation, the Scientific Revolution, the Enlightenment, all contributed to that most humanizing period in human history: the Industrial Revolution. Mankind quickly discovered that its well-being was not to be found in obedience to earthly powers commanding them through structured political forms, but in the release of their own creative energies. Industrialism helped us learn how to produce and exchange the economic values that sustain life; we learned how to maximize human well-being; how to produce the surpluses that provided the earliest evidence of this most prolific system: an increasing population.

Such productiveness did not occur without costs. Through this system, we expanded our capacities for converting natural resources into material goods, a process occasioned only by mankind "increasing its carbon footprint" in the world. It is a biological fact that life itself—at least on this planet—is based upon *carbon*, and its interchange among living beings. Plants produce oxygen that is breathed in by animals, and expelled as carbon dioxide which, in turn, is taken in by plants. Whatever the source of the energy that fuels human action—be it carbon, sunlight, wind, or some untapped element—a consequence will necessarily be that humans will be expelling carbon dioxide, a situation welcomed by our plant cousins. This symbiotic relationship will continue unless, of course, Homo Boobus can become convinced that the expenditure of energy—whether in play or the production of goods and services—is somehow a threat to the human species, if not the entire planet. What better way for those who want nothing more—or less—than a universal control over their fellow beings than to convince them that the essence of life itself (i.e., the vigorous and lively interaction of an organism with its environment) is anti-life. They will be reminded of the basic tenet of their conditioning: that only by submitting oneself to the authority of rulers—who will never moderate *their* energies on behalf of schemes to extend *their* power over others—can they *enhance* their lives by *renouncing* its very nature. The pursuit of individual preferences for living will come to be regarded as a secular form of original sin, to be dealt with most severely. Even school children will learn that as harmless an activity as running on the playground is to be prohibited, lest the energies that inhere in childhood be allowed to carry over into the stultifying atmosphere of the classroom. Free-spirited *dancing* will quickly evolve into well-ordered and supervised *marching*.

As Josie Appleton of the Manifesto Club in Great Britain has so well expressed it, "climate change" is the latest secular religion, with the "climate" serving as the new god.[1] What would otherwise be seen as the political opinions of humans, are transformed into the demands of outside forces. A scientific priesthood presumes to interpret the will of this new deity which, as Appleton puts it, comes down to hostility to individual freedom; "the antithesis of what people want to do." The aura of holiness with which true believers have endowed these secular clerics was illustrated when some of the enthusiasts stretched to touch the clothing of Al Gore upon his accepting an Academy Award for his indoctrinating film.

In Rudyard Kipling's *The Man Who Would Be King*, two Englishmen decide to swindle the priesthood and others in the country of Kafiristan, by one of the men posing as a god. Their scam succeeds for a time until it is discovered that the god-pretender was but an ordinary mortal. For his

---

1   From talk "Green Thinking and the Threat to Liberty and Happiness," presented at Paris Freedom Fest 2009, September 10-13, 2009. See, as well, Robert H. Nelson, *The New Holy Wars: Economic Religion vs. Environmental Religion in Contemporary America* (University Park: The Pennsylvania State University Press, 2010).

troubles, the man was sent to his death. Might such a fate await the modern pretenders to scientific "truth," whose ambitions for power were kept hidden only to be recently revealed either by hackers or a multitude of other scientists? Perhaps not. The institutional forces—both political and corporate—that have a vested interest in the "climate change" orthodoxy, may be resilient enough to overcome the embarrassing disclosures that "science" was not what was being done. The conservation of resources that members of the environmental collective—people I call "Gang-Green"—try to convince us they are protecting, has a purpose more akin to what Mark Twain told us decades ago: "Truth is the most valuable thing we have. Let us economize it."[2]

Be aware, my grandchildren, you may find yourselves besieged by people-pushing gangs of sociopaths who have ambitions over the very ownership of your lives. They will likely cajole and coerce you into minimizing your "carbon footprint" on this planet. But to give in to their importunities is to abandon the creative and joyous nature of life itself. Continue to direct your energies over what is yours to own, and make your footprints as grand and glorious as your imaginations are capable of generating. If I am still fortunate enough to be around in your young adulthood, I may help you to discover the most polite but insistent words with which to tell such misanthropic humanoids to "go to the devil; I have more dancing to do!"

---

2   Mark Twain, *Following the Equator* (1897).

CHAPTER 48

Overcoming Barriers
to Killing

Societies can be sunk by the weight of buried ugliness.

—Daniel Goleman

I n December, 2011, the Lincoln (NE) *JournalStar* newspaper carried a lengthy article discussing the problems the State of Nebraska was having administering lethal injections to condemned prisoners. The difficulties are related to the apparent shortages and/or quality of one of the three chemicals used to put a prisoner to death, as well as to legal challenges brought against the practice. The title of the article asks "Should Nebraska tweak execution rules?" I have enough to say against capital punishment without confining my objections to the space of an article. What grabbed my attention was this title itself.

If the State of Nebraska is seeking precedent for "tweaking" the rules that prescribe how it is to go about lawfully killing people, it need look no further than the content of what passes for "news" in our world. With the continuing collapse of the pyramidal power structure with which political systems exercise their coercive nature, governments have had to scramble to reinforce their authority. For along time, the appetites of the state—along with the corporate interests that direct the political machinery to their ends—have been disguised behind such liberalizing notions as "due process of law," individual "inalienable rights," and more general allusions to such principles as "life, liberty, and the pursuit of happiness."

Beginning in early childhood, schools inculcate young minds in the alleged virtues of obedience to the centralized authority of the state, without whose continuing supervision, we have been told, would render our lives "nasty, brutish, and short." Lest such teachings be lost in our adult pursuits, the institutional order reinforces them through its varied systems: the entertainment industry, political campaigns and elections, and those supposed organs of information I call the "lockstep media." The distrust of power that might otherwise exist in the minds of even the most gullible, is offset—by the chorus of establishment voices—with assurances that there are inherent limitations on both the range and methods by which state systems act.

The Constitution, we have been told, provides one such restraint upon the state. But it takes little time to discover that *words* do not carry with them the same meaning as what we use them to describe. The words "reasonable," "general welfare," "common defense," "due process," "probable cause," and the like, do not lend themselves to the demonstrable precisions of thought that we find in mathematics. The proposition "2 + 2 = 4" can be concretely demonstrated to any dullard in a matter of minutes. The content of what legal "process" is "due" an accused individual is another matter, inevitably tied up in the biases, self-interests, fears, and other subjective forces at work within the minds of those who are to decide such matters. In any political system, of course, it is the *state itself* that makes such determinations. Government officials—be they presidents, senators, judges, or administrative commissioners—will *interpret* the meaning of all the inherently vague and abstract words under which they act.

Lewis Carroll's Humpty Dumpty expressed this understanding in declaring: "When *I* use a word, it means just what I choose it to mean—neither more nor less," to which Alice replied "The question is whether you *can* make words mean so many different things." Humpty Dumpty's response goes to the essence of the political dilemma regarding words: "The question is, which is to be master—that's all."[1] In far less poetic fashion, I remind people that the Constitution is what keeps the government from doing all of the terrible things that it does!

---

1 Lewis Carroll, *Alice's Adventures in Wonderland* (1865).

Our institutional masters desperately react to the decentralization of social systems. The emergence of alternative information systems, such as the Internet, and a growing popular awareness that the political systems under which people are conditioned to subordinate themselves neither serve their interests nor recognize any limitations upon the exercise of state power. Even those who conduct so-called GOP presidential "debates" have struggled to sanitize the process from any questioning of the continuing need to preserve the status quo. The lockstep media continues to warn us of Ron Paul's candidacy—indeed, if they deign to acknowledge his existence at all—to "pay no attention to that man behind the screen."

Lewis Carroll, George Orwell, Thomas Pynchon, George Carlin, and numerous other thinkers, have advised us of both the power and the danger that reside in words. The Internet is a reminder of the lesson learned from the consequences of Gutenberg's invention of movable type: the free flow of information is a very liberating influence. The Internet—accompanied by technologies such as video cameras, tape-recorders, and cell-phones (particularly those with built-in video cameras)—has diminished the institutional order's erstwhile control of information. Political insistence on criminalizing the private video-recording of police behavior, Hillary Clinton's demands for a "gatekeeper" for the Internet, the persecution of Julian Assange and his Wikileaks system, are just the more visible examples of the establishment's war to preserve its power structures by preserving the ignorance of its subject people.

As the centrifugation of information continues its outward flow, institutional authority over the lives of billions of people will continue to erode. Just as with the rear-guard efforts of post-Gutenberg political systems to restrain the openness of ideas implicit in printing, the modern power structure will be unable to un-invent computer technologies—along with the numerous other information systems that continue to evolve. I watched one local television channel cover the Los Angeles Police Department descending upon peaceful "Occupy LA" demonstrators, to evict them from allegedly "public" lands. What was encouraging in this was the sight of many men and women, video-cameras or cell-phones in hand, recording and transmitting the event to others, thus preventing the confiscation of what was seen.

The establishment's efforts to maintain its authority over people have already gone beyond the reinterpretation of constitutional language that has long served its interests. The alleged guarantees of individual liberty we were bamboozled into believing were the *purpose* of the Constitution, were long ago thrown overboard in the interests of consolidating and expanding the powers of the state. Since 1942, the power structure has not seen fit to give attention to the constitutional requirement that only Congress can declare war. It is now enough that an imperial president chooses, from his Rolodex list of countries, to attack whom he will. Governments are now permitted to satisfy the First Amendment liberties of people by confining their speech and assembly to wired cages out of public view. The Fourth, Fifth, and Sixth Amendments have long been watered down by the political system, most recently in December, 2011, when the Senate voted to allow the military to exercise "battlefield" authority over whomever it or the president deems to be an enemy combatant. The policy of allowing torture and/or the assassination of persons considered a threat to American interests was previously announced by President Obama with few voices heard in opposition.

Following World War II, a system of "victor's justice" was inaugurated under the name "the Nuremberg Trials." The stated purpose of such trials was, *foremost*, to prosecute persons who had initiated acts of war against other nations. It was, at least in theory, to make the initiation of war such a crime against all of humanity as to justify punishing its fomenters. Intelligent minds were quick to point out that many of the *"victors"* in this war should also have been indicted for war-crimes (e.g., President Truman for his needless atomic bombing of Hiroshima and Nagasaki, along with those who orchestrated the bombing of such non-military targets as Dresden, Tokyo, Wurzburg, et al.). Despite the failure to include all criminals of war, there was a long-held popular sense that the Nuremberg principles stood for *something* worth embracing.

All of this changed, of course, when—following 9/11—the United States government decided to get into the war-crimes business by interpreting the word "defense"—what the Nuremberg principles permitted—into the doctrine of "preventive war." George Orwell would have understood this trick at once; the lockstep media and other institutionalists did not dare recognize it. From there, the processes of reinterpretation metastasized: "persons" protected by the Bill of Rights did not include foreigners or "terrorists" (even though a reading of these Amendments contain no such distinctions). The power of Congress to "provide . . . for the general Welfare" could be used to transfer hundreds of billions of dollars to the corporate owners of the state. The "due process" that must precede one's loss of "life, liberty, or property" may consist of nothing more—at least in the minds of one GOP presidential candidate—than having some government official secretly select his or her name from a file. Fourth Amendment "protections" against "unreasonable searches and seizures" do not prevent the state from entering and searching your home without your knowledge, and making it a criminal offense for you to tell anyone about this.

On and on go current examples of reinterpreting (i.e., twisting and contorting) fundamental principles so as to achieve the very opposite of their import. The Orwellian notion that "war is peace" keeps most Americans in passive acceptance of governmental policies. The sense that "freedom is slavery" prevents most of us from exercising the responsibility that comes from a condition of self-ownership. And when members of Congress are allowed to profit from "insider" information that would send the rest of us to prison, we are reminded of the *Animal Farm* premise that "all animals are equal, but some are more equal than others."

In our present culture, the aforesaid Nebraska newspaper along with the state government should have no difficulty finding ways to "tweak execution rules" that seemingly stand in the way of the state disposing of members of the criminal class. One could, of course, resort to the reinterpretation (or "tweaking") of the legal or moral principles that have heretofore been thought to constrain governmental action. I hesitate to offer any specific suggestions, fearing that even an unconventional hypothetical might, in this environment, speed up the "process" by which the State of Nebraska could kill a man; thus providing what is "due" him. But if all else fails, perhaps the state can send the names of its condemned prisoners to the White House, allowing the president to select those over whom he—and he alone—presumes the authority to select for assassination.

CHAPTER 49

What is to Become
of the State?

I f, as I strongly suspect, the American nation-state is in a terminal collapse, what is to become of its antiquated forms? Will they, like the government under the Articles of Confederation, or the Confederate States
of America, simply disappear? Or will they, like Ozymandias' empire,
dissolve into the surrounding sands?

We are discovering that our world is too complicated to provide us the
necessary understanding to control the future. This is particularly true in a
nation of some three-hundred millions people. As I continue to emphasize,
the American political system is in a state of turbulence, from which only
one of two outcomes seems likely: either to reorganize itself into a more
orderly system, or to experience entropic collapse. I see little likelihood of
the present state system acknowledging its causal connections to this turbulence and reforming itself. To self-correct one's behavior requires a sense
of resiliency, an attitude inconsistent with the arrogance and hubris underlying the American political system. The power of the state depends upon
a popular sanction for its rule, a legitimizing process that fundamentally
transforms people's thinking regarding the basis of their well-being. From
an economic system that focused on the liberty of individuals to control
their own lives and property as befit their respective self-interests, a conversion to a condition of dependency on state power occurred. The source of
one's well-being came more and more to rest upon momentary advantages
that appeared to derive from the transfer of wealth and restraints on the

liberty of others. Functionaries and other beneficiaries of political systems thrive by fostering such dependent and conflict-ridden thinking. As a consequence, the state feeds on and reinforces short-term time preferences, qualities that are incompatible with the longer term commitments upon which a productive, life-centered social order depends. Because of its inherently parasitic nature, no fundamental transformation can be expected to arise from within Leviathan.

Our current social and political disharmony has been brought on by an exaggerated commitment to the vertical structuring of society—under the micromanaged direction of a central state authority. Thus, one approach to reorganization might involve the decentralization of political power back to the level of individual states. Under this possibility, "America" might return to a system akin to the "Articles of Confederation," a model that has served Switzerland well for many years. The growing interest in political secession may presage such a change.

Another possibility would be for a fundamental transformation to replace the formal, vertically-structured, coercive political systems with more informal, horizontally-networked, systems grounded in voluntary relationships among individuals and associations. It is conceivable that this second condition might evolve, later, from the first confederation model.

Unless something along these or similar lines occurs, however, I believe that the American political system may well experience the same fate as the Soviet Union, with a rapid descent into entropy. I suspect the managers of the established order in this country sense the same dynamics at work within; and that recent efforts to exponentially increase government police and military powers reflect an intention to shore up, by the most forceful means necessary, the collapsing vertical structures that define the state. A healthy organism lives in symbiosis with those around it, nourishing and being nourished by one another. Such is not the case with the current state. Mutual distrust characterizes the relationship of the state and the public it pretends to serve. It is fear of the citizenry that causes state functionaries to demand more power over it.

I offer this as my best assessment of where American society stands at the moment. My visions of the future are as subject to the uncertainties attending complexity as anyone else's, and should be so considered. I have no special knowledge or secret information that is not available to anyone else who might take a focused look at events and pressures in our world and try to anticipate where we are headed. One thing does seem quite clear, however: the American society into which you and I were born and have lived is no longer viable in its present forms, and is in the process of major organizational change.

Whether the turbulence of our current society produces either a collapse or major metamorphosis of the state, it is likely that unforeseen social forms and practices will emerge. I trust in the self-interest motivations of most Americans to formulate organizational systems that will serve their practical needs. In a rapidly changing world which no longer tolerates the sluggishness of state systems that inhibit liberty, creativity, and productiveness, men and women will instinctively find ways to profit from the removal of restraints.

My experiences in the reading of history suggest that, even when major changes occur, remnants from the past often survive, albeit in altered forms. Thus, the English transformation to a parliamentary form of government did not result in the destruction of the monarchy, which has been retained—without genuine power—for the image of historic continuity.

I presume the same influences will accompany the decline and fall of statism in America, as the conservative nature of people finds expression in the preservation of governmental *forms*, even as they are deprived of power. Washington, D.C., may be turned into a new kind of tourist attraction—perhaps like the palace at Versailles, the Tower of London, or the acropolis of Athens. Years ago in Madrid, I watched a "sound and light" show, where bright lights played upon the palace as episodes of Spanish history were broadcast over loudspeakers. Perhaps the same spectacle will one day be performed at the U.S. capitol to inform visitors of American political history ("and in those primitive times, members of Congress would gather to deliberate what substances men and women could put into their bodies, or to cheer as presidents entertained them with lies and empty visions of national greatness").

The roles of the various branches of government might even be maintained—absent any coercive powers, of course—in a stateless world. Congress, which has long been intent on imposing its opinions as law, could continue this function as a nonbinding exercise. Unlike previous civilizations—whose epistemological bases were grounded in either divine revelation, reason, or empiricism—modern culture has adopted opinion polling as the standard for truth. Congress could perform this role in the future. "What was the best movie of last year?" "Should doctors be allowed to pull the plug on a brain-dead Uncle Willie?" "Does second-hand smoke cause cancer?" "Who is the 'number one' team in college football?" Hearings could be held, floor debates conducted, and congressional votes taken on these and many other questions about which "inquiring minds want to know." But, of course, such votes would have no more legally-binding significance than do college coaches' polls, the Academy Awards, or the results of questions asked by public opinion pollsters.

Congress has already prepared itself to be an arbiter of trivial inquiries. From rubber-stamping whatever police powers and tax revenues the president wants; to abandoning its war powers to the whims of White House occupants; to enacting administration-desired legislation without waiting for it to be drafted, members of Congress have expressed satisfaction with having a largely ceremonial role in Washington. Mindful that the folklore of "separation of powers" requires occasional compliance with the rituals of legislative deliberation, Congress has periodically devoted its attention to such matters of state as whether Bill Clinton should be impeached for lying about his sexual conduct, or whether Terri Schiavo's life-support system should be disconnected. As long as such isolated inquiries do not impede the establishment's agenda, Congress is allowed—and content—to play its token role, an attitude that will make it easy for members of this body to segue into a new form of insignificance.

What about the executive branch? The administrative agencies that have insisted upon managing even the smallest details of human existence may, stripped of coercive power, be relegated to purely advisory functions. The Consumer Protection Agency might offer product recommendations to consumers willing to consider its opinions. The Federal Communications Commission could provide reviews or ratings of upcoming television programs. You can see how this might play out in a stateless society.

But what of the presidency? We might have saved ourselves centuries of grief had we remembered the means by which our allegedly "primitive" ancestors inhibited the development of political power. In his book, *Society Against the State*[1], French anthropologist Pierre Clastres observed that such societies loaded their tribal chief with so many ceremonial duties as to deny him the time or inclination to pursue power over his fellow tribesmen. Should the chief fail to satisfy these ritualistic functions, he would lose face.

Such benefits could be recovered in a stateless society. Like the British monarchy, the role of the president would become a purely ceremonial one. The president could show up at shopping center openings to cut

---

1   Pierre Clastres, *Society Against the State* (New York: Zone Books, 1989).

the ribbon, or award the Congressional National Championship trophy to whatever college football team Congress has selected, or judge beauty contests, or be the Grand Marshal at various parades around the country, or even continue to throw out the first pitch in the opening game of the baseball season.

The only role I could see for members of the judiciary in a stateless world would be to become private arbitrators or mediators. By offering their services in the marketplace—where men and women would be free to accept or reject them—judges could get a realistic sense of their value to others. They could then get back to the mindset of earlier judges who spoke of "discovering" the customs and usages of society that were the basis of the "common law" system. Those who saw their roles as being to *impose* standards of conduct upon an unwilling society, would probably find themselves without a clientele.

And who, in a stateless society, would pay for these ceremonial functions? It is to be expected that there will be many who, cut loose from the state's umbilical cord, will insist upon retaining the empty forms of the state as a security blanket. Let these sad beings pay for their continuing addictive dependencies. Organizations could be set up to solicit donations from such men and women; or lotteries could be used to provide such funds. Without any coercive power to exercise, however, such donations are unlikely to be forthcoming from the corporate-state interests that now flood the pipelines to Washington.

What is the course that will likely follow the collapse of our present top-heavy, vertically-structured system? I have no greater talent for unraveling the entanglements of our world than does anyone else, and am thus unable to make definitive predictions. I have offered what is little more than personal speculation as to possibilities. But if we are to avoid being crushed beneath the fall of the ossified forms that are destroying human society, each of us had best undertake the speculations that precede all creative actions. When the decline and fall occurs, it is best not to be standing beneath an institution.

CHAPTER 50

Civilization Collapsing, or Transforming?

It is the business of the future to be dangerous. . . . The major advances in civilization are processes that all but wreck the societies in which they occur.

—Alfred North Whitehead

The study of chaos informs us that outcomes of complex systems are unpredictable, due to the inconstant and interconnected variables that underlie our behavior. Historians offer glimpses of the factors that have contributed to the lives and deaths of past civilizations, views always attended by the caveat of uncertainty that inheres in complexity. The *tendencies* that are found in causal relationships often lead us to conclusions regarding outcomes that do not materialize. Smoking three packs of cigarettes per day greatly increases the likelihood of a person developing lung cancer or emphysema, but such results are not inevitable. So, too, is the historian's effort to retrace Ariadne's cord often hindered by unexpected or unidentified influences.

So cautioned, it is nonetheless evident that Western Civilization in general—including the American version in particular—is in a very turbulent—and, perhaps, terminal condition. The dynamic forces at work on both the structures and processes of this once-vibrant culture go beyond the economic dislocations, the disruptions of social movements, political upheavals, wars, and other major fluctuations long associated with the history of any culture. The tumultuous and entropic state of our modern world has eroded the very core of what it means to be civilized.

To focus on Western Civilization—or any of its national subcategories—runs the risk of overlooking the global consequences of either the collapse or major transformation of this culture. Our world is dominated by highly-structured, interconnected political and corporate-state institutions, whose coercive powers extend far beyond American and European boundaries. The institutional order depends upon the existence of social conflict. At the very least, this division consists of the subordination of individual interests to collective systemic purposes. It also finds expression in the clash of institutional undertakings. In either case, it is evident that any significant changes in organizational thinking or behavior will affect *all* of mankind, including so-called "third world" countries.

As I have emphasized throughout this book, civilizations are created by individuals and are destroyed by collectives. As historians have shown, the collective means of destruction begin with the institutionalization of the systems that have created and sustained the culture. The organizational *forms* that were employed to generate the values that made the civilization productive and life-enhancing, become their own *raison d'etre*, superseding the *processes* that brought the forms into being. The liberty of individuals to act upon the world—which, in turn, depend upon such values as private ownership of property, respect for contracts, and the idea that societies exist for the enhancement of individual well-being—came into conflict with the structured systems that insisted upon their primacy over the affairs of mankind. The state, corporations, churches, universities, communications systems, and other organizations combined to condition and reinforce the minds of individuals to accept the formalized direction of their lives.

A complete assessment of organizational systems must include an analysis of *all* costs and benefits of such practices, not just those upon which institutional interests focus. Collective undertakings grounded in coercion tend to dismiss certain costs and presume non-existent benefits. The *utilitarian* doctrine is premised upon this thinking, with the preferences of the "greatest number" prevailing at the expense of others. Political systems, by their nature, impose externalities upon some in order to benefit those who enjoy the use of force. By contrast, in a *marketplace* system—premised upon the inviolability of property boundaries and contracts—costs and benefits are incurred/enjoyed by persons willing to invest their own resources. The presumption that a given political program provides a "social benefit" smuggles into the equation what is often not true, namely, that most people value such ends and, because of "free-rider" tendencies, are unwilling to pay for them. One sees this in so-called "public goods" arguments. While the free-rider motive can exist—particularly where large numbers of persons are involved—it is too often assumed that the non-participant is trying to enjoy a benefit at the expense of others. What if a neighbor refuses to pay for a street-light on the corner because he doesn't want the light shining into his bedroom? What is often implicit in the free-rider question is that a "public good" has some *objective* value to it—rather than it being the *subjective* value of the more numerous. What is further ignored—in presuming the rightful authority of the state to force some to pay for another's preferences—is the psychic cost associated with violating one's will (a topic to be explored in the following pages).

If our culture is to be transformed rather than destroyed, we need to examine our assumptions about how social systems are to be organized. In the course of human history, complex societies—particularly institutions—are a very late invention.[1] In our search for systems that sustain life, we should find encouragement in our history. Our ancestors lived without institutional masters, while more recent histories inform us of the destructiveness of our failure to do so. Wars, genocides, depressions, torture, and the general dehumanization of life have been occasioned by our thinking. Self-serving abstractions (e.g., *e pluribus unum*)—which become ends in themselves—ultimately bring down the civilizations that spawned them. This is where we now stand, living in a hierarchically-structured world in which institutional interests have become so dominant that the state can give to its corporate partners hundreds of billions of dollars with no greater justification than that they are "too big to fail"; that wars can be conducted against any peoples personally selected by an imperial president and for no stated purposes; that torture, imprisonment without trial, assassination, widespread surveillance, groping people's bodies, domestic SWAT teams, and other forms of police brutality can be carried out to reinforce the subservience of the individual to the state; that the creative, life-sustaining energies of the marketplace that have maximized our material well-being can be depressed or destroyed whenever it suits institutional interests to do so; that alternative systems not subject to institutional control (e.g., the Internet) must be regulated, or subjected to a "kill switch" in the hands of the president; and that those who insist upon informing the public of

---

1   Tainter, *The Collapse of Complex Societies*, p. 198.

governmental action the state prefers to keep secret will be prosecuted for high-crimes, reveal a civilization nearing its end.

The organizational design of our world is moving from the *vertical* to the *horizontal*. Whether our social systems will continue to be dominated by the top-down, externally-directed thinking that serves institutional interests, or by lateral networks of cooperation through which human beings pursue their varied purposes, is the question unfolding before us. The established order frantically and desperately works to reinforce the crumbling foundations of its pyramidal power-structure with increasingly draconian measures. The current "war on terror"—or what I prefer to label the "war to preserve the institutional order"—treats any challenge to the status quo as a "terrorist threat" to be forcibly resisted. In so doing, it has only hastened the collapse of the civilization upon which it has long been a parasite.

The "instrument of expansion" that defines our industrialized culture has been the *marketplace*, not that corruption going by the name of the "corporate-state." Perhaps a rational response to the bankruptcy of our present civilization can be found by looking at how the marketplace deals with bankrupt business firms. Instead of government bailouts, the market alternative is to allow the failed firm to collapse, and reinvest its resources in more productive, efficient undertakings. Might we find a parallel alternative for dealing with the collapse of our dysfunctional civilization? Might we search the substance of our culture to rediscover its creative, peaceful, life-enhancing qualities, and reinvest those values in fundamentally transformed social systems?

Is it possible to reverse the collectivizing practices that dehumanize people and destroy civilizations? To regard institutions as ends in themselves necessitates treating the liberty of others to generate destabilizing influences as a threat to be forcibly restrained. For established interests to be insulated from the vicissitudes of change, requires the *centralization* of authority through the *vertical* structuring of society. Such a condition, in turn, depends upon men and women adopting collective, mass-minded forms of thinking.

Carl Jung has probably done the best job of analyzing patterns of collective thought and action, and suggesting the means by which individuals may liberate themselves from such destructive influences. In the process he calls "individuation," people can discover how to withdraw their energies from the collective mindset. As the bulk of our collective inclinations arise from the mobilization of the "dark side" forces common to us all, Jung warns of the dangers of *projecting* such traits onto others, as well as *suppressing* them within. Only in acknowledging our own "dark side," can we separate ourselves from the mass-mindedness that is destroying us.[2]

The weakening of the institutional order is providing not only the opportunity, but the necessity, for fundamentally transforming our social thinking and practices. If mankind is to avoid destroying itself, we must learn how to decentralize the systems by which we organize ourselves. We must dismantle the engines of violence that reside in collective identities. In the process of doing so, we may be able to generate a new civilization premised on enhancing the lives of *people* rather than *institutions*. If we are able to liberate our minds from the chains of collective group-think, we will continue to discover the benefits of *decentralized* decision-making authority. Organizations that are grounded in cooperation, rather than conflict and coercion; in which voluntarism replaces violence; and in which the values of individual liberty and private ownership of property prevail, are principles that we need to inform our thinking and behavior. The fact that our world is presently experiencing the processes of centrifugation in the form of alternative social systems, provides encouragement.

Rethinking such matters might begin with our redefining the nature of a creative and peaceful society of free people living in liberty. Perhaps the words "civilization" and "civilize" should be replaced by "humanization" and "humanize." "Civilization" has too much of the political and other formal institutional connotations.

To better understand the nature of this social transformation, we might return to Joseph Schumpeter's analysis of the "process of Creative Destruction." Contrary to the status quo purposes that define the institutional order's insistence upon being an "end in itself," creative change depends upon the transformation of existing systems and practices. The vibrancy that characterizes and sustains life is incompatible with an institutional need to keep the world in a steady state, immune from the vicissitudes of uncertainty and variation. The metaphor of the cutting-and-filling function of a river system is recalled.

The new renaissance that seems to be emerging is fostered, in large part, by exponential increases in our capacities for communicating information to one another. Indeed, "information" may prove to be the "instrument of

---

2   C.G. Jung, *The Archetypes and the Collective Unconscious*, trans. by R.F.C. Hull (Princeton, N.J.: Princeton University Press, Bollingen Series XX, 2nd ed., 1968), pp. 275–354.

expansion" that will underlie a new culture. Because of the lies, deceptions, and contradictions upon which the institutional order has depended for maintaining its dominance over the rest of humanity, secrecy—along with the twisting of explanations of events—has long been inseparable from establishment policy-making. The final scenes, in both *The Wizard of Oz* and *Animal Farm*, in which the victims of systematic bamboozlement finally become aware of the games played at their expense, attest to the liberating powers of information decentralized into the hands of individuals.

We must recall how so much of the substance and the epochs of Western Civilization arose in the years following Gutenberg's contribution to the expansion of information: the Renaissance, the Enlightenment, the Age of Reason, and the Scientific and Industrial Revolutions. With even greater modern technological capacities for marshaling, analyzing, and communicating information, how prolific a culture might our children and grandchildren enjoy? They might also discover how to live in ways in which the material values for human well-being become fully integrated with the spiritual, emotional, and passionate dimensions that provide a deeper sense of meaning to life than an institutionally-dominant world can provide.

CHAPTER 51

A Cost/Benefit Analysis of the Human Spirit: The Luddites Revisited

nstitutional structuring of our lives has adverse consequences that reach far beyond the material costs that are harmful to us not only as individuals, but as they contribute to social conflict and the collapse of civilizations. The effect that such behavior has on the inner awareness of what it means to be human is something we rarely focus upon as we devote ourselves to our "practical" pursuits. I believe that each of us has a fundamental need for spiritual or transcendent experiences; a need to connect with the rest of the universe in ways that are meaningful to our innermost sense of who we are. We have been ignoring such needs, much to our detriment.

It is these costs to the human spirit that most threaten the well being of all mankind, and to which the attention of intelligent men and women must now be directed. As Viktor Frankl observed in his National Socialist concentration camp experiences, what hurt so much was not the physical pain inflicted by brutish guards, but the indignity, the lack of respect shown to one as a human being, the loss of a sense of individuality in being shorn of

Excerpted from The Murray N. Rothbard Memorial Lecture, given by Butler Shaffer at the Austrian Scholars Conference, The Ludwig von Mises Institute, at Auburn, Alabama, March 15, 2003.

everything—personal possessions, even one's body hair—that made them unique.[1]

The spiritual depletion of our lives can be identified in numerous ways. The anger, violence, and depression that have become commonplace in society; school children who have their sense of spontaneity and adventure numbed by drugs to make them more amenable to the control of parents and school officials; adults who drug themselves with legally prescribed tranquilizers, anti-depressants, amphetamines, or alcohol; or who resort to illegal drugs in order to seek, through chemistry, what they cannot find within themselves or their social systems. Why do we not grasp the message hidden in popular names for such substances: a synonym for "alcohol" is "spirits," while various drugs are referred to as "angel dust," "ecstasy," "paradise," "blue heaven," "upper," "joy powder," or "God's medicine"? Instead of condemning and criminalizing drug use—which only adds to the loss of control people have over their lives—intelligent people might ask why so many are unable to find spiritual expression in their institutionally centered lives and look for it in ersatz forms.

For those who doubt the power that the human spirit exerts over our sense of life, recall the impact of some of the visual news images from recent years: the naked Vietnamese girl running and screaming down a road following an American napalm attack; pictures of the Berlin Wall being torn down by individuals; or the photo of one of the many victims of American terrorism, six-year old Elian Gonzalez, with a machine-gun shoved in his face by one of Janet Reno's storm-troopers. Or consider that most powerful of photo images—one I have hanging on my office wall—of Wang Wei-Lin, confronting that row of impenetrable tanks in Tiananmen Square. Western journalists, trained to feed off leftovers thrown into the trough by their political masters, tended to see only *political* symbolism in this event. But it was not the American flag or the dollar sign around which these young Chinese rallied, but the Statue of *Liberty*. This man did not seem intent on overpowering the state—or even the tanks—but appeared to be making a declaration on behalf of *reclaiming the human spirit*. It was the spirit of mankind, represented in the form of a solitary human being, standing up to the faceless, dispirited machinery of state power, that sent a common chill up the spines of most of us.

---

1   Viktor Frankl, *Man's Search for Meaning* (New York: Washington Square Press, 1963).

Fragmenting ourselves into "physical" and "spiritual" dimensions has been a major source of social conflict. The discord may also become internalized within each of us, as we become increasingly beaten down by a sense of powerlessness over our own lives, and may eventually surrender to an inner despair that finds expression as "what's the use?" In the language of students of chaos, unless we reverse our entropic decline, unless we can rekindle the inner fire that has gone out through our neglect, we may collapse into spiritual bankruptcy. An experience I had a number of years ago provides a helpful metaphor. I attended a photographic exhibit in which a scientist displayed his experiences in observing the eye of a mosquito under a microscope. Initially, the eye was afire with brilliant, dancing colors of orange and green. But suddenly, the eye turned black; the fire had gone out of the system; the mosquito was dead.

Our well-organized war upon the human spirit is at the core of the crisis now being faced by all of Western Civilization.

Spiritual needs *are* central to our lives; they energize our inner sense of being through which we find meaning. But if institutions are to dominate our lives, would not these entities find it in their interests to satisfy these needs? Is this, in fact, not the professed role that churches play? At first glance, the answer might appear to be "yes," but upon closer examination we discover that such is rarely the case. Churches institutionalized God and, in so doing, have discouraged us from seeking our own godliness. The inadequacy of institutions to satisfy our needs for transcendence is found in the fundamental distinction between individual and collective behavior. Spiritual expression, like other forms of emotional experience, is peculiarly individualized. For the same reason that only each person can satisfy their own hunger or thirst, or feel fear, love, or any form of excitement; only individuals can experience their inner connection with the rest of the universe. Passion is confined to individuals. Institutions are but abstractions, the creatures of human thought. But the currency of thought is other abstractions—words—and spirituality is wrapped up in experiences that *transcend* thought. Institutions function only through individuals, and individuals can supply such organizations with abstract, secondary expressions of inner experiences, but they can never move beyond words. But words, as Korzybski reminds us, are never the "things" to which they refer. This is what makes it so difficult to communicate—much less to organize—our inner sensations.

Relating all of this to political systems, a given state may, with the best of intentions, associate itself with the abstraction of "liberty." Indeed, the

Bush administration defended its repressive, statist policies as "operation enduring freedom." But the word "liberty," being an abstraction, is always less than the experience of not having one's will violated with regard to one's person or property. Because "liberty," as a word, is less than the experience of liberty, it must—within a legal/political context—always be subject to interpretation. The inner experiences that we associate with our spiritual needs, do not translate into anything of value—or even comprehension—to institutions. This is why, in an institutionalized world, whatever is *non*material tends to be regarded as *im*material.

How are we to give up our attachments to abstract systems and reclaim the spiritual dimension of our nature? The answer to that question lies in returning to the point at which we lost contact with this part of our lives; namely, when we accepted the mind/body division of our nature and, as a consequence, became attached to—and made ourselves dependent upon—those institutional forms that promised us physical security in exchange for our subservience to their interests.

To get some insight into this question, I want to revisit those hobgoblins of the Industrial Revolution, the *Luddites*. Because I have long defended the Industrial Revolution as, perhaps, the most humanizing period in history, you may ask what possible message I could derive from the Luddites. The word, itself, conjures up images of collective ignorance, mob destructiveness, and the dangers of mass-mindedness. For the most part, the Luddite movement emerged from craftsmen whose economic interests were challenged by the developing factory system, and whose "machine-breaking" responses derived from the same kind of anti-competitive sentiments that later fired the "progressive" and New Deal eras. So as to relieve any sense of anxiety you may be feeling at my suggestion that we revisit the Luddites, let me assure you that I am herewith making no defense of machine-breaking riots, nor am I embracing the neo-Luddite sentiments favoring the technological dismantling of modern society.

I do believe, however, that the Luddites may have been about something more than the reactive destruction of machines. I suspect there was an awareness—exhibited, today, by members of the Amish subculture—that dependence upon technological systems portended an eventual loss of our sense of humanity; a fear that society would quickly become dominated by a technical imperative, in which everything, including human beings, would be little more than standardized, fungible, institutional servomechanisms. "Libertarian" and "anarchist" traditions have, at their very core, an insistence upon supporting the individuality, autonomy, and spontaneous nature of each human being, and to distrust any form of organization that threatens such values. Those who question the validity of these concerns might ask how and why a nation, so long steeped in the rhetoric of individual liberty, has so easily turned into a mass-minded collective.

The temptation of many who observe the dehumanizing nature of our modern world is to lash out at the technology that they perceive as the cause. But to do so makes no more sense than attacking gun manufacturers or gun owners for the violence committed by those few who use guns as tools of destruction. I recall—as a child at the end of World War II—hearing otherwise intelligent people arguing that dumping military weapons into the seas would end wars. Such thinking completes the vicious circle of mechanistic thinking: humans become machinelike, while machines take on the human attributes of will, directing our behavior. It is not technology that has turned human beings into dispirited mechanisms, but our willingness to think of our lives as dependent upon such machinery, and attaching our sense of identity to the systems that produce and control the technologies.

Those who reject technology outright make as big a mistake as those who allow themselves to become attached to technologies. Each dismisses an important aspect of our humanity. We are tool-makers. The machines we create are expressions of our nature; extensions of the human life process. To think otherwise is to fragment ourselves, and to imagine that evolutionary processes ought to have left us governed only by fixed instincts. Whether for good or bad, we have been the *creators* of the world in which we live. The Industrial Revolution; inventiveness; discoveries; the building of skyscrapers, bridges, and other cathedrals, have all been expressions of the human spirit. We should ask ourselves: what were the inner forces that drove Edison to continue inventing? Might they have been the same spiritual needs that kept Van Gogh painting and Beethoven composing? But to attach ourselves to the created forms is to institutionalize and petrify the very spirit that created them. It is to worship the structure by dissipating the process.

Furthermore, because we have created machines, they provide us an opportunity to discover a great deal about our sense of being. Have we projected onto their forms and systems a sense of how we think of ourselves? Are machines our cloned images, in which we see our own reflections? How else do we explain the machine-like ways in which we think of ourselves? We speak of getting "warmed up" for work, or "running out of gas," or being "turned-on" or "turned-off" by others; we imagine ourselves to be "big wheels" in life, or "cogs in the machine" who may, on occasion, get our "wires crossed." We suffer from "burn out," and "let off steam" so as not to "blow a gasket" or a "fuse" or become "unhinged." We speak of having a "screw loose," or "going to pieces," and resort to drugs or alcohol in order to "get fixed" and "get in gear." We speak of ourselves as "assets" or "resources" to our workplace or community, and are more likely to regard our brain as computer-like, than to think of computers as brain-like.

Those who do not understand the Amish often imagine that their resistance to new technologies arises from a sense of "evil" they see in such tools. But this is not the case. The Amish do employ tools, but if someone wants to consider bringing a new technology into the community, the Amish study it with this thought in mind: will acceptance of this technology make us dependent upon the external world, such that we will be tempted to change our ways? An automobile, for instance, would make the Amish have to rely on parts manufacturers, tire and battery sellers, and petroleum companies to keep it operative.

What if you and I began thinking this way? Can our work become what farming or carpentry are to the Amish, or what architecture was to Frank Lloyd Wright, namely, expressions of our inner sense in the material world? Rather than seeking employment primarily by the standard of how well the job pays, can we discover a kind of work that is so inwardly rewarding that we would pay someone to let us do it, and then figure out how to get well-paid doing it?

I assume that most readers have developed a strong dependency on computers—a tool that has managed to insinuate itself into our lives in recent years. How many intrusions and restrictions on our lives have we begun to accept [for example, government surveillance of our e-mail and Internet website visits and transactions] rather than give up the convenience of our computers? What if state or federal governments were to announce significantly greater inroads on our liberty as the price to pay for our being entitled to continue enjoying this technology? How many of us are prepared to walk away from these machines and return to pen and ink and Xerox machines?

Perhaps the Luddites—whose fears were machine-centered—have less to offer us in our search for the reclamation of our souls than do another group revered by my Irish ancestors and, perhaps for genetic reasons, by myself: the *leprechauns*. For those of you whose upbringing was so destitute that you cannot even imagine the existence of these wondrous beings, and for those of you who long ago gave up your childlike assurances of the enchanted nature of the world in which you live, let me introduce you to the leprechauns. According to Irish folklore—which is the only publication of record acknowledged by these beings—the leprechauns are industrious souls who place great value on two factors in their lives: [1] their accumulated gold, and [2] their individual liberty. No sack-clothed ascetics they: the leprechauns love their material wealth, and will do just about anything to keep it. If you manage to steal their gold, there will be hell to pay in their efforts to get it back. Many a tale has been told of these mysterious folk hiding in bushes and watching, with both sadness and anger, as thieves steal their hidden treasure. They nevertheless will not reveal themselves, for the one thing they will never risk in trying to protect their gold is their liberty.

If we are to end the material and spiritual division in our thinking, and learn to live with a sense of wholeness that most of our lives lack, can we learn from the Amish or the leprechauns how to value our material tools and other possessions without becoming attached to them? Can we understand that the greatest threat to individual liberty has always been in our willingness to value anything beyond ourselves more highly than we do our own sense of being? Can we end the practice of progressively lowering the price of our liberty as we negotiate for the preservation of our attachments?

Our well-organized world has become less and less relevant to the inner lives of most men and women. Those of us who have a passion for individual liberty have a wonderful opportunity to address these unfulfilled needs in ways that no others, of whom I am aware, have managed to do. When millions of human beings, throughout the world, come together in demonstrations to protest a war even before it has begun, you can be assured that the human spirit remains alive beneath the hardened surface of events in our lives; that the inner voices that define the essence of humanity have not been fully ground down by the dehumanizing machinery of state power. Wang Wei-Lin may have been silenced, but his spirit has not.

To communicate with others as to these concerns requires a totally new perspective. How we view economic systems or law, or the study of history, government, or sociology, is a subset of the question of how we view individual liberty. And whether we value individual liberty or not is a subset of our attitudes about the sanctity of life itself. As a consequence, if we are to understand any of these areas of human behavior with *wholeness* and *integrity*, we must learn to incorporate a spiritual awareness into our analyses. We must, in other words, abandon our fragmentary and divisive approaches to understanding the human condition. We must learn a *new language,* one that can translate our inner voices into conversations with the outer world.

We have figured out how best to provide for the satisfaction of our material needs. Those who understand the practical importance of reclaiming control over our lives, property, and transactions with others now need to focus on the question: *why* is it important to do so? Do we understand the significance of reclaiming the spiritual dimensions of our humanness? Can we learn to calculate *all* these factors into our thoughts and actions? Once we ask such questions with regularity, we may look to the day when the human spirit walks away from its self-imposed bondage. In that day, men and women may discover that death in service to the state is not heroic; that obedience to power does not confer meaning upon one's life; and that a lengthened leg-chain is not to be confused with liberty.

We must begin with the awareness that abstractions—such as institutions—are *spiritless, sterile* entities, able to pursue their ends only through the actions of individuals who identify themselves with institutional purposes; and that the interests of humanity transcend such artificial forms. Only individuals suffer pain, dream, experience love and joy, and eventually die. Only *individuals* make value judgments and act in furtherance of such values. Only individuals transport, through DNA, the future of mankind from one generation to the next. Each of us is biologically and experientially unique, and liberty is the only condition in which we can express our uniqueness. If we are to discover our connectedness with the world, we must understand that what we have in common with one another is the need to protect the conditions in which the liberty of each of us can be exercised. Only if we learn to respect the inviolability of each individual can mankind hope to survive. You and I *are* mankind, . . . its *present* and its *future.*

We must then declare to ourselves, as well as to our neighbors, that mankind, integrated in both body and spirit, will not only *survive,* but *prosper* in this world; that life belongs to the living, not to abstract collectives, regardless of their exalted trappings or the duration of their tenure over the minds of men and women. We must further declare that the *spirit* of mankind is going to survive on this planet, in the only place in which it can ever be found, namely, in the autonomous and spontaneous expressions of individuals. It is time for those who believe otherwise to stand aside, as we support one another in the effort to reclaim our souls!

Index